WHEN BORDERS DON'T DIVIDE:
Labor Migration and Refugee Movements in the Americas

WHEN BORDERS DON'T DIVIDE:
Labor Migration and Refugee Movements in the Americas

Edited by Patricia R. Pessar

*Published in association with
the Center for Immigration Policy
and Refugee Assistance
Georgetown University, Washington, D.C.*

1988

Center for Migration Studies
New York

The Center for Migration Studies is an educational,
non-profit institute founded in New York in 1964
to encourage and facilitate the study of socio-demographic,
economic, political, historical, legislative and pastoral
aspects of human migration and refugee movements.
The opinions expressed in this work are those of the author.

The Center for Immigration Policy and Refugee Assistance,
Georgetown University, Washington, D.C., was founded
in 1980, and through its Hemisphere Migration Project
sponsors policy-relevant research on migration in the Americas.
The studies featured in this selection were sponsored by the H.M.P.

WHEN BORDERS DON'T DIVIDE:
Labor Migration and Refugee
Movements in the Americas

First Printing

CENTER FOR MIGRATION STUDIES
209 Flagg Place, Staten Island, N.Y. 10304-1199

Library of Congress Cataloging-in-Publication Data

When Borders Don't Divide:
Labor Migration and Refugee Movements in the Americas

Includes index.

1. America — Emigration and immigration.   2. Alien labor — America.
3. Refugees — America.
I. Pessar, Patricia R.

JV7398.W47 1987   325.8   87-20856
ISBN 0-934733-26-0 (Cloth)   ISBN 0-934733-27-9 (Paper)

Printed in the United States of America

TABLE OF CONTENTS

PREFACE

Harold Bradley, S.J.

The chapters in this book are the result of research conducted under the auspices of the Hemispheric Migration Project (HMP). The HMP is a pioneering research and policy effort involving scholars from throughout the Americas who study the causes and consequences of international migration.

The inspiration for the HMP came in a speech delivered by Congressman Peter Rodino, Jr. (D-NJ) at the 1980 inaugural conference of Georgetown University's Center for Immigration Policy and Refugee Assistance (CIPRA). At that time Congressman Rodino called for policy-relevant research that might guide a more hemispheric approach to policy making on immigration and refugee matters.

We are gratified that many of Rep. Rodino's colleagues in Congress and officials in the Department of State shared his commitment to a sound research basis for policy making and program development in these areas. It was this commitment of support and resources that launched Georgetown and the Intergovernmental Committee for Migration to collaborate on the Hemispheric Migration Project.

Over the last three years there have been many individuals and institutions that have helped us to plan and coordinate the first phase of the ongoing Hemispheric Migration Project. Foremost among these individuals are Charles Keely and Elsa Chaney, who drafted the first proposal for the project. Our advisors, the Experts Review Group, and the Regional Research Coordinators helped us to realize our commitment to international collaboration in which research problems and designs emerge from the concerns and institutional strengths found in Latin America and the Caribbean rather than being imposed by foreign scholars or international agencies.

The following individuals served on our Experts Review Group: Vilmar Faria (Brazil), Charles Keely (USA), Lelio Mármora (Argentina),

Dawn Marshall (Barbados), Thomas Merrick (USA), Gabriel Murillo (Colombia), Alejandro Portes (USA), Helen Safa (USA), and Alan Simmons (Canada). These distinguished migration scholars helped set the HMP research agenda and later reviewed and selected the sixteen projects that the HMP funded in its first research round.

The Regional Coordinators were Edelberto Torres-Rivas for Central America, Elsa Chaney for the Caribbean, Ramiro Cardona for the Andean Region, and Jorge Balán for the Southern Cone. They not only strengthened the collaborative nature of the HMP by helping to recruit potential researchers throughout Latin America and the Caribbean, but they also consulted with the grantees at various stages of their research and write-up.

We also relied on the Regional Coordinators to encourage sometimes reluctant researchers to take the leap to draw out the domestic and international policy implications of their studies. This agreement on the part of HMP researchers to link research to policy had major payoffs at the international policy conference the HMP held on Capitol Hill in February of 1986. We were gratified that at this conference senior officials of sixteen Latin American and Caribbean countries joined their counterparts from the United States to consider whether, in light of new research findings, there were migration and refugee-related problems that might be resolved through bilateral and multilateral cooperation. Areas for future cooperation that were explored at the conference included joint border development programs in the Andean region and third country resettlement of Central American refugees in the Southern Cone.

In addition to bringing new research to the attention of policy makers in the Americas, the HMP has also been committed to bringing new voices from Latin American and the Caribbean into the scholarly debates on the causes and consequences of Western Hemispheric Migration. This edited collection accomplishes this latter goal. Many people contributed to the painstaking process of translating, editing, and typing the papers included in this book. I want especially to acknowledge Patricia R. Pessar, Mary Ann Larkin, David Lessard, Charles J. Becker, Isabel Benemelis, Graciela Mangasarian, and Debbie Charles.

INTRODUCTION: MIGRATION MYTHS AND NEW REALITIES

Patricia R. Pessar

Many migration myths prevail within the Americas. These myths treat such basic matters as where the migrants go, who they are, why they leave, and what the social and economic impact of migration is on sending and receiving countries.

The studies presented here challenge many of the myths and half-truths surrounding migration in the Americas. In challenging these myths through original research, the contributors to this volume present a valid portrait of labor migration and refugee flows in the hemisphere. To our knowledge, this is the first time that such a contemporary treatment of hemispheric migration/refugee trends and developments has been available to readers.

More Than a Fair Share

The frequent charge that U.S. borders are uncontrolled and perceptions of a heightened immigrant and refugee presence in the United States contribute to a sense that the United States is receiving a disproportionate share of newcomers from Latin America and the Caribbean. As the contributors document, however, border migration and trans-hemispheric migration are prevalent throughout the Americas as people seek economic opportunity and political security. For example, Palacio's chapter on Belize shows that as a result of massive undocumented migration, Belize ranks among the top five countries in the world in ratio of refugee to native population.

Challenges to policy-making accompany this massive population dislocation. As the chapters on Belize and on Colombian migration to Venezuela (Ungar) show, the United States is not alone in finding it necessary to formulate an amnesty program for undocumented migrants. In fact, within the Americas there have been earlier amnesty programs in Canada, the Virgin Islands, Belize, Venezuela, and Argentina. Similarly, in response to massive refugee flows, many countries throughout the hemisphere have been faced with the task of incorporating Central Americans into their economies and societies. The Central American region has been heavily impacted. However, as Mármora's study here documents, there are limitations to the hospitality many Central American countries can offer neighbors seeking safe haven and material assistance. In a time of escalating economic crisis, these countries of first asylum have had to weigh humanitarian aid for refugees against the responsibility to provide for the basic social needs of their citizens.

The Migrant as Peasant

A popular myth found throughout the hemisphere holds that most immigrants are peasants who have been recently displaced from their land by commercial agriculture. As several chapters demonstrate, the peasant-to-proletariat view of labor migration is inaccurate and misleading.

First, this view would lead us to believe that most international migrants in the Americas settle abroad permanently due to displacement from their rural base. In fact, a circular migration pattern is more common. This pattern is described and analyzed here in Dandler and Medeiro's study on Bolivian migration to Argentina. In this case, border migration by select household members is part of an overall household strategy for generating a diversified household income. Rather than migration leading to resettlement abroad, migrant households often manage to accumulate sufficient savings to permit all household members ultimately to reside comfortably in their home country.

These Bolivian households, like many migrant households throughout the Americas, are neither peasant nor proletarian. Rather, migrant households subsist by pooling both income-in-kind and wages. Such households have been termed, semi-proletarian. Some authors argue that the reason rural areas in many Latin American countries have not lost the bulk of their populations to internal and international migration is that poor rural households are able to survive by combining temporary migration for wages with local subsistence activities (de Janvry and Garramón, 1977).

This claim is controversial, however. There is a growing body of research on rural emigration that points to highly negative outcomes for rural households and communities (Rubenstein, 1983; Pessar, 1982). As Mills documents here for St.Kitts-Nevis, emigration from rural areas can lead to households abandoning local economic activities in favor of subsisting solely on remittances from abroad. Under these circumstances, international migration is itself a force for the impoverishment of productive options in rural areas and the displacement of workers from these areas. Moreover, in "remittance societies" such as St.Kitts-Nevis, one finds a tendency to confuse remittance-induced prosperity with real economic security and welfare. It is on these grounds that Mills urges his compatriots to look beyond migration as a solution to unemployment and underemployment in St.Kitts-Nevis. Clearly more research is needed to determine the local conditions which promote or undermine development within rural migrant communities.

The immigrant-as-peasant view is being challenged on another front as well. Recent findings suggest that the origin of international migrants has shifted from rural to urban over the last two decades. This holds for border migration (Pessar, 1986) as well as for emigration from Latin America and the Caribbean to the United States (Chaney, 1985; Urrea, 1985; Balán, 1985).

Immigrant Labor as Surplus Labor

One common view of labor migration holds that migrants are drawn abroad temporarily to fill short-term increases in labor demand — a demand that usually accompanies national growth spurts (Lebergott, 1964). Such a view led many policymakers and researchers to expect a massive return of labor migrants in the 1980s from economically troubled labor-importing countries, such as Venezuela and Mexico. As documented by Ungar's chapter, however, there was no massive return from Venezuela to Colombia.

Her findings add support to an opposing view of labor migration. This view holds that international migration is a permanent feature of our interdependent economies in the hemisphere, rather than merely a result of a temporary increase in labor demand on the part of expanding economies (Portes and Walton 1981; Bach 1985).

Apparently, even with the recession, those Venezuelan businesses that recruited immigrant labor continued to require — or perhaps came to require even more — the relatively cheap and docile work force Colombians represent in Venezuela. Furthermore, as Ungar's chapter shows, actions taken by Venezuela, such as currency devaluations and trade protectionism, helped the Venezuelan economy to rebound. By contrast, these steps further hindered Colombia's recuperation from the international recession owing to the interdependence between the two national economies. Consequently, with unemployment rates skyrocketing in Colombia, emigrants were left with little or no incentive to return.

If research findings continue to point to migration as an enduring feature of our interdependent economies in the hemisphere, certain policymakers and researchers will have to abandon the popular assumption which holds that migration is a temporary "anomaly" adjusted when development spurts subside or recession strikes. As the alternative view gains more adherents, we may find a greater willingness and determination among countries in the hemisphere to engage in bilateral and multilateral cooperation on international labor-migration issues.

Migration and Development

Conventional wisdom holds that countries in the region are underdeveloped due to a lack of well-trained, highly skilled workers. The reality, however, is that many developing countries are investing precious resources in the training of professionals, managers, and other skilled workers for export abroad.

Anderson's study in this collection describes why such training for export occurs. As part of a larger analysis of Jamaica's manpower losses, she considers the scarcity of health-care professionals in Jamaica. According to Anderson's calculations, the vast majority of Jamaican-trained physicians have been lost to out-migration. Over the 1978-1985 period, she finds, Jamaica experienced a net loss of 306 doctors — a figure equivalent to 78 percent of the training output. It should be noted that Jamaica is not alone in confronting the paradox of physician flight and a shortage of doctors. In the case of Grenada, one study found that "whereas in general, five Grenadians must be sent to (the University of the West Indies) to get one back; to obtain one doctor through that institution, 22 must be trained" (Cole, as cited in Marshall, 1984:103).

For the Jamaican case, Anderson attributes this costly emigration to structural factors as well as recent austerity measures which have jeopardized professionals' chances for social mobility and a secure middle-class standard of living. To account for the high rates of emigration by these professionals, she introduces two concepts: "social need" and "effective demand". By "social need", Anderson refers to the public's concern about the departure of well-trained and experienced workers. However, this "social need" does not necessarily mean there are appropriate jobs for these people — "effective demand". From the perspective of the potential emigrant, Anderson finds the lack of effective demand is experienced as employers' and consumers' inability to employ the service provider at levels of remuneration commensurate with the latter's investment and expectations about appropriate standards of living.

Policymakers must be urged to prioritize "social needs", to determine those skills which cannot be lost if specific social needs are to be met, and to create policies for holding on to such skilled workers. If these steps are not taken, developing countries in the region will continue to train for export the very individuals needed for social welfare and sustained economic growth.

Some officials of labor-exporting countries defend emigration by claiming that nationals will eventually return after having accumulated new skills. Most migration scholars challenge this optimistic view. Such scholars point to studies indicating, first, that many recent immigrants from Latin America and the Caribbean are found in unskilled jobs in secondary sector businesses; and second, many skilled and semi-skilled immigrant workers are employed in jobs that do not take advantage of their previous training (Piore, 1981; Portes and Bach, 1985).

An exception to the pattern of downward occupational mobility is revealed in Marshall's study in this collection. In this work, she documents that for many Argentine immigrants in the United States, there are more opportunities for higher-skilled jobs than is usually the case for Latin American immigrants. Marshall also contests the depiction of Argentine out-migration as a prototypical case of "brain drain". Her study of Argentine emigration to the United States documents that this flow is bimodal with high rates of migration for both professionals and semi-skilled manual laborers.

There is evidence that after many years abroad some skilled and semi-skilled workers do return home with the intention of settling permanently. Most settle in major cities where they are often self-employed in the retail, service, and transport sectors (Thomas-Hope, 1984; Baez and D'Oleo, 1985). Such "middle-strata" migration shares a feature with the pattern of circular migration from rural areas described earlier. Both seem to be oriented to the long-term goal of providing households with independent economic outlets that mitigate the need for further migration.

Nonetheless, there is reason to believe the return of such middle-strata migrants will not be permanent. Returnees with savings and skills will likely reencounter the same limits to social mobility and effective demand that led them to emigrate in the first place (*See*, Bray, 1984). A pattern of return and re-emigration is likely to prevail until returnees and other allies are able to redefine the terms of national development to meet the expanding needs of the middle and working classes.

We are reminded by another Argentine study in this collection that there is another type of return occurring in the hemisphere — the repatriation of political exiles. This return, too, seems to be precarious. Maletta, *et al.*, describe the repatriates' struggles to readjust and reincorporate into Argentine society. They show that repatriation is a slow and tentative process.

Contrary to what is generally the case with return labor migration — and which had been assumed to be the case with repatriation — the principal problem encountered by repatriates is not economic, Maletta's group finds. The returnees in this study claim that they anticipated downward mobility or a period of unemployment subsequent to their return. In spite of this negative outlook, exiles returned primarily to reestablish their identities as Argentines. Upon return then, it was not the real economic hardship they encountered that jeopardized their reintegration. Instead, they surprisingly found their claim to Argentine identity, or at least their loyalty to the *patria*, to be in question by friends, family, and members of the society at large who stayed at home. Thus, the researchers suggest, how repatriates are received by their compatriots determines, on the one hand, whether the returnees are free to contribute once again to their home country, or, on the other hand, whether they are stigmatized and therefore liable to emigrate once more.

This chapter warns us that it is perilous to forget the human factor as we press to establish assistance programs for the large numbers of refugees and repatriates caught up in the hemisphere's refugee crises. In the case of repatriation, government and private programs must meet more than the immediate reintegration needs of returnees. Equally important, they must find ways of promoting reconciliation and trust among those who stayed and those who sought temporary exile.

In presenting new research findings which challenge major migration myths, this book's Latin American and Caribbean authors bring new voices into the debates over migration in the Americas — debates that have been dominated largely by scholars from the United States. It must be stressed that this is not a collection written by outsiders looking in. Each author is a citizen and resident of the country or region about which he or she writes. In many of these works, one finds a license to question national policy — an opportunity that sometimes eludes or is denied foreign social scientists.

BIBLIOGRAPHY

Bach, R.
1985   *Western Hemispheric Immigration to the United States: A Review of Selected Trends.* Occasional Paper Series. Washington, D.C.: Georgetown University Center for Immigration Policy and Refugee Assistance.

Baez, Evertsz, F. and F. D'Oleo Ramírez
1985   *La emigración de dominicanos a Estados Unidos: Determinantes socio-económicos y consecuencias.* Santo Domingo: Fundación Friedrich Ebert.

Balán, J.
1985   *International Migration in the Southern Cone.* Occasional Paper Series, Washington, D.C.: Georgetown University Center for Immigration Policy and Refugee Assistance.

Bray, D.
1984 "Economic Development: The Middle Class and International Migration in the Dominican Republic", *International Migration Review*, 18(2):217-236.

Chaney, E.
1985 *Migration from the Caribbean Region: Determinants and Effects of Current Movements*, Hemispheric Migration Project Occasional Paper Series. Washington, D.C.: Georgetown University and the Intergovernmental Committee for Migration.

de Janvry, A. and C. Garramón
1977 "The Dynamics of Rural Poverty in Latin America", *Journal of Peasant Studies*, 4(3):206-216.

Lebergott, S.
1964 *Manpower in Economic Growth: The American Record Since 1800*. New York: McGraw-Hill.

Marshall, D.
1985 "Migration and Development in the Eastern Caribbean". In *Migration and Development in the Caribbean: The Unexplored Connection*. Edited by R. Pastor. Boulder, CO: Westview Press.

Pessar, P.
1986 "Border Migration in the Americas". Paper prepared for the Inter-American Dialogue, Washington, D.C.

1982 "The Role of Households in International Migration from the Dominican Republic", *International Migration Review*, 16(2):342-364.

Piore, M.
1979 *Birds of Passage: Migrant Labor and Industrial Societies*. Cambridge: Cambridge University Press.

Portes, A. and R. Bach
1985 *Latin Journey*. Berkeley: University of California Press.

Portes, A. and J. Walton
1981 *Labor, Class, and the International System*. New York: Academic Press, Inc.

Rubenstein, H.
1983 "Remittances and Rural Underdevelopment in the English Speaking Caribbean", *Human Organization*, 42(4):295-306.

Thomas-Hope, E.
1985 "Return Migration and Its Implications for Caribbean Development". In *Migration and Development in the Caribbean: The Unexplored Connection*. Edited by R. Pastor. Boulder, CO: Westview Press.

Urrea, F.
1985 "Características socioeconómicos de los hogares colombianos con miembros migrantes en el exterior y posible impacto de la migración internacional sobre los mismos". Hemispheric Migration Project. Intergovernmental Committee for Migration and Georgetown University, Center for Immigration Policy and Refugee Assistance, Unpublished manuscript.

TEMPORARY MIGRATION FROM COCHABAMBA, BOLIVIA TO ARGENTINA: PATTERNS AND IMPACT IN SENDING AREAS[1]

Jorge Dandler and Carmen Medeiros

This chapter analyzes temporary Bolivian migration from Cochabamba to Argentina. The development and importance of international migration from Bolivia to Argentina, principally to Buenos Aires, is placed within the context of demographic and economic changes that have occurred in Bolivia since the 1952 Revolution. We argue that migration to Argentina is a popular alternative selected by rural and urban households in their pursuit of a diversified domestic economy. In developing this line of analysis, we refine several traditionally static and formalistic concepts of labor migration analysis.

Contrary to conventional wisdom, which claims that peasants maintain themselves solely through subsistence agriculture, urban and tertiary activities have emerged in many rural areas of Bolivia particularly during the last two decades. This process of change also involves increasing spatial mobility. Such economic diversification and migration are related to the deterioration and shortage of lands in the Andean valleys and mountains. In the central valley of Cochabamba, non-agricultural activities have become the primary source of income for many peasant families (CERES, 1981; Dandler and Torrico, unpublished).

These activities (transportation, commerce, wage labor, and crafts) often require frequent, temporary migration in search of work and the development of household economies based on diversified income sources (Long and Dandler, 1978; Long, 1979). Industry is at an incipient stage in Bolivia; therefore, the permanent wage market only inte-

[1] The authors would like to thank Celio Alemán, assistant researcher, who worked with them both in the field and in the processing of data.

grates a small portion of the economically active population (Dandler *et al.*, 1985).

In this economic context, international migration to neighboring countries becomes important. Table 1 presents two estimates of the number of Bolivian migrants residing in neighboring countries. The 1970 data is based on official censuses of the countries. These figures probably include professional, technical, and some unskilled laborers. However, they do not take into account the time or length of residency in the country, nor do they consider other temporary or undocumented workers. The 1975 data, based on a study by the International Labor Organization (Breton, 1976), show a much larger contingent of Bolivian migrants in neighboring countries.

TABLE 1

Number of Bolivian Migrants Residing in Neighboring Countries

Country	1970	1975
Argentina	92,000	500,000
Brazil	10,000	45,000
Chile	7,694	70,000
Peru	4,115	60,000
Total	113,809	675,000

Source: OIT/PRELAC 1975, cited by Zuvekas (1977).

The general impression in Bolivia is that most workers migrate to sugarcane fields in the northern part of Argentina. Whiteford (1975, 1981) calculated that some 70,000 workers, mostly undocumented, migrated to the northern areas of Argentina in 1974. Ardaya (1978) attempted to quantify the various migration flows and identify the various places of destination. However, her estimates are based on the official Argentine census of 1970, which probably grossly underestimates more "permanent" migrants. On the basis of this census, she cites a total of 100,900 Bolivian residents in Argentina. Of these, 23,150 lived in Buenos Aires, 17,750 in Greater Buenos Aires, and 49,000 in Jujuy and Salta. Antezana (1969) observed that some 98,000 Bolivians worked in a migratory circuit throughout Argentina and that possibly 490,000 Bolivians lived in outlying areas around Buenos Aires and other cities.

These different estimates of the number of Bolivians residing abroad suggest certain tendencies: 1) the underestimation of the total number of migrants by official census data; 2) the underestimation of temporary migrants and; 3) the importance of Argentina as a receiving country for Bolivian migrants.

Migration and the Household: Preliminary Observations

Various studies indicate that a high proportion of permanent migrants from Cochabamba reside in metropolitan Buenos Aires (Mugarza, 1975; Ardaya, 1978). The networks of families who reside around Buenos Aires serve as a crucial link for temporary migrants (Mugarza, 1975; Anderson, 1981; Anderson and Dandler, 1983). The central hypothesis of this study is that migration to Argentina constitutes an important option in the diversified economic strategies of many rural and urban households in Bolivia.

A study on migration cannot ignore the household as a unit of analysis and decision-making; nor can the larger socioeconomic context be ignored (Balán, 1978; Roberts, 1978). In the anthropological and sociological literature, the concept of "household" has been variously defined as a co-residential grouping, a domestic consumption unit, a property-holding or production unit, or as a resource-management group (Goody, 1972, Laslett and Wall, 1972). The same difficulties of definition arise in the Andean literature (*See*, the discussion in Bolton and Mayer, 1977).

According to researchers, the Andean household controls and manages productive resources, deals with budgetary problems and livelihood strategies, and attempts to meet basic consumption needs. It is also the unit legally recognized for taxation and inheritance purposes, and through which individuals acquire community rights and obligations. Hence, it is argued households rather than individuals constitute the units of economic, community, and ceremonial participation. Households are largely composed of a single nuclear family. This domestic organization arises because of the prevalence of neolocal residency, whereby, upon marriage, adult children establish their own independent household units, usually receiving some land in the form of anticipatory inheritance, or they will have already mananged to purchase land themselves so that they can at least build a house. Divisible bilateral inheritance is a common pattern; all children, male and female, should receive some share of the property. Frequently, Andean households are tied together through a pattern of extended family relations, but they do not constitute a corporate group of the kind normally associated with the notion of a lineage or descent group. These extended family ties are reinforced through a series of exchanges of labor and products between households at certain times of the year when shortages arise. Such patterns of reciprocity and exchange frequently involve households with differential access to ecological niches where different crops and livestock are produced.

This dominant model of the household reported in Andean studies is, we suggest, problematic in several respects: First, ambiguities arise in existing accounts of household organization due to the failure to distinguish precisely between production, property, consumption and dwelling units, which should not always be assumed to coincide. Second, little attention is given to how these units and their interrelations change over time with respect to the family developmental cycle or to shifts in the fortunes of particular households and their members. Third, the pattern of exchanges between households is not so uniform as is often implied and, in fact, extends well beyond the field of agriculture and livestock production to embrace households and family members who live outside the rural milieu in mining towns and urban centers. Fourth, Andean households commonly do not correspond to the typical domestic unit of the traditional peasant community. Rather these households have been modified by the transformations that have occurred at the wider regional and national society. In a previous study, we suggested the importance of "confederated" household groupings which spanned different rural zones and the rural-urban divide, especially in areas where there was considerable household economic diversification (Long and Dandler, 1978; CERES, 1981).

In certain situations, we found groupings of a "confederated" type whose strategies coincided with a co-residential group organized as a unit of production and management, while in other cases we found that the activities of a household cover a wide area and involve individuals who live and work separately. There are situations in which economic diversification involves families with such small parcels of land that they cannot cover their basic necessities. Under these circumstances, some members of the household are obligated to migrate for extended periods of time. Economic diversification for many impoverished families is a prerequisite for assuring their social reproduction.

We purposely chose to use the notion of "livelihood" rather than "survival", "sustenance" or "subsistence". In our view, "livelihood" best expresses the idea of individuals or groups striving to make a living, attempting to meet their various consumption and production necessities, coping with economic uncertainties, and responding to new opportunities. Livelihood, then, is broader than the idea of simply surviving or meeting subsistance requirements, although for the very poor the problem of making ends meet, of course, remains central. The relevant resources for developing particular strategies often include not only conventional economic categories such as land, labor, and capital, but also less tangible factors such as timing, information, know-how, social networks, and identity.

For example, if we consider that a migrant from Cochabamba may arrive for the first time in Buenos Aires to find work in the construction industry, he will generally stay with a kinsman or "compadre" from his village who, at the same time, will guide him into a network of "cochabambino" contacts to secure a particular job.

Furthermore, he will need to obtain certain residence and work permits which he will get through the help of other kinsmen. Although it is possible that he may not have previously met some of these "kinsmen" and "compadres", he will nevertheless be able to activate the links and secure their assistance. Later, it is even possible that he will develop some joint economic activity with them, while in Buenos Aires. He can do all this because they share "common roots" and a common recognition of "belonging" to the same place of origin which carries with it certain moral obligations. For the villagers in Cochabamba, Buenos Aires is ever present in their minds because of the frequent arrival of returning migrants who tell of their exploits and bring evidence of their "success".

The notion of livelihood strategy allows for a broader analytical perspective on a dynamic social and economic process. For example, it puts into context the needs of rural peasant families to maintain their roots in the region where they can reside only when they first develop a wide range of specialized or diversified activities both within and outside the region. This implies a constant family mobilization that is expressed as a way to expand resources; e.g., the search for land in the tropical lowlands, travel to and from regional markets and fairs, access to a wage-earning urban job or self-employment, or migration for long periods of time to Buenos Aires.

The Region of Cochabamba

The region of Cochabamba is a highly diversified setting which includes not only valleys and highlands, but also tropical and semi-tropical production areas. Ever since the early colonial period, the region was integrated into a wider economy linked to the mines of Potosí and Oruro, and thus became an important source of labor and agricultural production. Centrally located within the Alto Peru (later to become Bolivia), the region's economy also became a hub of transport and commercial activities (Larson, 1987). Our setting for the present study includes the lower and upper valleys and the city of Cochabamba.

Intensive horticulture and dairy production are the principal farming activities in the lower valley. However, since the area is closely linked to the city and the regional and national transportation networks, it is becoming increasingly urbanized and supports an extensive system of local markets. Furthermore, there is a trend toward increasing economic diversification (trading, transport, auto repair shops, food provision, *etc.*) There are also some medium-sized dairy farms which hire temporary workers from the surrounding highlands. Since in the lower valley peasant holdings are generally less than one acre, women are often the principal managers of agricultural activities, whereas the men work in activities off the farm. Women are also deeply involved in trading at the nearby markets.

The upper valley, which comprises the provinces of Tarata, Cliza, Punata, and Arani, is also characterized by extreme land fragmentation. In contrast to the lower valley, most farming occurs on non-irrigated land, and therefore, only one yearly crop is possible, thus greatly limiting income and reducing labor demand for agricultural activities. Therefore, households develop a highly diversified economic strategy that includes temporary and permanent migration. Commercial and transport activities have evolved due to the valley's proximity to the city of Cochabamba, its dense population of towns and hamlets, and its network of local markets.

The principal problems for most peasant families in the upper valley are land fragmentation and the lack of irrigated land. Many young persons do not have a place to construct a house, a corral, or a small orchard. Potatoes and corn are not grown for the market economy and do not even meet the annual consumption needs of most families. Consequently, families must depend on food purchased in the market.

Agriculture in the area has become more mechanized in the last decade. Most families work the land with rented tractors. The decision to use tractors does not necessarily arise from the desire to increase production; rather, tractors save time for non-agricultural activities. Renting tractors often allows men to migrate and leave their wives and relatives in charge of agricultural activities.

There is a limited land market. When land is available prices are generally high, though prices vary according to the quality of the land. Preference is given to buyers who are close relatives or to others from the same locality. The value of the land is not commensurate with its agricultural use. Land has become over-valued precisely because its role has changed. A small plot, especially if located on the main road in a village, also serves as a platform for other economic activities (*e.g.,* a shop, a house where maize beer is sold, a seamstress shop, *etc.*) Land, above all, is the basis for the establishment and continuity of a household. It is difficult to think about establishing a new peasant family unit without access to a small plot to build a house. Owning a small plot of land assures a residence, an identity, and a social relationship with the area. It is also a base upon which to undertake a variety of economic activities.

The city of Cochabamba has a population of approximately 200,000 persons. Because of its central location in the country, it is an important commercial and transportation center. It is the principal regional market for farm products. The huge market place, La Cancha, is the principal distribution center for food and consumer products for Cochabamba's urban and rural populations (Calderón and Rivera, 1984). While the urban zone contains about one-third of the growing national industry, the majority of the manufacturing establishments are small shops and family enterprises. These small businesses comprise 73 percent of the city's manufacturing sector. The medium and large manufacturing firms employ about 4,000 wage laborers. Four industries contain 75 percent of the area's total industrial investment (CERES, 1981:7).

Many rural families settle in Cochabamba as part of a strategy of economic diversification. The majority are self-employed while in the city; women, in particular, are very involved in commerce. Those migrants from the central valleys have a more privileged position because of their geographical proximity to the city. They are much closer to their places of origin and have better access to lands under cultivation than persons who come from other areas of the country.

Methodology and Characteristics of Sample Group

Our study analyzed migrants from two rural areas and one urban area. The rural areas include Ucureña and bordering areas of the upper valley as well as various villages in the lower valley. The urban area comprises northern and southern neighborhoods of the city of Cochabamba and the towns of Quillacollo and Sacaba. We interviewed 143 families (93 in the upper and lower valleys and 50 in the urban areas).

A member of each household responded to a basic semi-structured questionnaire on household composition, activities, education, land tenure, and other matters. We also sought to interview female members of the household, especially the wives of those men who had migrated to Argentina. This questionnaire had a special section on migration that examined the situation of the household before, during, and after the first trip to Argentina. We collected a life and work history, including an account of the various migrations, applying the method developed by Balán, Browning, and Jelin (1973), which is an open-ended, codifiable technique especially useful for constructing a diachronic perspective on individual and household careers. We also developed special questionnaires for construction and transportation enterprises and the state oil refinery, to explore whether these industries had employed a significant skilled work force that had previously migrated to Argentina.

A significant proportion of persons we interviewed in the urban areas are originally from the rural region of the upper valley. That is, the majority of the residents of the outlying neighborhoods of the city of Cochabamba are first generation migrants. Many families maintained dual residences. Significantly, many household heads who live in the city originally migrated to Argentina from a rural area, returned to their place of origin, and then moved to the city of Cochabamba.

The majority of the rural and urban households we studied exhibited a wide range of economic activities, an intense spatial mobility and self-employment strategies linked to the informal sector within a framework of extended kin and wider social networks. In many respects, then, this population was representative of a wider phenomenon that characterizes the social sectors of the upper and lower valleys of Cochabamba, as well as the outskirts of the capital city.

A person or a household experiences different types of migration in a lifetime. Some undertake one trip; others migrate many times. Some Bolivian migrants stay only a few months in Argentina; others live there for twenty years. The definition of "trips" and migration periods presented some methodological difficulties. When does a migrant return just for a visit? If he stays for a long period back home in the village and then returns to Buenos Aires, does this break the period of migration, and thus, should one classify such actions as two separate "migrations"? For the purpose of this study, we have classified a migration as the period during which the migrant's principal focus of work is in Argentina. If during this time, the migrant returns to Bolivia but is not tied to a job, then the visit in Bolivia is purely a visit. If, on the other hand, the migrant works in Bolivia and travels again, then we consider that the work undertaken in Bolivia separates one migration from another.

Temporary migration cannot be studied through a static, synchronic approach. It must be analyzed through a diachronic process. Table 2 shows different durations of migration for various age groups. A short migration period lasted between a few months and 4 years; a long period lasted from 5 to 20 years (the longest duration we found). Table 2 shows that most Bolivian migrants (61 percent) have been in Argentina a short time, and most were between 25 and 40 years of age. This group could potentially migrate again.

TABLE 2

Duration of Migration to Argentina by Age Group

Current Age	0 - 4 Years		5 - 20 Years	
	No. of Migrants	%	No. of Migrants	%
20 - 24	8	5.7	1	.7
25 - 29	14	10.0	4	2.9
30 - 34	20	14.3	11	7.9
35 - 40	24	17.1	17	12.1
41 - 50	12	8.6	13	9.3
51 - 60	6	4.3	7	5.0
61 - 70	1	.7	2	1.4
Subtotal	85	60.7	55	39.3
Total	—	—	140	100.0

Among the migrants, we found the following marital situations: (1) migrants who are single and remained unmarried throughout their stay in Argentina; (2) migrants who were single when they departed but later married a Bolivian woman (usually from the same original village or the Cochabamba region) in Argentina or a woman in Cochabamba while returning to Bolivia for a short period (taking the wife with him or leaving her in the place of origin); (3) migrants who are already married prior to departure and take their wives to Argentina; and finally (4) those who are already married but leave their wives and the latter may never actually visit Argentina.

Most first-time migrants to Argentina are between 25 and 34 years of age (*See,* Table 3). Table 4 shows that most first time migrants — particularly those from urban areas — are unmarried. Furthermore, the longer the duration of the migration or the more trips made by a migrant, the greater the likelihood that the migrant would get married in Argentina or during a return trip to Bolivia. Our survey found that of those who migrated more than 4 years, about 25 percent got married during a migration, whereas only 2 percent of those with less than 4 years of migratory experience married during a migration.

The tendency is for temporary Bolivian migrants to leave their wives in the place of origin. Of our sample of 143 migrants, 104 wives had never been to Argentina; 26 accompanied or visited their husbands; and 13 women travelled unmarried (of these 8 got married in Argentina and 5 remained unmarried).

TABLE 3
Age of First-Time Migration for Urban and Rural Migrants

Age Group	Urban Number	%	Rural Number	%	Total Number	%
Less than 19	4	2.8	2	1.4	6	4.3
20 - 24	3	2.1	2	1.4	5	3.5
25 - 29	16	11.3	36	25.5	52	36.9
30 - 34	12	8.5	35	24.8	47	33.3
35 - 40	9	6.4	7	5.0	16	11.3
41 - 50	3	2.1	6	4.3	9	6.4
51 - 60	1	0.7	3	2.1	4	2.8
61+	1	0.7	1	0.7	2	1.4
Total[a]	49	34.6	92	65.2	141	99.9

Note: [a] Please note that due to rounding, not all percentage totals listed in this table and others will add up to 100 percent.

TABLE 4
Marital Status for First-Time Rural and Urban Migrants

Status	Urban Number	%	Rural Number	%	Total Number	%
Unmarried	32	22.7	53	37.6	85	60.3
Married	15	10.6	37	26.2	52	36.9
Free Union	1	.7	—	—	1	0.7
Separated	1	.7	—	—	1	0.7
Widowed	—	—	2	1.4	2	1.4
Total	49	34.7	92	65.2	141	100

The vast majority of the migrants (76 percent) travel directly to the metropolitan area of Buenos Aires. Most migrants travel to Argentina with relatives or friends and are housed in homes of relatives or friends. Table 5 shows the kind of residence in which migrants live according to the number of migrations. First-time migrants primarily live in relatives' residences without charge, and this pattern continues for those who migrate more than once. By the fourth migration, however, a sizeable proportion of the migrants live in their own homes. Thus, multiple migrations to Argentina do allow for increased economic independence.

TABLE 5

Residences of Migrants to Argentina by Frequency of Migration
(in percentages)

	Number of Migrations			
Residence	1	2	3	4
Own Home	5.7	9.3	16.7	30.8
Rent	2.1	—	3.3	—
Settlement/Camp	15.6	9.3	20.0	15.4
Hotel/Pension	—	—	3.3	—
Relatives (rent free)	49.6	57.4	43.3	46.2
Other (only pay food)	2.8	—	6.7	7.7
Not Reported	24.1	24.1	6.7	—
Total	99.9	100.1	100.0	100.1

The majority of the migrants travel by train to Argentina. Since Bolivians do not require a passport to enter Argentina, most migrants travel with a safe-conduct document, which permits them to remain in the country for 90 days. A small portion of the migrants travel by air when exchange rates are favorable and when they have residency documents.

The Role of Women in the Migratory Process

In order to understand how women participate in the migratory system, it is necessary to analyze the role of women in the Bolivian urban and rural economies. Various studies have demonstrated that women participate significantly in the family economy and are the principal administrators of the household (Jelin, 1984; and Jelin, *et al.*, 1983; Harris, 1984). Women residing in the urban and rural areas of Cochabamba enjoy a certain degree of autonomy *vis-à-vis* men in managing economic resources (León, 1984; CERES, 1981; Calderón and Rivera, 1984).

In the areas we studied, females, from a very early age, have always participated in domestic and agricultural tasks in both rural and urban households. These tasks have prepared young women to assume many of the roles required in the economic strategies of the household. As girls, they begin their activities in the domestic sphere and soon move into the complex inter-regional system of urban and rural markets. Women in the upper valley are not wage earners. In the lower valley and in Cochabamba, women are employed as domestic workers, blue-collar workers, and temporary migrants. This does not imply, however, that they have abandoned their normal domestic, agricultural, artisanal, or commercial activities.

The role of women in the areas we studied is also determined by the organization of the household; that is, by its division of labor and structure (nuclear or extended family). The domestic cycle of the household also defines the role and position of woman/daughter within the family, since older children generally have more responsibilities (Jelin *et al.*, 1983:160).

In rural areas, young girls (ages 5 or 6) begin participating in domestic activities by caring for animals. Some girls attend school until age 10; a few finish primary school; very few enter secondary school. At age 12 or 13, adolescent women begin to learn a trade with their mothers or in a shop. By age 15, they become involved in regional trade and commerce while they continue their domestic and agricultural duties.

Young women in the city of Cochabamba follow typical urban economic and cultural patterns. For the most part, they are responsible for fewer domestic tasks and economic activities than their rural counterparts and participate more in school.

Marriage marks an important transition for young women. It begins a long process of forming a new household without destroying ties and activities associated with the natal household. When two people marry, they generally live with the man's parents until they are able to build a house. The woman becomes integrated into the man's family and begins to undertake many household responsibilities. This does not mean that she has to abandon her own trade and commercial activities. In some cases, a husband may join his wife in the activities she developed before they were married.

When her children are first born, the woman dedicates most of her time to childcare. She undertakes activities which do not require leaving the household, *e.g.*, sewing, weaving, or embroidery of articles that others sell. When her children are grown, she returns to commercial activities and travels to markets throughout the valley and city.

The roles of women vary according to the nature of migration within the household, the composition and organization of labor in the household, and the women's occupations.

When a couple is first married, the woman stays in Bolivia while her husband migrates to Argentina. If he maintains a job in Argentina for many years, the household will become consolidated "at a distance" and children will be conceived during the husband's visits. On the other hand, if the husband migrates after they have been married for many years, the couple probably lives separately and the children remain with their mother. Nevertheless, separate residences and economic independence does not necessarily imply total autonomy for the woman. While her husband is away from the household, parents, relatives, and in-laws often visit her and exercise a certain degree of control and protection over her.

A central purpose of our study was to analyze how women organize daily activities of the family while their husbands are absent from the households. In general, it appears that the women are able to manage their households very easily.

Some 67 percent of the migrants indicated they did not send money home. Among those who did send remittances, very few sent funds on a regular basis; only two of the 143 migrants sent bank drafts; most sent money whenever they could with a friend, or took money home during a visit. Therefore, the majority of the families in Bolivia cannot depend on remittances for their daily support.

For the most part, women develop activities that generate income for the daily maintenance of their families. Any remittances sent by their husbands are used for purchasing materials to construct or amplify a house, for purchasing animals, paying debts, or for savings to be used as investments upon the husband's return.

In principle, the absence of the husband can destabilize the family. We discovered, however, that most families do not consider the absence of the husband to be a problem. When we questioned them about problems, families generally gave stereotyped answers. Thus, the maintenance and consolidation of the household are not the exclusive responsibility of the male household head. In some cases, the woman plays a more determinant role in acquiring income and making economic decisions. In some cases, the woman motivates her husband to migrate. Indeed, one woman stated: "I always told him: You have to go; here you will never make a good living. Your parents do not even own land. Perhaps you want to be as poor as they are? So I sold a cow to pay for his passage. He never gave me any money — I gave money to him."

If the decision to migrate is shared, the woman accepts the prolonged absence of her husband and the economic necessity of managing the household in his absence. We found only two cases in which migration and the absence of the husband influenced the dissolution of the marriage. In both instances the disruption was caused by infidelity on the part of the woman.

Of the 143 families we interviewed, only 39 women had traveled to Argentina. Of this subgroup, 8 got married in Argentina, 5 returned to Bolivia as unmarried women, and 26 had been married when they migrated.

In a discussion of the woman's role in migration, it is important to note Balán's (1985:61) distinction between primary movers and secondary movers. Primary movers or migrants are those whose decisions to migrate are linked to the labor market possibilities; their employment status, earnings, or career possibilities give rise to the decision to migrate. Secondary movers, who may or may not have economic activities in their place of origin or at their destination, migrate as a result of a decision of a primary mover.

Since migration to Argentina is fundamentally masculine, Bolivian women are secondary movers. The few unmarried women who migrate are also secondary movers, because their migration (always temporary) is closely tied to relatives who take and integrate them into their households. These women did not make a clear distinction between traveling to visit relatives and traveling in order to work.

Bolivian women who travel to Argentina generally work as street sellers, domestic laborers, or as artisans. Unmarried women are employed in machine-sewing and weaving by other Bolivian women who sign contracts with Korean and Argentine clothing manufacturers. These single women are paid on a piecework basis or by the hour as domestic workers. Women find employment through networks of relatives or through employment offices.

The act of migration does not disrupt women's traditional obligations and roles in the domestic economy. Rather, women migrants recreate an environment in Argentina that mirrors the one found in Bolivia. For example, the woman is always tied to the informal sector whether she works in a small business, shop, family business or domestic service. Unmarried women re-create and maintain family networks in Argentina. Married women establish eating places (*pensiones*) for other Bolivians, receive relatives, organize family labor networks, and replicate cultural patterns found in their place of origin.

Temporary Migration and Life Cycle

In order to portray distinct situations before, during and after migration, we developed a method of interviewing that allowed us to capture the diachronic character of migration. Temporary migration is best viewed as one of several possible life strategies aimed at fulfilling the needs of the family economy. There are many migrant families who, after working in Buenos Aires, manage to broaden their economic base. In many cases migration to Argentina permits them to invest in their children's education, to buy a vehicle, a lot, land, or build a house. Nonetheless, migration is but one economic option available to them. It is not the only source of savings or investment since, in the absence of the husband, other members continue to earn income for the household. While migration moves household members into the formal wage-earning market, it does not necessarily imply the destruction of that segment of the family economy which is supported by self-employment in the informal sector.

Therefore, migration can be interpreted as a sort of "parenthesis" in a process whose ideal outcome is self-employment, the accumulation of some capital, and sufficient control over a social and geographical space to maintain economic diversification. Access to a wide range of information and social relations, to residences at key locations or a vehicle, and the preservation of identity with one's place of origin are the basic resources required to maintain a dynamic and diversified domestic economy.

The following sketches will illustrate some of the significant tendencies we have been discussing throughout the study.

Bonifacio is 36 years old and lives in a village in the upper valley. He attended primary school and one year of secondary school. Like many other young men, his household duties included feeding and caring for the animals and assisting in diverse agricultural activities.

At age 15 he traveled to Argentina and stayed there for nine years. He returned to his village every two years. On one visit he was married in a civil ceremony; on the next visit, he was married in a religious ceremony. During his entire stay in Argentina, his wife and children lived with his family in the upper valley.

Bonifacio had many jobs in Argentina: he worked in a toy factory, was a night guard in a high school, and was employed as a construction worker. When he returned to Cochabamba in 1975, he continued working in the construction industry. He returned to Bolivia, "because I had a family to raise and besides, Argentina was not prosperous then; I couldn't save money".

When his father died in 1980, Bonifacio left his construction job and opened a livestock business. His father had been in the livestock trade and Bonifacio wanted to pursue the same career. He was able to start the business with the salary and savings he acquired from the construction job.

In 1982, Bonifacio and his family moved from the upper valley to the city of Cochabamba. "My wife and I wanted our children to get a better education in the city". After 1982, he became a trader in agricultural products. He traveled throughout the region buying and selling local products with a truck he was able to purchase. His business forced him to be away from home often.

To summarize, the skills Bonifacio acquired in Argentina as a construction worker were useful in Cochabamba. His wages and savings from jobs in Bolivia allowed him ultimately to establish his own business. Today, Bonifacio owns land, a truck, and has a house in the valley and the city.

Juan is 41 years old and is from a village in the upper valley. He attended primary school until the sixth grade. He quit school due to economic problems. He learned hat-making from his father and assumed more responsibility for agricultural chores. At age 15 he worked in a small shop where he learned how to make women's skirts.

He migrated to Buenos Aires when he was 18 and at first lived with one of his brothers. During a four year period in Buenos Aires, he worked as a laborer in a concrete business and later as a journeyman carpenter.

He returned a few times to Bolivia and in 1965 was married in a civil ceremony. He and his wife lived with his family for four years during which time Juan was an agricultural worker and also worked as a hat maker with his father. His wife sold pork. By 1969 he and his wife had two children.

Juan and his family migrated to Argentina in 1969 and lived with his brother for seven years. Juan again worked as a carpenter for various contractors; his wife sewed clothes on a piece-rate basis for Koreans. During a visit to Bolivia, Juan bought some land near Santa Cruz.

When Juan and his family were repatriated in 1976, they returned to their village in the upper valley. They had a house built on a lot given to them by Juan's father while they were in Argentina. Upon returning to the region, Juan and his wife renewed their artisanal, agricultural, and commercial activities, and they were able to purchase farmland in the valley.

Juan returned alone to Buenos Aires in 1980 where he worked for two years as a skilled construction worker. When Juan returned to Bolivia in 1982, he and his wife sold their land in Santa Cruz and bought a lot in Cochabamba where they built a second house. In 1984 they moved permanently to Cochabamba and became coca merchants. This business allows Juan and his family to maintain contact with the upper valley.

Hipólito, 47 years old, is married and has eight children. He lives in Cochabamba and is a self-employed mason. Hipólito was born in the upper valley and attended primary school there until third grade. At the age of 10 he learned how to manage and care for animals by working closely with his father, and he also helped his mother make *chicha*.

When he was fifteen, Hipólito and his uncle traveled to Argentina but were not permitted to cross the border. They stayed in Santa Cruz for two years and both worked as masons. Hipólito returned to live and work with his parents in the upper valley, then joined the Bolivian military at age 19, and got married at age 22.

In 1959, Hipólito migrated to Buenos Aires; his wife and child stayed in Bolivia. He worked for 16 years in Argentina and returned to Bolivia 12 times during this period. His wife and family (by 1975 they had six children) always lived in Bolivia. He was employed in Argentina by the Ford-Alfali motor company on the assembly line and later worked as a mason and a construction foreman. In 1967, he started his own construction and contracting business. His oldest son joined him in 1972 in his small construction business. After his son returned to Bolivia in 1974, Hipólito remained in Buenos Aires and worked as a contractor until 1976. During his 16 years in the city, he first lived with relatives in a squalid neighborhood, then lived in a pension, and later moved into a rented house in Buenos Aires province.

Hipólito had sent regular remittances to Bolivia, although there were some variations. In the first few years, he generally brought money with him. During his last period of residence in Buenos Aires he sent money every three months through the Banco Argentino. These funds were used to buy a lot and build a house in Cochabamba. Hipólito returned to Bolivia in 1976 and brought his savings and masonry tools. He and his family moved into the house in Cochabamba. Hipólito works as a contract mason but still maintains contact with the upper valley, especially during planting and harvest times.

The oldest of five children, *Eulogio* is 22 years old. He and his parents are peasants from Ucureña. He is married and has two children. He has worked as a tailor since he was 17 in order to help his family earn money.

In Argentina, he worked for a construction firm which employed nearly 1,000 Bolivians from the valleys. His Bolivian contact in Buenos Aires gave him the name of a friend with whom he first lived. His work crew took turns preparing meals and has used part of the first floor of the building under construction as their housing. This allowed them to save money used normally for meals and transportation and to work longer hours. Eulogio has moved up in status and pay as a mason and has assumed more responsibilities.

Eulogio returned to Bolivia after 17 months in Buenos Aires. As soon as his first child was born, he returned to Argentina in order to work and save more money. His wife stayed in Bolivia and lived in a house he built on a lot given to him by his father.

This case history is quite typical of recent Bolivian migration to Argentina. Eulogio obtained a job through a Bolivian contact and was able to enter a more established enterprise. He began as a day-laborer without much experience and managed to increase his skill, rank, and salary. He is registered as a worker, "married with four children" in order to obtain social benefits for his family.

These four vignettes of the migrants and their families show some of the tendencies we have been describing. A general pattern emerges from the occupations the Bolivians had before migrating to Argentina and upon returning to Bolivia. Table 6 shows the occupations rural migrants had before migrating to Argentina. Nearly one-half (49 percent) worked in agriculture. Two-thirds of these workers worked on their own land, one-third worked on family land. Another significant proportion of the migrants were employed in the traditional artisan trades (*e.g.*, hat-making, tailors, barbers, bakers) and in technical trades (*e.g.*, plumbing, mechanics, and carpentry). Most of the artisans were skilled workers in their trades or shop owners. Another small proportion worked as day laborers in masonry. In short, most Bolivian migrants were self-employed in diverse occupations before they traveled to Argentina.

Table 7 shows the prior occupations of urban Bolivian migrants. Many worked initially on their family's land in rural areas before migrating to Argentina. They settled in urban areas in Cochabamba after they had worked in Buenos Aires. These migrants also worked in traditional and technical trades before migrating to Argentina.

The different occupations held by Bolivian workers in Argentina are shown in Table 8. The majority of the workers were employed in a wide range of jobs in the construction industry. Most migrants started as day laborers in construction and were able to ascend to other positions including foreman during the same period of residency in Argentina. Those who migrated more than once managed to enter the construction industry at a higher status. Furthermore, they tended to work in only one job probably because they had come to know the contractor.

The current occupations of migrants who have returned to Bolivia are presented in Table 9. Rural migrants work primarily in agriculture, but they have managed to become more independent by investing in land, lots, and homes. They have been able to establish more autonomous households after returning from Argentina. Table 9 also shows that more rural migrants have entered commercial activities, while fewer are involved in artisan trades.

Urban workers, on the other hand, are less likely to work in agriculture after returning from Argentina. Most of the urban migrants were originally from a rural area and moved to an urban area when they returned to Bolivia. Thus, migration to Argentina for these workers contributed to a later urban migration in their native country. While they may no longer be agricultural workers in the strict sense, many still maintain ties to their rural places of origin by working on the family's land or even by obtaining their own land. Finally, there is a significant

TABLE 6

Occupations of Rural Bolivian Workers Before Migrating to Argentina

Occupation	Number	%
Agriculture	45	48.9
Own Land	30	32.6
Family Land	14	15.2
Day Laborer	1	1.1
Traditional Trades	14	15.2
Apprentice	1	1.1
Skilled	3	3.3
Shop Owner	10	10.9
Technical Trades	6	6.5
Apprentice	2	2.2
Skilled	1	1.1
Shop Owner	3	3.3
Mason-Day Laborer	5	5.4
Student	7	7.6
Military	3	3.3
Musician	3	3.3
Teacher	3	3.3
White Collar	2	2.2
Blue Collar	1	1.1
Transportation-Chauffeur	1	1.1
Commerce	1	1.1
Other	1	1.1
Total	92	100.1

increase in the number of urban workers involved in commercial activities, especially in marketing coca. Urban workers are more highly represented as masons than are rural workers. These workers transferred the skills they obtained in masonry and construction in Argentina to the labor market in Bolivia. To be sure, the construction employers reported that they actively recruit workers with previous experience in Argentina.

TABLE 7

Occupations of Urban Bolivian Workers Before Migrating to Argentina

Occupation	Number	%
Agriculture	13	**26.0**
Own Land	4	8.0
Family Land	9	18.0
Traditional Trades	5	**10.0**
Apprentice	1	2.0
Shop Owner	2	4.0
Technical Trades	5	**10.0**
Apprentice	1	2.0
Shop Owner	4	8.0
Student	6	12.0
Transportation-Chauffeur	5	10.0
Blue Collar	5	10.0
White Collar	1	2.0
Musician	1	2.0
Mason-Day Laborer	3	6.0
Military	1	2.0
Commerce	2	4.0
Other	3	6.0
Total	50	100.0

Tables 10 and 11 show the occupational categories of Bolivian migrants before they migrated, immediately upon their return to Bolivia, and their current occupation. Table 10 shows that 11 percent of the rural migrants worked in a family enterprise without pay immediately upon their return, while 7 percent were directly dependent on their families. Nevertheless, the proportion of those who were dependent on their families declined from 12 percent before migration to 4 percent at the present time. A great increase occurred in the proportion of self-employed workers. Whereas 56 percent of the workers were self-employed before they migrated, 79 percent are currently self-employed. Migration not only increased independence but also created new households.

TABLE 8

Occupations of Bolivian Migrants in Argentina

| | First Trip | | | | | |
Occupation	First Job		Second Job		Third Job	
Mason-Day Laborer and Semi-Skilled	80	56.7%	23	16.3%	1	0.7%
Mason-Skilled and Foreman	11	7.8	25	17.7	17	12.1
Contractor	1	0.7	—	—	3	2.1
Day Laborer	14	9.9	7	5.0	1	0.7
Technical Trade Assistant	8	5.7	1	0.7	—	—
Technical Trade Skilled	2	1.4	2	1.4	1	0.7
Agricultural Day Laborer	11	7.8	3	2.1	—	—
Other	12	8.5	8	5.7	2	1.4
Without Employment[a]	2	1.4	72	51.1	115	82.1
Total	141		141		140	

	Second Trip					
Mason-Day Laborer and Semi-Skilled	17	31.5%	3	5.5%	—	—
Mason-Skilled and Foreman	24	44.4	5	9.1	2	3.7
Contractor	—	—	—	—	—	—
Day Laborer	2	3.7	—	—	—	—
Technical Trade Assistant	2	3.7	—	—	1	1.9
Technical Trade Skilled	1	1.9	1	1.8	1	1.9
Agricultural Day Laborer	3	5.5	—	—	—	—
Other	4	7.4	—	—	—	—
Without Employment[a]	1	1.9	46	83.6	50	92.6

TABLE 8 (Continued)
Occupations of Bolivian Migrants in Argentina

Occupation	Third Trip					
	First Job		Second Job		Third Job	
Mason-Day Laborer and Semi-Skilled	6	20.0%	1	3.3%	—	—
Mason-Skilled and Foreman	17	56.7	1	3.3	—	—
Contractor	2	6.7	—	—	—	—
Day Laborer	3	10.0	—	—	—	—
Technical Trade Assistant	—	—	—	—	—	—
Technical Trade Skilled	1	3.3	1	3.3	—	—
Agricultural Day Laborer	—	—	—	—	—	—
Other	1	3.3	2	6.7	—	—
Without Employment[a]	—	—	25	83.3	30	100.0%

Note: [a] The percentages listed here do not reflect unemployment, but rather the fact that most migrants retained their first jobs.

The occupational categories of urban workers presented in Table 11 also show marked increases in workers who are self-employed. The proportion of unpaid family workers has decreased. Urban workers are more likely to be wage earners and day laborers than are rural workers. Those who are dependent on their families also decreased in the case of urban workers.

Finally, Table 12 compares the occupations that both rural and urban migrants had in Bolivia, Argentina, and those that they currently hold. Two-thirds of the migrants are currently self-employed in Bolivia; only 43 percent were self-employed before they migrated. While only 14 percent of the migrants were wage workers in Bolivia, some 83 percent became wage workers in Argentina. Many of these workers may not have been able to enter this category upon their return to Bolivia; thus, they may have decided to become self-employed. In short, migration did change the occupational status of Bolivian workers.

TABLE 9

Current Occupations of Bolivian Migrants Who Returned from Argentina

Occupations	Rural Workers		Urban Workers	
	No.	%	No.	%
Agriculture	54	65.8	1	2.2
Own Land	52	63.4	1	2.2
Family Land	1	1.2	—	—
Day Laborer	1	1.2	—	—
Commerce	7	8.5	11	23.9
Coca	2	2.4	2	4.3
Chicha	3	3.7	5	10.9
Other	2	2.4	4	8.7
Masonry	6	7.3	11	23.9
Day Laborer	5	6.1	8	17.4
Contractor	1	1.2	3	6.5
Traditional Trades	—	—	3	6.5
Shop Owner	—	—	2	4.3
Skilled	—	—	1	2.2
Technical Trades	3	3.7	6	13.0
Shop Owner	3	3.7	3	6.5
Skilled	—	—	3	6.5
Student	1	1.2	1	2.2
Military	1	1.2	—	—
Blue Collar	—	—	3	6.5
White Collar	3	3.7	1	2.2
Teacher	5	6.1	1	2.2
Musician	1	1.2	—	—
Transportation	—	—	7	15.2
Chauffeur	—	—	3	6.5
Owner	—	—	4	8.7
Other	1	1.2	46	100.0
Total	82	100.0	46	100.0

TABLE 10

Occupational Categories of Rural Workers Before Migrating, Upon Return and Currently

Category	Before		Return		Current	
	No.	%	No.	%	No.	%
Family Worker-Paid	11	12.0	1	1.1	—	—
Family Worker-Unpaid	4	4.3	10	10.9	1	1.1
Wage Worker	8	8.7	7	7.6	8	8.7
Day Laborer	7	7.6	12	13.0	7	7.6
Self-Employed	51	55.4	56	60.9	72	78.3
Dependent	11	12.0	6	6.5	4	4.3
Total	92	100.0	92	100.0	92	100.0

TABLE 11

Occupational Categories of Urban Workers Before Migration, Upon Return and Currently

Category	Before		After		Current	
	No.	%	No.	%	No.	%
Family Worker-Paid	—	—	—	—	—	—
Family Worker-Unpaid	12	24.5	7	14.3	—	—
Wage Worker	13	26.5	15	30.6	16	32.0
Day Laborer	4	8.2	9	18.4	5	10.0
Self-Employed	9	18.4	13	26.5	25	50.0
Dependent	11	22.4	5	10.2	4	8.0
Total	49	100.0	49	100.0	50	100.0

Table 13 compares how rural and urban workers have invested their wages and savings in Bolivia upon returning to their home country. Many rural migrants invest their money in land, while urban migrants often invest in housing. Both types of migrants also utilize their resources for household goods, debts, savings, *etc.* That rural migrants invest in land and housing reveals the importance assigned to consolidating the rural household. Urban migrants tend to invest in housing or in amplifying their existing homes. Both situations show that investments in one way or another serve to stabilize the migrants' household.

TABLE 12

Occupational Categories of Rural and Urban Workers Before Migrating, in Argentina, and Current Category

Category	Before		Argentina		Current	
	No.	%	No.	%	No.	%
Family Worker-Paid	11	7.8	5	3.5	—	—
Family Worker-Unpaid	16	11.3	—	—	1	0.7
Wage Worker	21	14.9	117	83.0	25	17.7
Day Laborer	11	7.8	16	11.3	12	8.5
Self-Employed	60	42.6	3	2.1	95	67.4
Dependent	22	15.6	—	—	8	5.7
Total	141	100.0	141	99.9	141	100.0

TABLE 13

Investments Made by Rural and Urban Migrants Upon Returning to Bolivia

Investments[1]	Urban		Rural		Total	
	No.	%	No.	%	No.	%
Land	2	2.0	27	14.3	29	10.0
Agriculture[2]	—	—	12	6.3	12	4.2
Housing[3]	25	25.0	13	6.9	38	13.1
House Improvement	5	5.0	6	3.2	11	3.8
Pre-Marital Expenses	6	6.0	8	4.2	14	4.8
Other Family Expenses[4]	9	9.0	15	7.9	24	8.3
Other Household Expenses[5]	15	15.0	37	19.6	52	18.0
Motor Vehicle	6	6.0	1	0.5	7	2.4
Commercial[6]	2	2.0	3	1.6	5	1.7
None	30	30.0	67	35.4	97	33.6
Total	100	100.0	189	99.9	289	99.9

Notes: [1] Calculated on the basis of each trip taken.

[2] Livestock, equipment, other.

[3] Purchase of a lot, house, construction of house.

[4] Children's education, assistance for parents, burials.

[5] Household utensils, debts, savings, transportation.

[6] Shop, commercial equipment.

Methodological and Conceptual Problems

An important consideration in studying international labor migration is determining whether a migrant is "permanent" or "temporary". Our investigation found a variety of different types of migrants; for example, a migrant who worked in Argentina for 20 years while his family remained in Bolivia; unmarried migrants who returned after 10 or 15 years and established families; migrants who traveled with their families to Buenos Aires, bought a house there, and then returned some years later to begin anew in Bolivia.

What distinguishes a temporary migrant from a permanent one are the ties maintained with the place of origin and the continual reinforcement of family relations. Many migrants visit their families on a regular basis, but the determining characteristic of a temporary migrant is not the short duration of a trip but the type of strategy that gives meaning to the migration. In this sense, perhaps, migration is best considered as a decision "to go to work" instead of a decision to "migrate".

In order to understand the true dimensions of temporary migration, it must be situated within the context of households which develop strategies aimed at the goal of self-employment. The head of the family or other member decides "to go to work", *i.e.*, migrate as part of this household strategy.

Methodological problems also arise over the difference between a permanent return and a visit. For example, some migrants work in Argentina and return to Bolivia frequently for long periods of time. Over the duration of their years in Argentina, the migrants work for more than one firm and generally change jobs. In these cases, we ask ourselves whether we are dealing with one trip abroad with numerous vacations home or various migrations and returns. In other cases, migrants do not have a steady job in Argentina but maintain contacts there and keep their options open; trips are the result of a contingency plan to travel in search of employment after having evaluated other possibilities in Bolivia.

These considerations and examples lead us to think that what remains permanent is the maintenance of social networks — while the period of residence in Argentina may be temporary. The migrants and returning migrants manage these networks as their fundamental strategy. Considering that rural and urban households develop diversified strategies, it would not be sensible to think that migration to Argentina becomes the only alternative. Rather, it is always an option open for some, a recourse for others. Thus, migration to Argentina, as an option, is no different than the spatial mobility and social networks that these households develop within the region of Cochabamba.

An integral part of this migratory system is that Argentina offers flexibility of income, return, and residency. It does not require visas or return trip passage in order for Bolivians to enter the country. At the border, a traveler can obtain a 90 day permit to enter the country by presenting an identity card and a safe-conduct pass.

The construction industry in Buenos Aires offers great flexibility for Bolivian migrants. Despite the economic deterioration of the construction industry, there is a well established demand for Bolivian workers since workers without families can live on the job-site or in a camp and work with greater intensity and longer hours. The construction industry also provides laborers with a specific job for a fixed period of time. This allows the migrant to return to Bolivia with the relative assurance that another job will await him upon returning to Buenos Aires. Labor contracts in the construction industry are flexible. Migrants without proper documents cannot be hired directly by construction companies; instead, they are recruited by contractors and referred to as Argentines. The contractors often allow the migrant to negotiate absences from work which can be covered by friends or relatives.

Many studies about temporary migration become too tightly bound by formal methodologies to analyze why a person migrates. Migrants consider themselves workers. To go to work or to get a job does not necessarily imply migration in the formal sense. Whether a migrant moves within the country or abroad, his/her disposition is that of moving when it is convenient. An old muleteer from the highlands of Capinota (in Cochabamba) who traveled with his herd to Uyuni (Potosí) and later migrated to Buenos Aires to work in construction, told us how easy it was to move from one job to another based on social and family contacts. For this man, migration to Buenos Aires was just one of many options, no different than those available to him in Bolivia.

The majority of those we interviewed did not decide beforehand how long they would stay in Argentina. In fact, our very questions sometimes provoked the respondents to a more elaborate discussion of their decision-making than we suspect actually occurred at the time of migration. Often answers to our questions did not reflect a causal decision to migrate; many times workers departed suddenly. Women often were not able to recount the length of time their husbands were in Argentina, where they were working, or when they might get news from them. Nonetheless, women were certain that their husbands would find jobs, would live with family, and maintain contact from Buenos Aires.

It is difficult to elaborate with any specificity on the reasons for migrating. De Oliveira and Muñoz (1972:9-11) mention that migrants rationalize their motivations for migration *a posteriori*. Singer (1981:58) places migrants' motivations in a broader context:

Migration is probably a social process whose active unit is not the individual but the group (family). When one wants to study social processes, the data obtained from individuals lead in the majority of the cases to a psychological analysis in which the principal macro-social conditions are distorted if not omitted. In the case of internal migrations, the collective nature of the process is so pronounced that almost always the reasons for migrating fall into two categories: an economic motivation or to accompany a spouse. The stereotypical form of the answers indicates that the investigation did not focus on those who could have offered an answer capable of elucidating the factors that caused migration.

While it is certain that economic factors enter into the decision to migrate, other factors surrounding the household are also important. The reason can be related to a certain moment in the individual's or family's life. A young adolescent man, evidently, can afford to be absent from the household, and his decision to migrate can be related to acquiring work experience, saving money, and, upon returning, getting married and starting a family. The head of an older family leaves with the assurance that his wife can rely on fixed supplies and savings and can thus continue to maintain diversified economic activities. At the same time, situational factors may motivate the immediate departure of a worker. Examples of these situations are the return of a friend or relative from Buenos Aires, and news about available jobs.

In our field research, we included a specific question about why persons migrated. In general, almost all of the answers were formal or standard responses. When we took life and work histories of the migrants they expressed their reasons more spontaneously, for example:

"I wanted to make money".
"Work was scarce here and my brother sent for me".
"I couldn't live like this any longer".
"To prove that one could make a good living".
"My brother asked me to go with him".
"Not to get mixed up in problems".
"To earn money to pay a debt".
"To earn money to buy land".
"To take medicine to my brother".
"To earn money in order to get married".
"To pay for the construction of my house".

Returnees explained their decision to return from Argentina in the following terms:

"I applied to the Military College".
"I came to set up a shop".
"My mother needed me".
"I rejoined the teaching profession".
"So my wife would not be alone".
"I wanted to experience Argentina; not to remain there".
"To have a better time than in Argentina".
"My feelings for my family didn't let me stay".
"I worried about my family".
"My sister died".
"My family did not get used to living in Buenos Aires".
"My father gave me an inheritance".

State Migration Policies

International labor migration from Bolivia to neighboring countries
and its impact on sending areas should be understood in the following
context. Bolivia has a national economy in which the majority of urban
and rural workers are not incorporated into wage earning jobs in the
formal economy. Industry is still at an incipient stage. The mining industry relies largely on a surplus labor force that lives in mining camps.
The industry and workers confronted a brutal crisis after the fall of tin
prices and other metals. Faced with massive dismissals, the labor force
had to use its own creativity to survive.

A significant proportion of the economically active population in Bolivia are self-employed. For example, some small landowners complement their agricultural activity with non-agricultural activities such as
trade, transportation, and commerce. Wage-earning miners, factory
workers, and day laborers whose average monthly salaries do not reach
U.S. $50 also resort to self-employment activities. This phenomenon re-
quires a carefully organized and coordinated effort among members of
the household. Nevertheless, the existence of a large self-employed
labor force is not a simple consequence of the current economic crises;
historically, many sectors of Bolivian society have been involved in self-
employment activities. This historical fact makes Bolivia quite different
from more developed countries that have a large wage-earning and
formal labor force or where the welfare state has created public assistance programs for the unemployed.

The phenomenon of self-employment in the informal economy has
been ignored by governments, economic planners, and political parties.
These sectors are generally more concerned with the wage-earning
labor market, salary demands, and the urban family's economic situation. Likewise, the government has ignored the fundamental role that
the peasantry plays as the principal producer and supplier of the basic

food commodities for the country. There is an erroneous impression
that the peasantry is homogenous. The government does not realize
the regional and local differences that exist within this sector of
society nor the different ways peasants are inserted into the economy.
In the valleys of Cochabamba, peasant economies cannot be
understood without recognizing the important extra-agricultural activities including migration which form an integral part of the peasant
economy. Without these diverse economic activities, the so-called "rural
exodus" would be much greater in Bolivia. What differentiates Bolivia
from other countries is that the majority of the peasants have developed
economic and social strategies to support themselves in the countryside,
notwithstanding the lack of state assistance, the poor economic base,
and the absence of a solid infrastructure.

The government has been inefficient and weak in generating employment and in providing basic services. If the government does not
provide the population with essential services such as education, pre-
ventive health care, medical assistance, basic services of water, electricity, and sewage, an adequate road system, credit and other facilities,
we can hardly imagine how it could exercise an effective presence in
extensive areas of the country, especially in rural zones.

To plan and recommend specific state policies to adddress the issue
of temporary international labor migration presents special difficulties.
One example of the state's policy was the repatriation program carried
out by the governments of Banzer (Bolivia) and Videla (Argentina) in
1976. After the eradication of "villas miserias" in Buenos Aires and the
massive relocation of the population to outlying areas, a controversy
arose in Bolivia over the discrimination against immigrants in Argentina. Thus, the governments reached an agreement for the return of
Bolivian migrants and their families. The Bolivian government allowed
duty-free imports, and promised house plots, credits for housing, and
the possibility of obtaining employment; the Argentine government arranged for transportation, provided that the migrants forfeit their residency papers. As was expected, soon after 1,000 families returned, the
Bolivian government reneged on its promises. Nearly 200 families in
Cochabamba organized a repatriates' cooperative in order to pressure
the government to grant urban lots for housing. The repatriates
achieved their objectives after a few years, but the government never
extended credits or other services.

The Bolivian government apparently had good intentions with this
program, but it did not consider that migration was a complex process.
It assumed that there existed "permanent" migrants who would easily
choose, with minimal incentives, to return to Bolivia. It did not realize
that migration to Argentina was just one of many options. Thus, many

families were attracted by the incentive to import duty-free household goods back to Bolivia, but they did not consider their return to Bolivia permanent. Restrictive migration policies or repatriation incentives cannot achieve their objectives if, at the same time, broader economic transformations are not forthcoming in the country.

CONCLUSIONS

International migration is an important option among a wide gamut of activities in both rural and urban economies in Cochabamba. Temporary migration to Buenos Aires and other Argentine cities consolidates the family economy. Migration provides capital that supports households and permits them to develop certain productive activities that do not depend necessarily on wage-earning strategies but rather on self-employment and economic diversification.

From the point of view of rural migrants, a journey to Argentina permits them to strengthen their agricultural activities within a diversified economic framework that is also common to other households that do not migrate to Argentina. For urban migrants, the ability to go to Argentina is one of many options and allows them to cope with the precarious urban living situation. It also provides resources and certain "know-how" in adapting to urban employment patterns and in managing multiple resources and businesses.

For many rural migrants, the trip to Argentina is a bridge to the city of Cochabamba. This does not mean that rural migrants abandon the countryside. In maintaining a double residency, they preserve family ties, access to land and produce, and contacts that are crucial for their commerical enterprises.

Urban and rural migrations to Argentina are not very different. Many of the inhabitants of Cochabamba who live in marginal neighborhoods are recent migrants from rural areas. They tend to participate in the large segment of the urban economy that is characterized by self-employment in diverse activities. Many households are economically, socially, and culturally attached to their place of origin and utilize a family strategy to combine resources, unite efforts, or complement the economic roles of their members.

Both rural and urban women develop a variety of economic activities outside of their domestic sphere and maintain strong ties to their places of origin. They demonstrate a considerable degree of specialization, particularly in commerce, which reveals a degree of economic autonomy that permits them to maintain the daily subsistence of their families without relying upon remittances from their husbands. It also permits men to be away for long periods of time and to develop a long-term orientation to employment in Argentina. For this reason, a prolonged absence of the husband does not necessarily destabilize the household; the extended family serves to maintain and support it.

As a result of the low labor demand in the Bolivian industrial and construction sectors and the marked wage differentials between Bolivia and Argentina, migration will remain a viable economic option. It is significant that the majority of the migrants we interviewed consider their self-employment activities as a marketable resource and a better option than being tied to a fixed job, despite the benefits of social security and job stability. Migrants continue to find Buenos Aires attractive, despite growing unemployment and a decline in the construction industry in that city. They perceive a labor demand, although it may be in smaller enterprises that require a variety of activities. Other migrants who have returned are now involved in the coca trade which they find more economically viable than remaining in Argentina.

REFERENCES

Anderson, B.
1981 "Importancia de la migración temporal desde áreas rurales a las ciudades argentinas; un estudio de caso sobre el valle de Cochabamba, Bolivia y Buenos Aires". Buenos Aires-La Paz: Centro de Estudios de Estado y Sociedad (CEDES) y Centro de Estudios de la Realidad Económica y Social (CERES).

Anderson, B. and J. Dandler
1983 "Spatial Mobility and Peasant Economy in Bolivia: The Case of Cochabamba Valley". Report presented to UNESCO. La Paz: CERES.

Antezana, F.
1969 "The *Braceros* of Bolivia: The Human Tragedy of Thousands of Bolivian Migrant Workers in Argentina", *International Migration in Latin America Series*. Geneva: Secretariat of the World Council of Churches.

Ardaya, G.
1978 "Las migraciones bolivianas hacia la ciudad de Buenos Aires, Argentina", Tesis de Maestría. Buenos Aires: Facultad Latinoamericana de Ciencias Sociales (FLACSO).

Balán, J.
1985 *International Migration in the Southern Cone*. Hemispheric Migration Project Occasional Paper Series. Washington, D.C.: Georgetown University and the Intergovernmental Committee for Migration.

1978 *Estructura agraria, desarrollo capitalista y mercados de trabajo en America Latina: La migración rural-urbana en una perspectiva histórica*. Buenos Aires: CEDES.

Balán, J., H. Browning and E. Jelin
1973 *Man in a Developing Society*. Austin and London: University of Texas Press.

Blanes, J. and G. Flores
1984 *¿A dónde va Chapare?* La Paz: CERES.

Bolton, R. and E. Mayer, Eds.
1978 *Andean Kinship and Marriage*. Washington, D.C.: American Anthropological Association.

Breton, F.
1976   "Working and Living Conditions of Migrant Workers in South America", *International Labor Review*, 114(3).

Calderón, F. and A. Rivera
1984   *La Cancha: Una gran feria campesina en la ciudad de Cochabamba*. La Paz: CERES.

Centro de Estudios de la Realidad Económica y Social (CERES) (Mimeo)
1981   "Programa de investigación sobre economía doméstica y desarrollo regional en Cochabamba". *Serie Estudios Regionales*. No. 1. La Paz.

──────────

1980   "Migración rural-rural: procesos de migración desde zonas rurales o zonas de colonización en Bolivia". La Paz.

Dandler, J., *et al.*
1985   *Apuntes generales sobre economía 'informal' y su importancia en Bolivia*. Trabajo presentado al Seminario sobre Economía "Invisible", Proyecto "Hacia una Economía a Escala Humana", La Serena, Chile: Centro de Estudios para Alternativas de Desarrollo (CEPAUR)/Fundación Dag Hammarksjold.

Dandler, J. and J. Torrico
Unpublished   *Ucureña: Campesinos diversificados*. La Paz: CERES.

De Oliveria, O. and H. Muñoz
1972   "Migraciónes internas en América Latina y crítica de algunos análisis". In *Migración y Desarrollo*. Buenos Aires: Consejo Latinoamericano de Ciencias Sociales (CLACSO).

Goody, J.
1972   "The Evolution of the Family". In *Household and Family in Past Time*. Edited by P. Laslett and R. Wall. Cambridge: Cambridge University Press.

Harris
1984   "Complementariedad y conflicto: una versión andina del hombre y de la mujer", Cuzco: *ALLPANCHIS*, XXI(25):17-42.

Jelin, E.
1984   *Familia y unidad doméstica: mundo público y vida privada*. Cuadernos CEDES. Buenos Aires: CEDES.

Jelin, E. and C. Wainerman
1983   *El deber ser y el hacer de las mujeres*. México: El Colegio de México Programa de Investigaciónes Sociales Relevantes para Politicas de Población en América Latina (PISPAL).

Larson, B.
1987   *Colonialism and Agrarian Transportation in Bolivia: Cochabamba 1550-1900*. Princeton: Princeton University Press. (In press).

Laslett, P. and R. Wall, Eds.
1972   *Household and Family in Past Time*. Cambridge: Cambridge University Press.

León, R.
1984   *Minera, campesina y comerciante: Tres dimensiones de la participación de la mujer en Cochabamba*. La Paz: CERES-U.N. Research Institute for Social Development (Mimeo).

Long, N.
1979   "Multiple Enterprise in Central Highlands of Perú". In *Entrepreneurs in Cultural Context*. Edited by S.N. Greenfield, *et al.* Albuquerque: University of New Mexico Press.

Long, N. and J. Dandler
1978   "Diversified Household Enterprise and Labour Processes in the Andes: The Montaro Region (Perú) and Cochabamba Valleys and Highlands (Bolivia)". Proposal submitted to the Social Science Research Council, London.

Mugarza, S.
1975   "Características demográficas, económicas y sociales de un barrio de migrantes bolivianos a la ciudad de Buenos Aires". *Migración*, 5:11-13.

Oficina Internacional de Trabajo (OIT), Programa Regional del Empleo para América Latina y el Caribe (PRELAC)
1979   "Distribución del ingreso, migraciones y colonización: una alternativa para el campesino boliviano", *Documento de Trabajo*. No. 176, Santiago.

_____
1975   "Empleo y recursos humanos en Bolivia". *Documento de Trabajo*, No. 85. Santiago (Mimeo).

Rivera, A. and F. Calderón
1984   *La mina urbana*. La Paz: CERES.

Roberts, B.
1978   *Cities of Peasants*. London: Edward Arnold.

Singer, P.
1981   *Economía política de la urbanización*. México: Siglo XXI.

Whiteford, S.
1981   *Workers from the North: Plantations, Bolivian Labor and the City in Northwest Argentina*. Austin: University of Texas Press.

_____
1975   "Urbanization of Rural Proletarians: Bolivian Workers in Northwest Argentina" (Mimeo).

Zuvekas, C.
1977   "Unemployment and Underdevelopment in Bolivian Agriculture". *General Working Document*. No. 3. La Paz: U.S. Agency for International Development.

DETERMINANTS AND CONSEQUENCES OF THE MIGRATION CULTURE OF ST. KITTS-NEVIS

Frank L. Mills

St. Kitts-Nevis can lay claim to a dubious distinction: In recent years, it surpassed every Commonwealth Caribbean country in the rate of net emigration as a percent of the natural rate of growth of its people. This twin-island state has had a history characterized by periodic mass departures of its natives for foreign shores. Despite a relatively high crude birthrate and (since 1950) a low mortality rate, St.Kitts-Nevis experienced zero population growth over a sixty-five year period. Between 1960 and 1970 the rate of emigration was 42 percent higher than the rate of growth in population. The size of the populace has been shrinking at a quicker pace than in any other Commonwealth Caribbean territory or state (Watson, 1982).

However, the exodus of people from St.Kitts-Nevis in recent years is not unique to that country. The demographic history of the region shows that microstates of similar size have been subjected to the same centrifugal forces that disperse their people. The neighboring island of Montserrat lost 31.5 percent of its total population to the United Kingdom between 1955 and 1961; Dominica lost 13.3 percent, Grenada 8.6 percent, and St. Lucia 8.5 percent (Watson, 1982:187). In terms of actual numbers, the larger territories such as Guyana, Jamaica, Trinidad and Tobago, and Barbados account for more than 80 percent of the total emigrant population. However, the larger percentage loss to the smaller states exerts a much greater social and psychological impact on them than it does on the larger states. While the focus of this paper is on St.Kitts-Nevis, several of the findings and conclusions are applicable to other Caribbean states.

This study consists of five broad sections. The first deals with methodological issues. The second section is devoted to a discussion of the characteristics of migration from St. Kitts-Nevis, including the testing of hypotheses that are based on quantitative analyses. The third section is concerned with "explanation". Here the attempt is to provide reasonable answers to the "How" and "Why" questions relating to emigration from St.Kitts-Nevis. The fourth section examines the impact of migration on the social and economic life of the twin-island state. In the final section, the long-term migration policy of the government is examined, and recommendations dealing with the diaspora are suggested.

METHODOLOGY

The data collected for this study came from a household survey. A probability sample of 495 households was selected from a total of 11,600 housing units in St.Kitts-Nevis.[1] About 78 percent of the housing units were in St. Kitts and 22 percent in Nevis. The survey design produced a complex probability-cluster sample. The multi-stage area design insured that every housing unit had a known probability of selection into the sample, irrespective of social class, ethnic or national origin, political affiliation, level of education, or any other characteristic that defines a group in the country. The total number of households was stratified by island, then by geographic location. The strata consisted of clusters or enumeration districts. A pair of unequal clusters was randomly selected from each of 20 strata by probabilities proportional to their sizes. About 12 housing units from each cluster were selected systematically after a random start. The means and proportions were computed with the ratio mean estimator, and accompanying standard errors were also computed.[2]

The questionnaire had two major goals: to collect data relevant to specific aspects of migration and to derive such information with as

[1] The design calls for a target of 400 completed interviews. This target sample size is based on the need to keep sampling errors within tolerable limits. The final number of units — 495 — is derived from the following equation; the completed interview and dwelling-use rates are estimated from information provided by the Statistics Unit in the Planning Office in St. Kitts:

$$\frac{\text{Completed Interviews}}{400} = \frac{\text{Completed Interview Rate}}{(0.95)} \times \frac{\text{Dwelling Use Rate}}{(0.85)} \times \frac{\text{Dwellings to be Selected}}{x}$$

Solving for x produces a sample size of 495. (*See*, Warwick and Lininger, 1975:112).

[2] Kish (1965:223) suggests that paired selection of primary sampling units (PSUs) frequently provides the best design for selecting clusters, and is probably the single most important key to design in survey sampling, for it facilitates stratified multistage selection with probability proportional to size from unequal clusters.

much accuracy and validity as possible.[3] In relation to the first goal, questions were classified according to subject areas: perception of economic conditions of the islands, employment of the respondent, mobility of household members, characteristics of migrants, income of the household. In relation to the second goal, the questionnaire was first tested in both islands with a 10 percent subsample in order to evaluate the questionnaire items, the adequacy of the sampling instructions, the quality of the interviews, the rate of and reasons for refusals, and the overall appropriateness of the survey method.

Several aspects of the questionnaire that relate to content and methodology deserve mention. First, the collection of information on the characteristics of migrants at the place of origin necessitated a retrospective approach since the move had already taken place at the time of the interview. This approach influenced the types of questions respondents could be asked about the migrant household member. Second, the continual movement of population from St.Kitts and Nevis required the establishment of a time frame. The year 1955 was chosen as the base year. It effectively separates two migrations: the "old" pattern, mainly to Curaçao and Aruba, Venezuela, the Dominican Republic, and the United States (under the *Bracero* program); and the "new" pattern to the United Kingdom, the U.S., and British Virgin Islands, and later to Canada, the U.S. mainland, and the Dutch Windward Islands (mainly St. Maarten). Third, information from the respondent was required for one migrant only. If there were more than one migrant from a household, one was selected on a probability basis, and information about this individual was sought. This selection procedure maintained the statistical rigor of the research design.[4]

CHARACTERISTICS OF MIGRATION

The questionnaire elicited information on five related areas: socioeconomic conditions of the islands as perceived by heads of households; employment status of these individuals; potential mobility from the islands; characteristics of migrants; and the perceived effects of migration.

Conditions in St.Kitts-Nevis which promote migration were measured. Responses were provided to the question: "What do you think is

---

[3] A number of questions are designed to maintain comparability with questions used in the Man and Biosphere (ISER) project in four Caribbean countries. Appreciation is acknowledged to Dawn Marshall for sharing with me her experience on that project and other insights on the general topic.

[4] Kish (1965) describes a rigorous statistical method for selecting a single person from a household in a probabilistic way.

the main condition in St.Kitts-Nevis that causes people to go and live overseas?" From Table 1, it is clear that the majority of household heads, 62 percent, consider that the lack of opportunities in St. Kitts-Nevis is the main reason most people migrate. This result shows that a once popular assertion that internal political strife, particularly in the 1960s and 1970s, was a major reason for the emigration of Kittitians and Nevisians is no longer so compelling; only one percent of the householders thought that internal politics contribute to migration.

TABLE 1

Main Conditions that Cause Kittitians-Nevisians to Migrate

Conditions Promoting Migration	Percent
Limited Opportunities (Unspecified)	16
Limited Job Opportunities	46
Limited Educational/Training Opportunities	2
Higher Prices in Relation to Wages	31
Politics	1
Lack of Social Prestige	1
Other	3

The question which provides the information on the "pull" factors to the metropolis is: "What do you think is the main condition overseas that attracts most people?" The responses given in Table 2 tend to support the data in Table 1. Forty-two percent hold that employment, educational and other opportunities constitute the main attraction, and another 40 percent identify "making money" as the compelling reason. It is also noteworthy that almost one out of every five householders considers that the main condition that attracts Kittitians and Nevisians abroad is that of a "better life". In the explanation section, I will examine what the concept of a better life means for island residents and how emigration is tied to this pursuit.

Some significant characteristics of migrants are listed in Table 3. It shows that throughout St. Kitts and Nevis, about one out of every two households has family members abroad. In all, 44 percent of all households in the country have had at least one of their family members living overseas since 1955. Of these migrants, half are female. This finding appears to be consistent with evidence from the rest of the Caribbean

TABLE 2
The Main Conditions Overseas that Attract Kittitians and Nevisians

Conditions Promoting Migration	Percent
More or Better (Unspecified) Opportunities	11
More or Better Job Opportunities	28
More or Better Educational/Training Opportunities	3
Making Money	40
Better Life/Standard of Living	17
Higher Social Prestige	1
Joining Family/Spouse	0
Other	0

TABLE 3
General Characteristics of Migrants

Characteristics	Response	Standard Error
Households with Emigrant Members	44%	2.0%
Year of First Departure:		
1955 - 1962	19%	3.8%
1963 - 1971	36%	3.5%
1972 - 1980	30%	3.8%
1981 - 1985	15%	3.2%
Sex of Migrant:		
Female	51%	4.1%
Male	49%	4.1%
Average Age of Migrant	24.6	0.79
Average Migrant Members per Migrant Household	2.6	0.16
Average Return Migrants per Migrant Household	1.1	0.06
Average Migrant Members over 16 Years per Migrant Household	2.4	0.12
Rural Component of Migrant Stream	63%	3.0%
Employed in Agriculture	18%	2.2%
Percentage Sending Remittances in 1984	63%	3.7%

and Latin America (Chaney, 1985). Again, like many migrants from underdeveloped countries, those of St.Kitts-Nevis are comparatively young. The average age is 24.6 years. Most sources indicate that the majority of Caribbean migrants are between 20 and 30 years of age (Roberts, 1974:8; Segal, 1975:71).

For those households sending migrants abroad, the average number is 2.6, with 1.1 members returning. This latter figure only indicates the average number per household who returned and stayed for at least three months. In fact, most of these do leave again, having become accustomed to living abroad. The average number of migrants over 16 years of age per sending family is 2.4, indicating that only about one in five sending families has a member abroad 16 years old or under. This suggests that most young children are left behind in St.Kitts-Nevis. This finding has far-reaching social implications that are discussed later in this chapter. Two-thirds of this migrant stream departed St.Kitts-Nevis in the decades of the 1960s and 1970s. This occurred despite the 1962 Commonwealth Immigration Act of the United Kingdom, which significantly curtailed emigration to the British Isles.

The educational level of Kittitians and Nevisians is considered a crucial variable in the decision to migrate. Todaro (1976:63) cites the specific case of Tanzania in concluding that "there seems to be a close association between the level of completed education and the propensity to migrate; *i.e.*, those with more years of schooling, everything else being equal, are more likely to migrate than those with fewer years". These conditions seem to hold in St. Kitts and Nevis when one examines the distribution of migrants according to their educational level (Table 4).

TABLE 4

Educational Level of Migrants

Educational Level	Percent
No Schooling	2
Primary (4 Years or Less)	3
Upper Primary	39
Secondary	44
Secondary (Vocational/Technical)	8
College/University	2
Other	2

Only two percent of emigrants are without formal schooling, while an overwhelming 91 percent are educated at the upper primary, secondary, or secondary/technical level. This finding has grave implications for the development of St.Kitts-Nevis. Unlike some other emigrants from Third World countries, this stream of emigrants is not uneducated. It is argued below that the educational structure in the island-nation inherently promotes migration.

Given the inveterate state of underdevelopment and grinding poverty that has prevailed in these two islands since Emancipation, the large-scale migration during the twentieth century has been determined less by conditions at the source than by the easing of restrictions in the metropolis and the peripheral states. About one-third of the post-1955 migrations from St.Kitts-Nevis flocked to the U.S. Virgin Islands (and Puerto Rico) to work in the construction of hotels and housing, to work as hotel service personnel, and to perform myriad other tasks which native Virgin Islanders were unwilling to carry out for the bourgeoning tourist industry (*See*, Table 5).

TABLE 5

Destination of Migrants, 1955-1985

Destination	Percent
England	15
U.S.A. (Mainland)	9
Canada	14
U.S. Virign Islands/Puerto Rico	30
British Virgin Islands	13
Dutch Antilles	14
Other	1

Table 6 illustrates that in 1980, 6,523 of the 30,731 foreign-born persons in the U.S. Virgin Islands were from St. Kitts-Nevis. Apart from the demand for "H-2"[5] workers in the tourist industry in the U.S. Virgin Islands,[6] the U.S. immigration law of 1965 mandated that immi-

---

[5] The H-2 classification was used to categorize nonimmigrant "workers [who] perform services of labor for which qualified labor cannot be found...(and who require certifications by the Department of Labor)" (INS, 1975:9).

[6] The INS report (1975:10) states further that "the unusually large increase [of petitions approved] is attributed mainly to H-2 petitions for workers in the U.S. Virgin Islands".

TABLE 6

Migration to the U.S. Virgin Islands

Year of Migration	Migrants
Before 1950	139
1950 - 1959	337
1960 - 1964	1,375
1965 - 1969	2,161
1970 - 1974	1,348
1975 - 1980	1,163
Total	6,523

Source: U.S. Bureau of the Census.

gration be regulated by a certification requirement. Of this total, 92 percent are from the Commonwealth Caribbean. About 75 percent of the Kittitian-Nevisians migrated between 1960 and 1975, and 93 percent between 1960 and 1980. From these two tables it is estimated that in the period 1950 to 1980, St. Kitts-Nevis lost about 21,800 of its native population.[7]

In the process of uncovering the determinants that induce migration, researchers often include questions about the source of information that helped emigrants to make the decision. One survey question, "Who or what was the main source of information that helped [the migrant] to live abroad?", produces the results in Table 7. It is clear that the family is the main source of information about migration. Hence, the mobility index would tend to be higher in households in which there is at least one migrant. The estimate of 17 percent for spouse/family supports the finding of the Man and the Biosphere (MAB) project in St. Kitts-Nevis where it was found that among potential migrants, 19 percent planned to join their families (ISER, 1982:140). Nonetheless, having friends abroad also appears significant in the migration process.

[7] The total emigrant group of 21,800 is estimated as follows. If the survey in St. Kitts-Nevis has reliably measured the proportion of Kittitian-Nevisians migrating to the U.S. Virgin Islands as 0.299 with a standard error of 0.036, and the 1980 census in the U.S. Virgin Islands is reasonably accurate with a count of 6,523 Kittitian-Nevisians (with perhaps a slight undercount of illegals), then the estimated total seems a good working estimate. Further, the survey estimated a proportion of 0.091 with a standard error of 0.015 to represent the number of Kittitian-Nevisians migrating to the U.S. mainland. The Bureau of the Census in a release (CB84-179) in 1984 listed 1,903 foreign-born Kittitian-Nevisians in the United States. This is computed to be 0.087 of the estimated total of 21,800. If these estimates are tolerable, fully one-third of all Kittitians and Nevisians live abroad.

TABLE 7

Sources of Information About Destinations

Source	Percent
Spouse/Family	17
Relative(s)	37
Friend(s)	23
Media	8
Government	4
None	7
Other	4

TABLE 8

Employment Status of Migrants

Employment Status	Percent
Employed Full-time	46
Partly Employed	13
Unemployed	34
Student	4
Retired (Not Employed)/Disabled	1
Housewife	1
Other	1

It is commonly believed that unemployment is one of the major reasons people emigrate, that is, Kittitians and Nevisians migrate in search of employment because they are unemployed at home. Retrospective information on the employment status of migrants at the time of their departure does not support this view. Table 8 shows that 59 percent of all migrants from both islands are either fully or partly employed at the time of their leaving. One out of every 25 migrants leaves to study abroad, and 34 percent, or about one of every three migrants, is without employment. The notion that migrants from St. Kitts-Nevis constitute a horde of unemployed is therefore not substantiated. This

finding is consistent with the results of the MAB study, which found
that in general in the four Commonwealth Caribbean countries studied
(*i.e.,* Barbados, St.Kitts-Nevis, St. Lucia, and St. Vincent), "the potential
migrant is not likely to be...unemployed" (ISER, 1982:138).

Given the fact that most migrants are relatively young, it is to be expected that most of them are unmarried. This appears to be the case. In
Table 9, about one out of every five is married, but the overwhelming
majority — 76 percent — never married. However, this number includes many who lived in common law unions or in visiting relationships, often with children as a product of these informal unions. In most
of these cases, the children were left behind in the care of others, often,
as we shall see, with negative impact on the youth.

TABLE 9

Marital Status of Migrants

Marital Status	Percent
Married	21
Never Married	76
Divorced	1
Separated	1
Other	1

In Table 3 we saw that 63 percent of the post-1955 migrants send remittances to their relatives and others left behind. This variable is intrinsically
difficult to measure, primarily because remittances are often sent back
in a variety of forms: in cash by mail, money orders and checks,
food items, clothing, household appliances and furniture, and so forth.
Some effort was expended in the survey to arrive at dollar values for
items like food, clothing and other household items.

Table 10 presents estimated data with many households having more
than one member overseas. It is estimated that each household takes in
about US $2,525, a relatively large sum in St. Kitts-Nevis. The 1983
GNP per capita is estimated at US $820 by the World Bank. The remit-
tances maintain many families, and in fact, they are the only means of
support for many. Foodstuffs amount to about 22 percent of the total
remittance, and this suggests the dependence of many on this kind of
contribution. Cash constitutes about 57 percent of the total.

TABLE 10

Remittances to St. Kitts-Nevis in 1984

	US$	
Remittance Type	Average per Household	Standard Error
Cash	1,435	440
Food	568	239
Clothing	337	128
Household Items	185	89
Total	2,525	896

By making use of the mean contribution and the number of households with emigrants abroad in 1984, it is estimated that St. Kitts-Nevis received approximately U.S. $18.6 million in total remittances. When compared with the GNP of St.Kitts-Nevis in 1983 of U.S. $61.9 million, it is clear that the intake of remittances not only has a tremendous impact on the economy, but it obviously contributes to the well-being of many islanders. As discussed in the fourth section, the effect of this huge sum on the fabric of Kittitian-Nevisian society is great, and negative consequences predominate.

To determine how remittances were expended, respondents were asked: "On what did you spend most of the cash received: food, rent, conveniences, house and land, household items, education, or health? Or did you save most of it?" The responses appear in Table 11.

Remitted cash is allocated primarily to foodstuffs, as stated by two out of every three household heads. It is noted that this is in addition to the average of U.S. $568 received in food items by each household (Table 10). The second most important category — 15 percent — consists of modern conveniences; appliances and utilities for the home. Only 10 percent of all remittances go to savings. How remittances affect social and economic development in St.Kitts-Nevis is examined in the penultimate section.

TEST OF HYPOTHESES

Portes and Walton (1981:25) imply that the reporting of survey data on migration, with accompanying elaboration, is useful as a first approximation to certain meaningful questions on population movement. Goldstein and Goldstein (1981:32), in referring to survey data, decry

TABLE 11

Primary Items on Which Remittances are Spent

Items of Expenditure	Percent
Food	69
Rent	1
Utilities/Conveniences	15
House and Land	1
Household Items	2
Education	0
Health	2
Savings	10
Other	0

the fact that "only a small fraction of the material collected has been analyzed, often not going beyond simple cross-tabulations..." With this admonition in mind, we go beyond the presentation of empirical data collected on migrants to test hypotheses.

The first purpose is to establish the veracity for St. Kitts-Nevis of a set of hypotheses about migration. The second purpose is to provide the opportunity for making comparisons with the outcome of similar hypotheses advanced for other Caribbean microstates, such as are found in the MAB project (ISER, 1982). From these comparisons, generalizations about the migration process can be made. The third, and perhaps, the most important goal is to begin the arduous task of testing and retesting hypotheses geared to the ultimate establishment of a body of migration theory that could be used by regional policy makers.

The following hypotheses about the new emigration from St. Kitts-Nevis are examined:

1) More migrants are likely to have been employed than unemployed at the time of emigration;

2) More emigrants are likely to have been skilled than unskilled;

3) More emigrants are likely to have come from rural than from urban areas;

4) More males are likely to have emigrated in early years, and more females in later years.

The hypotheses that are tested in relation to the impact of emigration include the following:

5) More emigrants who were employed in agriculture are likely to have worked in the field sector than any other sector;

6) More of the households with migrants abroad are headed by females than by males.

The first hypothesis suggests that a majority of the migrants are likely to have been employed at the time they migrated. Much of the literature on migration generally would suggest otherwise. Newton (1984:5-6) records that the traditional reasons given for British West Indian emigration are unemployment and underemployment and a shortage of job opportunities. Stahl (1982:869) writes that "the relief of unemployment and underemployment" is a potential benefit perceived by those who remain behind. In this author's opinion, the fundamental reason for emigration from St.Kitts-Nevis has less to do with unemployment than with the quality of work and the quality of life. Having a job implies a certain level of education; it suggests the evolution of a need for personal development not easily obtainable in St. Kitts-Nevis, and it implies the eventual departure in search of that improvement.

Table 12 provides the statistical information for testing this first hypothesis. The proportion of all employed migrants is 0.586, and unemployed is 0.337. About 75 percent more Kittitians and Nevisians in the migrant stream were employed than unemployed.

TABLE 12

Statistics to Test the Employment/Unemployment Hypothesis of Migrants

Employment Status of Migrant	Proportion	Standard Error
Employed/Partly Employed	0.586	0.040
Unemployed	0.337	0.034
Difference	= 0.249	0.072
	p = 0.0003	

A putative characteristic of migration is that unskilled laborers constitute the majority of migrants, but the second hypothesis states that skilled migrants from St. Kitts-Nevis form the bulk of those who go to work overseas. Here we refer to higher professionals, managers, civil servants (such as teachers, nurses, police, secretaries), and skilled or semi-skilled manual workers (such as mechanics, masons, and carpenters). This position rests on the fact that emigration is held in high esteem by the majority of Kittitians and Nevisians; the employed and the unemployed, the skilled and unskilled. While conditions in St.Kitts-Nevis do not displace the skilled any more than the unskilled, demand for the skilled is built into the migration policies of the metropolis. This promotes the selection of skilled migrants.

In Table 13, the estimate of the skilled among the migrants is 0.739, and 0.261 unskilled. Thus, among the migrants, there are almost three times as many skilled workers as unskilled ones.

TABLE 13
Statistics to Test the Skilled/Unskilled Hypothesis

Skill Level of Migrant	Proportion	Standard Error
Skilled	0.739	0.036
Unskilled	0.261	0.036
Difference	0.477	0.073
	$p = 0.0000$	

The third hypothesis asserts that the majority of migrants from St.Kitts-Nevis are from rural areas. Conditions in the rural sectors of many countries often generate low standards of living, and there is little to engage the services of the working-class poor meaningfully. This is no less true in St.Kitts-Nevis, and there is virtually nothing to restrain the rural workers from seeking work overseas. Unlike many Third World countries where there is a first-stage movement to an urban center, then another stage to a metropole, there is no intermediate stop before the capital in St.Kitts-Nevis. The rural areas in St.Kitts-Nevis offer even fewer prospects for personal development than the urban areas; therefore, direct migration to the capital is more probable. The information from the study presented in Table 14 shows that the proportion of migrants who were living in the urban centers before departing is 0.360 and that from the rural districts is 0.640. There are about 80 percent more migrants from the countryside than the two towns and urban centers. The statistics lend strong evidence to the statement that rural migrants are much more numerous than urban ones.

TABLE 14

Statistics to Test the Urban/Rural Hypothesis

Previous Home of Migrant	Proportion	Standard Error
Urban	0.360	0.033
Rural	0.640	0.033
Difference	0.280	0.066
	p = 0.0000	

The fourth hypothesis relates gender to time of departure. The proposition is that males dominated the early streams while women surpassed men in later years. There is historical evidence to confirm that males primarily responded to the demand for labor in the canal works of Panama, the fruit plantations of Central America, the sugar cane estates of Cuba, the Dominican Republic and St. Croix, and the industrial cities of the United Kingdom. This was from 1885 until 1962. Since then, an increasing number of women have journeyed to Canada as domestics on bilateral government labor schemes, and to the tourist havens and service industries of the Dutch Windward Islands (St. Maarten principally) and the U.S. and British Virgin Islands.

As revealed in the last section, there is now a larger percentage of females in the migrant group — 51 percent. The data are arranged in a contingency table (Table 15) to show gross relationships: In the first and second periods, male migrants exceed female migrants by four and five percentage points respectively. In the third period both groups are equal, and by the fourth period females exceed males by nine percentage points. Although these percentage differences are not statistically significant, they reveal a trend in which females have come to outnumber males in the migrant outflow.

The continual movement of population from St. Kitts-Nevis cannot occur without direct impact on the social and economic structure of the country. As pointed out above, most migrants from the microstate are likely to be of rural origin where the primary activity is agriculture. This leads us to the fifth hypothesis: Of the migrants who work in the agricultural industry, the majority come from the field side. The mainstay of the twin-island economy is production and export of sugar, but the landowners are largely expatriates. The great variations in the price of world sugar have wreaked havoc on the local economy. When the returns from sugar production are low, the rural sugarcane workers are the most directly affected, and they often

TABLE 15
Relationship of Time of Departure to Sex

| | Sex | |
Time of Departure	Male (%)	Female (%)
1955 - 1962	18	14
1963 - 1971	35	30
1972 - 1980	35	35
1981 - 1985	12	21

TABLE 16
Statistics to Test the Hypothesis of Laborer Majority Among Agricultural Workers

Agricultural Work	Proportion	Standard Error
Supervisory/Technical/Clerical	0.343	0.077
Laborer	0.657	0.077
Difference	0.314	0.154
	$p = 0.0216$	

respond by traveling to sell their labor. Table 16 illustrates that of the migrant agricultural workers, about two out of three come from the field side of the industry. The other statistics in Table 16 confirm that a significantly larger proportion of laborers are lost than are other workers from the industry.

The loss of these workers is more critical economically than is the case for most other sectors. A scarcity of workers in the sugar sector is not easily met, for local laborers only work in the cane fields out of absolute necessity. In addition, the loss of food producers mandates the import of foodstuffs for many local residents who are becoming less and less capable of paying for imported foods.

Another forceful effect of migration on local society is embodied in the sixth hypothesis: The majority of households with migrants abroad are headed by women. In the first round of out-migration, males departed to perform the heavy labor of building canals and railroads, picking fruit, or cutting cane. The women were then left to manage the households with the children. In the second round, the majority of women with children who migrate left them in the care of grand-mothers, aunts, female cousins or other relatives, and even with neighbors and friends.

Table 17 shows that in those households from which there are no migrants, the number of male householders (*i.e.*, household members) is just equal to the number of female householders. Among households with family members abroad, the proportion of male householders de-creases to 0.354 while that of female householders increases to 0.646. When the statistics are used in the traditional way to construct approxi-mate confidence limits, they support the proposition that female house-holders are dominant among those with family members overseas.

TABLE 17

A Test of the Hypothesis of the Female Householder Majority

Type of Householder	Proportion	Standard Error
Non-Migrant Households:		
Male Householder	0.504	0.029
Female Householder	0.495	0.029
Difference	0.009	0.057
Migrant Household:		
Male Householder	0.354	0.029
Female Householder	0.646	0.029
Difference	0.292	0.059
	$p = 0.000$	

Let us move now from testing hypotheses about emigration to an ex-planation of the factors which determine migration from St. Kitts-Nevis.

EXPLANATION

A conscious distinction is made in this study between the explication of migration from St.Kitts-Nevis—that is, making it more understandable through description and illustration—and its explanation, which seeks to account for its origin and development. While it is useful to employ the positivist perspective to preserve the rigor in testing propositions, this author identifies with the position of the historical-structuralists in presenting an explanation of emigration.

In the discussion that follows, the internal processes in St. Kitts-Nevis that have created a migration culture are described. The explanation then focuses on the determinants of the phenomenon and sociocultural consequences that arise.

From Process to Culture

The movement of people from St. Kitts-Nevis may conveniently be referred to as a migration culture. This term was probably first used in the Kittitian-Nevisian context by Richardson (1983). In discussing the greater impact of migration on smaller Caribbean islands compared to the larger ones, Richardson says that "it is the smaller places where a migration ethos, as well as more tangible attributes of migration, underpin entire island communities". He describes migration culture as "locally adaptive traits pertaining to the particular island society in question [where] migration is economically and socially fundamental to insular ways of life" (Richardson, 1983:23-24).

In the context of this study, migration culture is redefined to refer to a way of life that was born in immigrant slavery and indenture, and which after Emancipation until today is acknowledged as a successful — and for many, the only — strategy for defeating the social and economic pressures of underprivileged status. Thus, successive generations of West Indians have been socialized in this tradition. Even for the wealthy and the educated, the status of being a (temporary) migrant enhances social importance in one's native society. In order to understand how this culture developed and why it continues to thrive, it is essential that one examine the socio-historic causes and effects of the phenomenon of migration.

Three West Indian scholars of migration have provided chronological accounts of inter-island, regional and extra-regional migration from the Commonwealth Caribbean (See, Thomas-Hope, 1978; and Newton, 1984). Marshall (1982) conveniently divides the post-Emancipation period into four phases of migration: inter-territorial (1835 to 1885), inter-Caribbean (1885 to 1920), crisis (1920 to 1940), and movement to the metropoles (1940 to the present). These four phases serve as the temporal basis for an examination of the period.

There is perhaps no other region in the world where colonial peopling was largely through forced immigration or indenture, and where a continual and persistent diaspora is as marked as in the Caribbean. Emancipation in 1834 in this analysis is significant not only because it marked the end of almost 200 years of slave life but also because it ushered in a period of freedom of movement, which initially and continually expressed itself in migration.

Indeed, it was only through this movement that many former slaves could achieve the freedom yearned for during bondage. The emancipated slaves of St.Kitts-Nevis never knew more than the plantation and its oppressive and sociocultural conditions. In St.Kitts and Nevis, particularly where the sugar- and cotton-plantation owners controlled all the land, there developed no peasantry as in the other larger islands or in Guyana. Thus, despite the freedom that the Act of Emancipation promised, the ex-slaves were initially coerced into serving their former owners on the very plantations and in the very fields which they shunned with inveterate bitterness. Nor did conditions in the local economy improve. These conditions were a function of the near total dependence on sugar revenues which in turn were dependent on the market value of sugar in London. The worsening economic conditions and the stultifying sociocultural environment of plantation life provided an impetus for migration. Such opportunities became available after 1835 in the newly acquired British territories of Trinidad and Guyana; and Kittitians and Nevisians responded by instituting a movement that marked the beginning of a tradition.

The economic history of the 1885-1920 phase was characterized by two phenomena: a deteriorating economy in St. Kitts-Nevis and throughout the Caribbean; and emigration from the British colonies to foreign countries in the Caribbean Basin. The economy was first hit when the United States gave preferential sugar duties to Puerto Rico, Cuba, the Dominican Republic and Brazil, thus ending the preference given to the British colonies. This was followed over the years by cane disease, widespread bankruptcies and abandonment of estates, a low demand for labor (expanded sugar plantations in Cuba and the Dominican Republic; the banana plantations and railway construction in Central America; a dry dock in Bermuda) were conducive to emigration from the islands. But it was the Canal Zone, with its lure of the "Yankee dollar", that attracted the overwhelming majority of the migrants between 1880 and 1914. The harshness of life in the islands led Marshall to conclude that "for the majority of the population, labor emigration must have seemed the only practical alternative to poverty and distress" (Marshall, 1982:8). Another writer on that phase of St.Kitts-Nevis history wrote: "It is safe to say that at no such time since the eighteenth century have either St.Kitts or Nevis been places of opportunity for significant numbers of people" (Merrill, 1958:95).

Despite the construction of a modern centralized sugar factory in St. Kitts in 1911 and a notable increase in productivity and production of sugar, the lot of Kittitians did not improve in the third phase. In fact, labor violence escalated and was repeated in other island colonies. Some relief was obtained through migration to the oil fields of Venezuela and the oil refineries in Curaçao in the 1920s, but the Great Depression not only ended the human flow, but caused a wholesale repatriation to an already depressed environment. The rioting that resulted was a clear indication of the economic misery of the time. Marshall (1982:9) writes:

> The series of disturbances which began in St.Kitts in January 1935 and ended in Jamaica in 1938, and occurred throughout the West Indies, signaled a crisis in West Indian history. The general consensus . . . was that the period was one of especially bad economic conditions caused by the persistence of adverse market trends for export crops, the closure of emigration outlets and the rapid increase in population. More than one contemporary observer commented on the need for emigration opportunities at this time while the Commission which investigated the disturbances stated: 'this extreme difficulty of movement . . . creates a sense of being shut in, of being denied opportunity and choice. . . .' But the commission did not see a possible solution within the West Indies. The solutions lay not within the island systems, but outside: in capital supplied from without, in a reduction of birthrates, and in securing, somehow, new outlets for emigration.

In 1948, a bitter labor dispute over wages led to St.Kitts-Nevis' longest labor strike. With adult suffrage in 1952, local labor leaders won political control of the islands, but they soon found that economic independence was beyond their grasp. Sugar production peaked in 1960 at 50,000 tons; thereafter, it experienced a steady decline. The vagaries of world market prices and a protracted dispute with local sugar barons led to a near collapse of the industry by 1970. Despite the fact that in 1986 a new business-allied government added to the economic base of the monocrop economy, some diversification of local conditions are perhaps no more compelling now to Kittitians and Nevisians than they may have been immediately after Emancipation. The evidence lies in the search for opportunities by the "new nomads" in the 1950s to the United Kingdom, in the 1960s to the U.S. Virgin Islands, Canada and the United States, and since then to the British Virgin Islands and Dutch Antilles as well.

Notwithstanding the relevance of the economic conditions in the establishment of a migration culture in St. Kitts-Nevis, this writer takes issue with the view that "there now seems to be widespread agreement among economists and noneconomists alike that migration can be explained primarily by the influence of economic factors" (Todaro, 1976:26). Even though Todaro admits to the relevance of social factors, there is no question that he considers "economic factors" to be the dominant explanatory variable.

The perspective of this writer differs from that of metropolitan scholars who see the improvement in the material welfare of immigrants as evidence of the great contribution of Atlantic societies to West Indians. Yet social welfare is equally important. It is believed that even if economic conditions rapidly change in St.Kitts-Nevis to provide jobs for everyone, it will not significantly reduce the human stream outward. It was shown above that employed persons predominate among the migrants. A more convincing explanation for migration lies in the social, cultural, and psychological factors that prevail in the class structure of the plantation society. Even more critical is the fact that these socio-cultural and other noneconomic variables are largely influential in the economic behavior of individuals and groups in society. Hence, it is necessary to understand the overarching role of these variables before accepting that economic factors contribute the primary impetus to the out-migration process.

The monocrop plantation economy that exists in St. Kitts-Nevis today has evolved from a system of rural agriculture that dates back to early colonization. The plantation system was so pervasive as a rural institution that it completely dominated the social environment. It was at once a unit of authority with control that permeated the lives of all its chattel, and at the same time, a system that demarcated the locus and rules of accommodation between its various ethnic groups. It classified its people with different statuses and formally defined the relationship between them. It exercised its authority through legal compulsion, and was reinforced by a class structure which completely restricted mobility from a lower to an upper status. Race was the basis of the caste system, and with little adjustment the system persists until today: At the top of the social hierarchy were the European landowners; in the middle were the white businessmen and artisans; and at the bottom were the blacks.

Even after Emancipation, memories of the brutality and inhumanity of slavery led the free bondsmen into a total rejection of the plantation. The ex-slaves naturally endeavored to find an existence that was independent of the plantation. Where there was available land in the larger islands, a "peasantry" developed; but this was not the case in St.Kitts-Nevis. All arable lands were owned by Europeans. Thus the freed men were forced to stay on the estates which they found abominable, or migrate to regional destinations when opportunities overseas were available. Beckford admirably identifies the inherent conditions in the plan-

tation society that created the initial compulsion to migrate, and which
in fact largely persist to the present.

> Society as a whole was rigidly stratified by race and color, and di-
> rectly correlated with occupational status . . . and without any kind
> of social mobility whatever. . . . There was little that black people
> could do to improve their lot. . . . Barring emigration, the only sig-
> nificant scope for social mobility open to them was education
> (Beckford, 1972:62, 64).

Since local education today is significantly related to emigration, it
seems useful to examine this factor further. Educational opportunities
opened up somewhat at the beginning of this century, but they were
primarily for half-castes rather than for blacks. As blacks took advantage of education and became upwardly mobile, they soon recognized
that the limited social mobility they could achieve was largely a function
of the distance they could place between the culture of black people and
the degree of assimilation into the dominant European culture. Beckford (1972:65) again captures the essence of this phenomenon at work:

> This set the stage for a dynamic process by which black people
> sought social mobility by aspiring continuously to a European way
> of life. Education, residence, manners of speech and dress, reli-
> gious beliefs and practice, social values and attitudes, and general
> lifestyle all served to distinguish the blacks who had "made it"
> from those who had not....All black people in these societies regard
> the white European culture as superior and, in a dynamic sense,
> they all aspire to it. Those still fully immersed in the plantation
> subculture aspire to getting their children away from it, even if
> they see no possibility of getting "out" themselves.

By and large, this last sentence helps to explain why older Kittitians
and Nevisians make enormous sacrifices to help their children migrate.
While it has been true that education has been the predominant avenue
for blacks to move out of the lower class since the middle of the century,
education alone was not enough. The broadening of the black middle
class has meant that something else is required for upward mobility and
social prestige: emigration, if only on a temporary basis (Thomas-Hope,
1978).

Additional corroboration of the noneconomic benefits that derive
from, and motivate, migration is provided by Thomas-Hope
(1978:76,77):

...higher wages and material possessions never became the only measure of migration success nor the sole migration motive. Virtually anything acquired overseas, even the new 'walks' and new 'talks', came to be regarded by the home society as superior to local forms. Migration and its related attributes had not only made its social and economic impact felt in the islands, but it had become incorporated into the entire fabric of lower class values.... Foreign travel was accompanied by such an aura of accomplishment that it came to be regarded as a necessity in order to 'become a man', to know the world and to understand life. Thus for several reasons emigration became highly desirable and sought after, even for its own sake; and as a channel to success it became for many sectors of society a social imperative.

In summary, socio-cultural, psychological, and economic factors underlie emigration from St.Kitts-Nevis. An understanding of the historical process of the plantation system is necessary to grasp the processes at work today. The harshness of the slave period, the total lack of arable land for independent small-scale agriculture, the vagaries of the sugar market after 1850 and concomitant depressed economic conditions together with a general shortage of employment opportunities, all created a culture or a tradition of emigration. The class and caste system that was based on race and reinforced by the plantation as an institution contributed as well to a migration ethos. The structural rigidity of the system prevented upward mobility for blacks until education in this century provided a route to the middle class, albeit with the necessary acquisition of North Atlantic cultural values. Yet education requires the mandatory varnish of overseas residence to claim the badge of social importance in St.Kitts-Nevis.

Having explored the socio-economic conditions that have given rise to and perpetuated large-scale emigration, let us now examine the effects of this mobility on the microstate.

THE IMPACT OF MIGRATION

Perhaps the most obvious impact of migration on the twin-island state is the infusion of relatively large sums of remittances on a continuing basis. The consequences for St. Kitts-Nevis may be conveniently classified into three categories: economic, agricultural, and social. An estimated contribution of US$18.6 million (in 1984) in remittances to an economy with a GNP for 1983 of US$61.9 million is quite substantial. At the national level, remittances undoubtedly contribute to balance-of-payments. At the household level, they may increase the living standards of individuals. Yet a number of scholars are uncertain about the salutary effect of remittances.

The survey data reveal that 64 percent of all respondents consider that "the main obligation of people who have gone away" is to send back money or parcels to family members. The survey also shows that 69 percent of remittances is consumed in foodstuffs. Brana-Shute and Brana-Shute (1982;279) observe that "we cannot say if a household's real standard of living has increased or if the money serves only to fill in the gap left behind by an individual who has emigrated". In rural St.Kitts-Nevis, general community standards appear to have been lowered. There is widespread evidence that low-paying (nonagricultural) jobs are spurned, or only part-time labor is sought, when remittances can be counted on to provide sustenance. Survey evidence further indicates that only 10 percent of remittances are invested. Metropolitan scholars often view remittances as contributions to the economic self-sufficiency of sending countries (Richardson, 1983:48; Brana-Shute and Brana-Shute, 1982:269). In St.Kitts-Nevis, however, there is little evidence to support this belief.

The first serious impact on agricultural production by the "new" migration occurred in the latter half of the 1950s after the McCarran-Walter Act of 1952 reduced the flow of migrants to the United States to a trickle while the floodgates were opened to the United Kingdom. The vast majority of the emigrants were from the rural areas, and most were agricultural workers. The shortage of labor was so acute in 1960 that seasonal workers were brought in from Barbados, St. Vincent and St. Lucia to harvest the cane that year. But throughout the 1970s and up to the present, workers have been nonchalant about agricultural work and their economic conditions because of their receipt of remittances. Management often expresses its frustration at workers who work part-time or slovenly or not at all because they can depend on cash, foodstuffs, and other parcels from abroad. This decline in production and productivity also serves to remove land from small-scale farming, create local food shortages and drive up prices, and it results in increasing imports of nutritionally poor frozen and canned foods. Over the years, management has resorted to various incentive programs to increase labor output particularly at harvest time, but the competition from remittances is beyond the inducements offered.

The government finds itself in a paradoxical position. On the one hand, it does nothing to discourage migration, and even participates in seasonal labor programs with the United States and Canada. On the other hand, it needs labor to harvest the cane from which it derived, until recently, more than 90 percent of its gross domestic product (Mills, 1974:3).

It is perhaps in the social arena that remittances and migration in general are having the greatest impact: The targets are the community

in general, household organization and behavior. A primary consequence of migration, especially in the rural areas, is the removal of the
more ambitious, educated, and progressive young people. These natural community leaders create a vacuum that is not easily filled. Evidence of this shortage abounds in both islands. It removes leaders from
rural communities and urban-based teachers, nurses, other civil servants and those others with skills who lack opportunities at home.
Households must tolerate the painful exile of fathers, then brothers,
and then sisters, for whom no amount of remittances can compensate.
Normal family development is thus destroyed or at best retarded. The
absence of bread winners in turn creates an anxiety for the regular
calling of the postman with postal money orders from abroad. The
legacy of the migration culture has instilled such a psychological dependency on this way of living that nothing short of a shocking restructuring of society can break its persistence.

Emigration has also had a negative impact on the islands' youth, according to all the welfare officers interviewed for this study. Empirical
data presented above show that female-headed units predominate
among migrant households. Welfare workers cite numerous cases of
children who are left in the care of grandmothers, aunts, uncles,
neighbors, and friends. Truancy among these youths is pervasive. Much
energy is expended by welfare agents in contacting similar agents in
destination countries in an effort to obtain support for minors left at
home. Youths in the care of friends and neighbors are often abandoned. Working mothers are forced to leave children on their own for
most of the day or night, and thus cannot monitor a child's school atten-
dance or help with homework. Even worse, education officials are frus-
trated by students who protest the need to achieve in school, since they
are biding their time until emigration documents are in order for them
to migrate to the "Promised Land". Such an attitude is a recent phenomenon that shows no sign of diminishing.

Most troubling to educators, welfare agents, and legal officers is the
widespread delinquency among youths. Empirical evidence shows that
these youths come from migrant working class families. The overwhelming majority of the cases occur in households where parental
control is minimal or absent. Youngsters often run afoul of the law for
all kinds of petty criminal activity. Truant and probation officers, as well
as senior police officers and magistrates, express very serious concern
with this rising social menace to which government leaders appear am-
bivalent. Young girls without caring parents are often abused by older
men. There are no facilities to incarcerate convicted female youths, and

authorities reluctantly imprison young males with seasoned criminals.

The enormous price which these youths have to pay should not be ascribed to indifferent and indigent parents, nor even to an unresponsive government. It must be seen against the overarching failure of a colonial and post-colonial society to defeat the socio-cultural and psychological conditions that cause migration to thrive until today, for the present society has its roots sunk deeply in the past. It is very clear that after 150 years of migration and remittances, St. Kitts-Nevis is nowhere close to the achievement of economic equilibrium. Emigration from this micro-state is neither accidental nor fortuitous, nor is it simply the act of individual decision making in households. It is sometimes argued that these islanders exercise their free will when they choose to emigrate, and their right to do so cannot be abridged (Maldonado-Dennis, 1982:19). But Maldonado-Dennis (1980:39) effectively neutralizes that argument when he asserts that:

> [it is] 'necessity' that serves as the principal motive for the massive emigration to the metropolis; and that the freedom not to do so in these cases is hollow and spurious. It is due to displacement and underdevelopment, unemployment and underemployment, and the 'necessity' of having to provide for their means of subsistence...It is not, therefore, a mere individual, voluntary act, but rather a real and objective process which takes power over the individual wills of those affected.

MIGRATION POLICY

If one accepts that economic factors are among the most decisive in determining economic processes, then, given the economic history of St. Kitts-Nevis, it is not surprising that only one piece of legislation (in 1910) was ever passed in an attempt to control migration. In this, the twin-island state may not be unique, for as late as 1880 there was no emigration legislation in force in the Commonwealth Caribbean. This attitude appears to have been fostered by Great Britain. When Barbados during the 1840s tried to restrict recruitment of laborers for overseas, it was "disallowed in Britain on the ground that they imposed undue restrictions on the right of free labourers to seek employment where they could find the best market for their labour" (Newton, 1984:51). As the successive governments of St.Kitts-Nevis deemed it beneficial to the islands to have its citizens migrate to seek relief from economic depression, it seems in character that public funds should

have been expended in 1889 to repatriate its natives from the Canal
Zone when the contracting company went bankrupt (Newton, 1984:58).
In fact, it appears that the island's government was at one time the most
accommodating in the flight of its natives. Newton (1984:72) records
that:

> The only Leeward Island government which made no at-
> tempt to regulate or restrict emigration to Panama between
> 1904 and 1909, when it would have been heaviest, was that of
> St.Kitts-Nevis-Anguilla. In fact during these years, the gov-
> ernment was confident that the movement would not se-
> verely deplete the islands' labor force. Not until 1910 was an
> emigration ordinance passed, and it was designed to control
> an exodus to Costa Rica rather than Panama. As a result of
> the liberal attitude adopted by the government of St.Kitts-
> Nevis—Anguilla, this was the only Leeward Island in which
> the I.C.C.'s agents hired laborers directly.[8]

The "new" migration which began around 1955 derived its impetus
from the English, whose London Transport had relations with Commonwealth Caribbean governments. There were active local agents who
recruited for the steamship lines. The exodus that started at this time
was given tacit support by government leaders who personally helped to
finance the emigration of some political supporters to the United
Kingdom. The government also cooperated directly with the Canadian
government in a training scheme of domestic workers, and still coop-
erates in the Canada-Caribbean Farm Workers Seasonal Employment
program. Just as the government responded to repatriate workers in
1889, two government leaders travelled to the U.S. Virgin Islands in
1972 to obtain information from incarcerated Kittitian-Nevisian emigrants. These workers were arrested in a reputed brutal round-up and
deportation of thousands of illegal immigrants (Goodwin, 1971). The
question of any action to deter or prevent migration to the U.S. Virgin
Islands never seems to have arisen.

The only act in recent years that is directed against migration began
in the mid-1970s with the government's attempt to prevent natives who
were educated by government funds or through government sponsor-
ship from emigration with impunity. It took action to contact immigration officials in some countries in which emigrants were violating terms
of bonds. The government attempted to recoup some of its investments
in its natives by placing a one percent tax on remittances, but the

[8] I.C.C., the Isthmian Canal Commission, was appointed in 1904 to direct the newly
acquired canal project which the United States bought from the French. Its agents at times
travelled to various Caribbean islands to recruit labor for building the Panama Canal.

present government repealed this Foreign Currency Tax Act. The fundamental point is that there is not now, nor ever has been, a written official policy in St.Kitts-Nevis that deals with the post-1955 emigration.

Additional statements by government leaders help to define the implicit policy toward migration. There is "a passive acceptance of migration as a contributor to local income [which explains] the benignly passive official policy that still now exists".[9] In the island of Nevis where jobs are more generally in short supply than in St.Kitts, emigration is seen as very necessary. Despite the constant loss of trained personnel, "emigration has served a useful purpose in providing employment opportunities for our people".[10] Another minister of government in St.Kitts laments the loss to the country of educated nationals and the disintegration of the family structure, but would not seek laws to enforce the return of nationals educated abroad at government expense.[11]

Throughout this period of the "new" migration, it is clear that government's implicit policy toward migration is one of near total acceptance. Its direct involvement in seasonal workers' schemes and its removal of a tax on remittances and on remitted foodstuffs, are clear indicators of the official recognition of the importance of migration to the economy and to the well-being of a large proportion of its citizens. Therefore, one has no reason to anticipate any policy changes in the near or foreseeable future from the incumbent government. Nevertheless, there are still a number of initiatives that the government can take to begin the serious work of establishing a meaningful policy on emigration. These can only help to ameliorate the less disturbing shortcomings of migration, however.

First, there is a need either to establish an agency to collect data on migration systematically or to improve the effectiveness of present offices or agencies that record migration statistics. The tasks include a marked upgrading of data collected on emigration and immigration forms from which a much more reliable estimate could be made of out-migrants. Another improvement could be made by including specific questions on emigration in the questionnaire used in the decennial census. Still another area of data collection could be improved by a definite attempt to monitor the level of remittances which are received in the country. These baseline data are fundamental to any explicit policy which might be developed in the future.

Second, a much more serious effort needs to be made to ensure that students who are financed or sponsored by the government are made to

[9] Personal interview with a former head of state.
[10] Personal interview with the chief government official in Nevis.
[11] Personal interview with a minister of government in St.Kitts.

contribute to the national welfare by repaying adequately through service to the state. This should also be extended to employees who have been trained at government expense on the job.

To suggest measures beyond these, particularly in the latter case, is to imply a degree of restriction of movement which the present government and similar ones in the Caribbean would find intolerable. This writer does not subscribe to the view that Malthus' ghost walks the Caribbean and that family planning will do wonders for the region. Population control is important, but it must be seen in its proper context; population density has little association with the waves of migration from the Caribbean. To suggest that the core countries should tie aid programs to the periphery as part of their immigration policy is to foster a continual reliance of the periphery on the metropoles. These benign efforts are tantamount to a band-aid on a leprous spot. For the ultimate question is: What kind of long-term development planning can take place in the periphery when the human resources needed for nation-building can be siphoned off at will by the labor needs of the core countries? The answers for dealing with migration should come from government leaders in the Caribbean and not from the metropoles.

The position of this writer is clearly at variance with the implicit policy attitude. Chaney (1985:102) is mildly critical of some U.S. researchers and policymakers who tend to view migration as a problem when "there is no disposition in the Caribbean to regard migration in anything but positive terms, and concomitant reluctance to frame and enforce any restraining policies at all". Yet this writer does regard migration as an enormous problem, no doubt in terms quite different from those of the scholars and policymakers she mentions. Even mindful of the driving necessity to which Kittitians and Nevisians have had to respond by exile from their homelands, and recognizing the contribution that remittances make to the economy and to the basic food and domestic needs of several households, the conclusion arrived at here is that the total economic, social, and psychological costs are far greater than the benefits received.

At this stage of political independence in the youthful state of St. Kitts-Nevis, the great dependence on migration is merely replacing the long-term dependence on the plantation system. The core countries permit immigration at levels they consider appropriate because of their singular drive toward capital accumulation, and not because of any genuine willingness to help St.Kitts-Nevis or the Caribbean with its development problems. It is not at all sufficient to say that Kittitians and Nevisians benefit from migrating, for it is patently dehumanizing to have to be so dependent on another. Any social system that denies the majority of its people any real stake in their country, or encourages dependency on others, deserves to be permanently transformed in the interests of its people. Such a transformation can only come about through an excruciatingly painful process; that is, a restructuring of the social, economic and political arrangements which sustain it. Kittitians and Nevisians are making, and have been making, sacrifices for over 150 years. They may well be prepared to make the ultimate sacrifice by choosing to be temporarily poor but free, rather than serfs living in material comfort.

REFERENCES

Beckford, G. L.
1972 *Persistent Poverty*. New York: Oxford University Press.

Brana-Shute, R. and G. Brana-Shute
1982 "The Magnitude and Impact of Remittances in the Eastern Caribbean: A Research Note." In *Return Migration and Remittances: Developing a Caribbean Perspective*. Edited by W.F. Stinner, K. de Albuquerque and R.S. Bryce-Laporte. Washington, D.C.: Research Institute on Immigration and Ethnic Studies (RIIES), Smithsonian Institution.

Chaney, E.
1985 *Migration from the Caribbean Region: Determinants and Effects of Current Movements*, Hemispheric Migration Project Occasional Paper Series. Washington, D.C.: Georgetown University and the Intergovernmental Committee for Migration.

Goldstein, S. and A. Goldstein
1981 *Surveys of Migration in Developing Countries: A Methodological Review*. Papers of the East-West Population Institute, No. 71. Honolulu, Hawaii: East-West Center.

Goodwin, I.
1971 "Virgin Islands' Expulsion of Aliens Creates Problems", *Daily News* (June 29):5.

Institute of Social and Economic Research, (ISER)
1982 *Project Report to the Government of St.Kitts-Nevis*. UNESCOUNFPAISER. Man and the Biosphere Project: Barbados.

Kish, L.
1965 *Survey Sampling*. New York: John Wiley and Sons.

Maldonado-Dennis, M.
1982 "Puerto Rican Emigration: Proposals for Its Study". In *The New Nomads: From Immigrant Labor to Transnational Working Class*. Edited by M. Dixon and S. Jonas. San Francisco, CA: Synthesis Publications.

1980 *The Emigration Dialectic: Puerto Rico and the USA*. N.Y.: International Publishers.

Marshall, D. I.
1982 "The History of Caribbean Migrations: The Case of the West Indies", *Caribbean Review*, 11(3):6-9, 52-53.

Merrill, G. C.
1958 *The Historical Geography of St. Kitts and Nevis, The West Indies*. Mexico: Instituto Pan-Americano de Geografía e Historia.

Mills, F. L.
1974 "The Development of Alternative Farming Systems and Prospects for Change in the Structure of Agriculture in St. Kitts, West Indies", Ph.D. dissertation, Clark University.

Newton, V.
1984 *The Silver Men: West Indian Labour Migration to Panama 1850-1914*. Jamaica: Institute of Social and Economic Research, University of the West Indies.

Portes, A. and J.W. Walton
1981 *Labor Class, and the International System*. New York: Academic Press.

Richardson, B. C.
1983 *Caribbean Migrants: Environment and Human Survival on St. Kitts-Nevis*. Knoxville: The University of Tennessee Press.

Roberts, G. W.
1974 "Working Force of the Commonwealth Caribbean at 1970 — a Provisional Assessment". Mona, Jamaica: Department of Sociology, Universtiy of the West Indies.

Segal, A. L.
1975 *Population Policies in the Caribbean*. Lexington, Massachusetts: D.C. Heath and Company.

Stahl, C. W.
1982 "Labor Emigration and Economic Development", *International Migration Review*, 16(4): 869-899. Winter.

Thomas-Hope, E.M.
1978 "The Establishment of a Migration Tradition: British West Indian Movements to the Hispanic Caribbean in the Century After Emancipation". In *Caribbean Social Relations*. Edited by C.G. Clarke. Liverpool: Center for Latin-American Studies, University of Liverpool.

Todaro, M. P.
1976 *Internal Migration in Developing Countries*. Geneva: International Labor Office.

U.S. Bureau of the Census.
1985 *1980 Census of Population: Detailed Population Characteristics of the Virgin Islands of the United States*.

U.S. Immigration and Naturalization Service (INS)
1975 *Statistical Yearbook of the Immigration and Naturalization Service*. Washington, D.C.: Government Printing Office.

Warwick, D.P. and C. A. Lininger
1975 *The Sample Survey: Theory and Practice*. New York: McGraw-Hill Book Co.

The World Bank
1985 *St. Christopher and Nevis: Economic Report*. Washington, D.C.

Watson, H.A.
1982 "Theoretical and Methodological Problems in Commonwealth Caribbean Migration Research: Conditions and Causality", *Social and Economic Studies*. 31(1)(March):165-206.

IMPACT OF THE VENEZUELAN RECESSION ON RETURN MIGRATION TO COLOMBIA: THE CASE OF THE PRINCIPAL URBAN SENDING AREAS

Elisabeth Ungar Bleier
with the collaboration of Helena Useche Aldaña

There are a number of commonly held assumptions about the function of immigrant labor at times of reduced international demand. The assumption that economic recession leads to decreased demand for immigrant labor led many policymakers and researchers to expect a massive return of immigrants in the 1980s from troubled labor-importing countries, such as Venezuela. Observers also feared a serious increase in unemployment as return migrants entered stagnating domestic labor markets. This chapter on Colombian-Venezuelan migration examines the effects of the recession on the principal labor-exporting communities in Colombia and explores why large-scale return migration did not occur.

The chapter begins with a discussion of the economic trends in Colombia and Venezuela over the last three decades. This is followed by brief case studies of the five principal labor exporting cities for the period of the recession in Colombia and Venezuela. We will see that recovery was directly influenced by the degree and range of economic interdependence each city had with Venezuela. The rates of return migration, however, did not impact these cities as much. The case studies graphically show that it was not only labor exchange, but also trade in commodities, that linked Colombia and Venezuela. Those labor exporting cities that were most dependent on trade with Venezuela were hit hardest by the Venezuelan recession. As we shall see, the marked increase in unemployment in these cities was caused much more by a reduction in export sales and by recession than by return migration.

The theoretical premises that guide our analysis are as follows: In general, the penetration of capitalism into peripheral regions has produced disequilibrium in their internal social and economic structures. While these inequalities were induced from outside, they have been internalized over time to produce migration pressures. In other words, the attraction to migrate to advanced, or relatively more advanced, economies is based not only on the advantages they offer but also on the fact that migration is presented as a solution to the internal problems of sending societies (Portes and Bach, 1985).

This relationship is clear in the case of Colombia and Venezuela: The crisis of world capitalism which started at the beginning of this decade deeply affected the economies as well as the labor markets of the two countries and, consequently, altered the expulsion and attraction factors which had characterized migration flows in the past. Therefore, the effects of the crisis on migration must be seen not only as a result of the changing economic opportunities in Venezuela, but also as a consequence of the economic crisis in the national and regional economies of Colombia.

The information in this chapter, particularly that related to the impact of recession on return migration, was compiled when the phenomenon was still undergoing profound change. Consequently, it was necessary to use indirect methods to approach the problem, since reliable statistical information on Colombian international migration was lacking.

In order to document the impact of the Venezuelan recession on the principal urban sending areas, and more specifically on return migration, 65 in-depth interviews were conducted in the five cities. They were administered to people of both the public and private sectors who, due to their political and socioeconomic activities, were highly knowledgeable about the phenomena. Although some of the interviews were also conducted with people who either had migrated in the past or who had a migrant family member, the purpose was not to obtain statistically representative data. Rather, we adopted a qualitative approach in order to illustrate a process and gather enough elements for future research.

This information was complemented by the analysis of data and studies on the socioeconomic characteristics of the sending areas (i.e., employment and unemployment rates, development of economic activities, etc.) These materials are used to buttress the findings obtained through the interviews and to enrich the conclusions about the impact of recession on return migration.

Regional Economies, the Recession, and International Labor Migration

We begin with a brief discussion of the ties between the Venezuelan and Colombian economies in order to clarify the incentives for workers to migrate. The development of both countries over the last three decades will be considered within an international context in order to specify the global forces that led to variations in their respective labor supplies and labor demands and to differences in their adjustments to the recession.

In general, the two economies have been suppliers of primary resources for more industrialized countries: oil in the case of Venezuela and agricultural products, principally coffee, for Colombia. This characteristic has a large effect on the foreign trade policies of the two nations and influences their economic development.

Venezuela was able to launch a program of industrialization financed by the foreign exchange obtained through oil exports. The emphasis on import substitution worked to the detriment of the agricutural production and commerce in Venezuela. Consequently, these two sectors were unable to supply the internal market. The relative lack of attention paid to agricultural modernization by the Venezuelan state considerably increased migration to the cities where large industries were being developed. Thus, the economy of the country became vulnerable to international changes in oil prices and more dependent on imports of agricultural and manufactured products from countries such as Colombia in order to cover the growing internal demand.

In the case of Colombia, the promotion of exports and import substitution were used to relieve the shortage of foreign exchange. The promotion of exports was based on fiscal subsidies. The policy of import substitution, conceived as a means to achieve industrialization, was characterized initially by domestic production of consumer goods and later, intermediate and capital goods. However, while the Colombian economy was more or less diversified, it still was highly dependent upon its key international export, coffee.

In exploring how Colombia's economic development has been linked to the larger capitalist system, it is essential to consider an additional regional feature. The economic dislocation Colombia experienced toward the end of the 1970s was due not only to the world economic recession, but also to the economic crisis in Venezuela and Ecuador. In recent years these two countries had constituted important markets for Colombian exports of agricultural, manufactured, and industrial goods. At the start of the 1970s, Venezuela accounted for only 3.7 percent of the minor exports from Colombia. By the end of this period, exports, other than coffee, from Colombia to Venezuela rose to 27 percent.

The process of industrialization in Venezuela and Colombia had an important effect on labor migration from Colombia to Venezuela, not only in terms of its magnitude, but also with respect to the destinations and the types of migrants. The increased migration of Colombian workers to Venezuela in the 1970s was caused by the rapid development of the Venezuelan economy during the oil boom when there was a shortage of labor, especially in agriculture and commerce, and by wage differentials between the two countries. While real wages declined in Colombia, they increased by an annual rate of 4.5 percent in Venezuela between 1972 and 1979.

Colombian Economic Development

We begin this discussion of the Colombian economy over the last three decades with a retrospective view. That is, we consider the impact of the recession (late 1970s and 1980s) by placing it in the context of earlier, positive economic indicators. We then examine the evolution of specific sectors over the last three decades.

Until the decade of the 1970s, the Colombian economy was characterized by high rates of growth. During the 1960s the Gross Domestic Product increased at an annual rate of 5.2 percent which indicated an increase of 3.1 percent per capita. Throughout the 1970s the rates of growth of the Gross Domestic Product and GDP per capita reached 5.5 percent and 3.3 percent respectively (OAS, 1984). By 1979, however, the Colombian economy had suffered the effects of the economic recession. According to data from the Economic Commission on Latin America and the Caribbean, the rate of growth of the GDP began to decline; it reached 4.1 percent in 1980, 0.9 percent in 1982 and one percent in 1983 (CEPAL, 1984). This development was associated with the stagnation of commercial and agricultural sectors and with the regional and worldwide economic recession. The results of these developments were a decline in production, employment, and exports.

During the first four years of the 1980s, the rate of growth for the Colombian economy was at its lowest in the history of the country. Among the most important manifestations of this deteriorating situation were the crisis in the balance of payments,[1] the fall in international reserves,[2] and the

[1] The disequilibrium in the external sector was manifested in increasing deficits in the balance of payments. These increased from U.S.$876 million in 1982 to approximately U.S.$1.9 billion in 1983 (CEPAL, 1985).

[2] The international reserves of the country fell from U.S.$5.6 billion in 1980 to U.S.$3.1 billion in 1983. In 1984 the amount fell to U.S.$1.9 billion (CEPAL, 1985).

increase in the external debt. The internal sector was characterized by industrial recession and an increase in unemployment and underemployment.[3]

Industrial output in Colombia was not consistent between 1970 and 1980. Production expanded in the early years but decreased in 1974 and 1975. After a ten percent recovery in 1976 and 1978, the economy again began to experience signs of depression. By 1981 industrial output decreased by 2.6 percent, and this trend continued in 1983 as manufacturing declined by 4.2 percent (DANE, 1983).

During the 1970s, the agricultural sector experienced an annual growth of 4.6 percent. By 1981, however, its growth was slower than the average of the economy as a whole, and less than its historical average (DANE, 1983b). This situation was caused by the fall in the international prices of cotton and fluctuations in the price of rice.

Aside from the traditional export products (coffee and flowers), Colombia was not able to promote exports from ranching nor sustain a policy of import substitution that would be capable of satisfying internal and external demand. In the past, exports from the ranching sector had been concentrated in regional markets and more specifically in the border economies, but in 1979 they began to lose relative importance within the total amount of exports to border countries. For example, these products represented 57 percent of the total exports to Venezuela in 1975 and then fell to 43 percent, 46 percent, and 34 percent respectively for 1976, 1977, and 1978. After 1979 the rates continued to fall and reached an average of only 20 percent of total exports between 1977 and 1983.

Other sectors of the economy were not as negatively impacted as industry and agriculture. For example, the construction industry grew at the beginning of the 1980s basically as a result of the state policy of investing public funds in infrastructure. The housing policy of President Betancur also contributed significantly to the growth of the construction industry. Finally, the mining sector experienced a great expansion in recent years and is becoming the most dynamic economic activity of the country. Its contribution to the GDP (in constant pesos of 1975) showed an average annual increase of 13.7 percent between 1982 and 1984. This expansion was predicated upon increases in the production of oil, coal, and gas.

[3] The rate of unemployment in the four principal cities of the country was 8.2 percent in 1981, 9.3 percent in 1982, 11.8 percent in 1983, and 13.5 percent in 1984 (DANE, *Boletín de Avance Estadístico*, 1985).

Economic Development in Venezuela

The recent evolution of the Venezuelan economy can be divided into three periods. The first period, which began in the 1960s, was characterized by import substitution. "During the decade of the 1960s, oil income was relatively stagnant which made the policy of import substitution politically and economically viable. These two factors stimulated the movement of private capital towards industry" (CORDIPLAN, 1984:3-4). During the second period, which comprises the decade of the 1970s, economic expansion was favored by increases in the international price of oil (1973 and 1978-1979) and by growing private and public investment in industry. In the third period, which began in 1980, the economy entered into a recession owing largely to the decline in oil prices.

During the last two decades, the Venezuelan economy generally experienced high rates of growth. In the 1960s GDP grew at an annual average rate of 6.1 percent, while GDP per capita grew at an annual average rate of 2.6 percent. During the 1970s, economic growth was sustained, but it was less than the level attained in the previous decade. The GDP grew annually at a rate of 4.2 percent while GDP per capita grew at an annual rate of 1.5 percent (OAS, 1984).

The current recession in Venezuela resulted from a series of internal and external factors which have produced substantial changes in the social and economic structures of the country. The great dependence of the Venezuelan economy on oil exports has made it vulnerable to cycles in the international market, since the amount of both public and private investment in various economic activities has been closely related to income generated by oil exports. For example, between 1969 and 1978, the level of production of crude oil decreased by 40 percent and the exports of oil by 50 percent. The latter, relative to total exports, dropped from 68.9 percent in 1969 to 57.4 percent in 1978; finally, notwithstanding the reduction in the exports, a nine-fold increase in the price of crude oil was reflected in an increase of 414 percent in the value of oil exports between 1969 and 1979 (Ruiz, 1980).

During the 1970's the service sector acquired a greater importance in the GDP. During 1971-1973, the activities of this sector accounted for an average of 27.4 percent of the GDP, while in 1976 and 1978 they accounted for 30.7 percent. The increase in the relative contribution of the service sector to the GDP was caused by the high rates of growth in transportation, communications, and government (Ruiz, 1980).

The commercial sector also grew in the 1970s. This increase "is as much a consequence of its physical growth as of the structural changes which occurred and which changed an important part of the economy

from that of a barter system to a monetary system" (Ruiz, 1980:809).
Finally, manufacturing expanded after the first increase in oil prices
and became a leading sector of the economy. Its activity grew at an annual average rate of 8.2 percent between 1974 and 1978.

The Venezuelan economy entered into a recession at the beginning of
the 1980s. In effect, a decrease in the rate of growth of the GDP started
in 1980. It fell 1.6 percent from the 1979 rate. Although the GDP increased in 1981-1982, it declined by 1.3 percent in 1981 and 0.7 percent
in 1982 with respect to 1979. The situation deteriorated in 1983 when
the GDP declined by 4.5 percent in relation to 1982 and 5.2 percent
in relation to 1979. GDP per capita fell by 2.3 percent in 1982 and 7.1
percent in 1983 in relation to 1981. GDP per capita in Venezuela is now
approaching the average for Latin America. Whereas in 1960 this rate
was two times greater than the average for Latin America, in 1983 it was
only one and a half times greater than the average.

According to statistics from the Organization of American States
(1984), the fall in GDP was marked by declines in mining and construction. The loss of production in the mining sector started in the 1970s
and reached a critical point in 1982 and 1983. In 1982, annual production fell 9.2 percent below the previous year and 8.5 percent the following year. While the construction industry had registered one of the
greatest rates of growth due to strong state investment by 1978, it
reached its lowest level in 1983 when it fell some 20 percent. In general,
all sectors of the Venezuelan economy, save agriculture, declined in
1983.

The external sector of the economy, which registered an unprece-
dented increase in 1979 (f.o.b. exports of goods increased from U.S.$9
billion in 1978 to U.S.$14 billion in 1979), continued to grow until 1982.
In that year, exports fell by 18.2 percent, and they continued to fall in
1983 (OAS, 1984). At the same time imports increased between 1979
and 1982, leading to a deficit in current accounts in 1982 of some
U.S.$4.2 billion and in the overall balance of payments of U.S.$8.1 billion (CEPAL, 1984).

The situation was aggravated by two major factors: greater rates of
interest charged by international financial markets; and the eventual
devaluation of the bolívar (the Venezuelan monetary unit), which produced large amounts of capital flight.

> The fiscal and monetary policies implemented in the period
> 1980-1982, far from reactivating the economy, facilitated the
> flight of currency abroad and pressured the balance of payments.
> Moreover, in 1982 the decrease in oil income affected commercial
> accounts by producing a deficit of such magnitude in the balance

of payments that it forced the centralization of the PAVSA reserves and the revaluation of the gold standard (CORDIPLAN,
1984:6).

The growing instability in the Venezuelan economy created a crisis in
the external sector at the beginning of 1983 which necessitated adjustments in the rate structure. According to Treasury Minister Arturo
Sosa, the principal factors that unleashed the crisis were the weakening
of the oil market which forced OPEC to reduce worldwide production
to 17.5 million barrels per day. This step then led in Venezuela to the
subsequent reduction in oil prices by U.S.$5.00 per barrel, the loss of
capital, and the growing external debt. Sosa indicated:

> In the case of Venezuela, the adverse effect of the world crisis
> caused a reduction of 17.1 percent in the oil revenues with respect
> to 1982 and the loss of U.S.$1.6 billion in the value of exports of
> crude. The loss of foreign exchange reached U.S.$10 billion in the
> eighteen months prior to the application of monetary controls.
> The depressive situation of the economy was exacerbated by the
> difficulties in refinancing the external debt due to the refusal of
> lending banks to continue to renew annual expirations of the debt.
> Venezuela had to confront the payment of its massive external
> debt precisely when incomes from the sale of crude experienced
> their greatest decline due to the dual reduction in prices and pro-
> duction (Pezzano, 1984:15).

The modification of the single exchange rate, which was maintained
for twenty years at a level of 4.30 bolivares to the dollar, into a system of
multiple exchange rates produced a new process of economic adjustment in the country. The economic policies adopted by the government
in 1983 centered basically around the control of imports, capital flight,
and internal prices in order to maintain international reserves and to
negotiate the external public debt which had amounted to approximately U.S.$25 billion by 1983.

Nevertheless, the adjustment measures were palliative and the "economic policy became a defensive plan without reaching the desired results. Thus, the crisis was prolonged and the country remained artifi-
cially trapped between recession and inflation" (CORDIPLAN, 1984:6).
That is to say, the economic measures did not attack the structural
problems within the Venezuelan economy and the process of adjustment was only intended to resolve the problems of the balance of payments and international reserves. Regardless of whether there was a
recovery of national reserves, the crisis in the general economy worsened. In other words, the intentions of the Venezuelan government to

solve the problems generated by the crisis were limited in relation to the determinants imposed by the dependence on the capitalist international market, specifically on the petroleum market.

Thus, the Venezuelan crisis was characterized by economic stagnation in all productive sectors. Unemployment rates increased from 4.8 percent to 8.2 percent between 1979 and 1982, and reached their highest level of 9.8 percent in 1983. The increase in unemployment was most critical in the industrial and construction sectors where the rates reached 12 percent and 21 percent, respectively. Finally, in spite of the policy of price control, the weakness of the overall economy also led to a fall in real wages for the Venezuelan workers.

Summary

This brief description of the development of the crisis in Colombia and Venezuela shows that both nations were tied closely to the international economy by being dependent on the financial markets of the major economies. It was almost inevitable for Colombia and Venezuela to fall into the debt crisis, notwithstanding the fact that remedial actions could have been taken four or five years earlier such as the prudent handling of foreign reserves and the export of oil. Given their interdependent economic relations, the Venezuelan crisis acted as an accelerating factor for the Colombian crisis. As a result, Colombia has had to confront problems resulting from the devaluation of the bolívar, the reduction in formal trade with Venezuela, and the increase in smuggling activities, particularly in the border area. These negative impacts have been felt to a greater or lesser degree throughout Colombia. Before discussing the differential effects of the crisis in particular cities in Colombia, however, we will describe the Colombian migrant workforce in more detail.

Characteristics of the Migration of Colombian Workers to Venezuela and Their Labor Market Participation[4]

In this section, we review the characteristics of Colombian migration to Venezuela and the nature of the labor market participation of these workers in Venezuela from two perspectives. First, we review the numbers, the destination, and location of the migrants as well as their demographic and labor force characteristics during the period of crisis.

---

[4] The information in this subsection is derived from the 1983 study of Michelena and Betancourt, entitled "Características económico-laborales durante los años setenta" (Economic and Labor Characteristics of Immigrants in the 1970s). The authors' principal sources were the 1980 General Registry of Foreigners carried out by the Foreigner's Division (DIEX) and data from the Central Office of Statistics and Information of Venezuela, particularly the National Census and sample household surveys.

Second, we will describe reactions in Venezuela to the recent Colombian migration.

Statistical Data

There are no accurate data on the number of Colombian workers in Venezuela. This limitation is evident in the Venezuelan studies on international migration and the immigrant workforce. Estimates of Colombians in Venezuela in 1979 range from one-half million (Papail, l985) to 1.5 million (Bello, 1979). The 1980 General Registry of Foreigners (MGE), the 1981 National Census, and the National Household Survey all conducted in Venezuela estimated that there would be 466,000 Colombians in the country by the end of 1981 (Papail, 1985).

Such varying estimates could be the result of difficulties in measuring such a highly mobile population that travels back and forth across the border in search of work. The illegal and undocumented nature of much of this migration is another element that makes quantifying workers difficult. Lastly, the political implications of this migration and conflicting political interests also play a role in the widely disparate estimates.

Still, Colombians represent the largest group of foreigners in Venezuela, as confirmed in a number of studies on this issue (Papail, 1985; Mora, 1985; Michelena and Betancourt, 1983).

Geographic Location of Migrants

Several studies on the geographic location of Colombian migrants in Venezuela concur that they are concentrated in the Venezuelan border zone, particularly in the states of Táchira and Zulia. Following these destinations, in order of importance, are the Federal District and the states of Miranda and Barinas in the Central and Andean regions (Mora, 1985; Pellegrino, *n.d.*). These destinations have been confirmed in the results of questionnaires applied to Colombian deportees (Mansilla, 1979).

The locations listed above also correspond directly to labor demands in various sectors of the Venezuelan economy. As an example, there is high demand for workers in the sugarcane and other agro-industries in the mentioned areas, as well as in commerce along the border (Gómez and Díaz, 1983).

Demographic and Occupational Characteristics of Colombian Migrants[5]

In 1981, the economically active population of Colombians in Venezuela was just over 200,000, or 4.9 percent of the Venezuelan labor force and 40.5 percent of foreign-born labor (Michelena and Betancourt, 1983).

[5] This subsection is also based on Michelena and Betancourt (1983). (*See,* Footnote 4).

Approximately, three-fourths of the Colombian migrants are employed in urban areas, and one-fourth in rural areas, where, according to Michelena and Betancourt, " [the Colombian migrants] appears to have taken over the jobs left by the Venezuelan workers who have migrated to the city" (1983:45).

In analyzing labor participation by sector, we can see that from 1976-1980, at least one-half of the Colombian migrant labor force was employed in the tertiary or service sector especially in the category "community, social, and personal services". However, during the same four-year period, there was an increase in those employed in the secondary sector (especially in construction). By 1980, the secondary sector employed 30 percent of Colombian workers in Venezuela; and 19 percent of the Colombian migrant labor force was employed in the primary sector (mainly agriculture). Moreover, most of the Colombian migrant labor force (66 percent) worked in the informal economy (*i.e.*, "off the books" or in self-generated employment), and this trend prevailed even more in urban than rural areas.

Michelena and Betancourt also note a tendency toward feminization (39 percent in 1981) and toward younger participants in the Colombian migrant workforce.

In comparing the various nationality groups in Venezuela, it was found that open unemployment was highest among Colombians. In the urban sector, 54.6 percent of Colombians were underemployed. From 1976 to 1980, Colombian workers in the cities fell into the lowest salary bracket in the country.

In summary, we can say that in the period just prior to the Venezuela crisis, the Colombian workforce was generally found to be among the least privileged in Venezuela. Venezuela's economic development policy allowed for a high degree of labor absorption. Colombians competed with Venezuelans for jobs, with a consequent general reduction in wages. Once the labor market became saturated in the sectors employing Colombians, an increase could be seen in unemployment and underemployment indices and in repressive and discriminatory practices. An important part of the Colombian workforce was forced to move from agricultural work to new employment in the cities. Nonetheless, in comparative terms, conditions in Venezuela were more favorable than those in Colombia.

Reactions in Venezuela to Colombian Labor Migration

Obviously, a phenomenon of the magnitude of the Colombian labor migration to Venezuela caused a series of repercussions in the receiving society. Thus, we present a snapshot of how the migration is seen from various social, political, and economic vantage points in Venezuela.

As has been noted by migration scholars, Venezuelan immigration policy has changed over time, according to the intensity and volume of the migration flows and, even more, to the needs and interests of the various economic sectors that at one time or another affect decision-making.

In the 1960s, selective immigration policies were put in place. However, it was during this period that a great number of illegal Colombian migrants entered the country to fill jobs in agriculture (Torrealba, Suárez, Schlocter, 1985).

During the 1970s, there was an even greater emphasis on controlling unskilled immigration and promoting the immigration of skilled labor by means of selective policies. But, the Colombians continued to migrate, both to the rural and urban sectors.

Currently, Venezuela has established the following criterion for labor migration: "In order to enter the country as a foreign worker, one needs to have a higher level of education than one can get in Venezuela" (López, 1984:19).

Since 1980, when the recession began in Venezuela, employment and immigration policies began to exert greater control over foreign workers, opening up the way for selective legalization, limited "to those activities that because of the nature of their economic and technological development" cannot be carried out by Venezuelans (López, 1984:l9).

Such a policy stance was reiterated by the Venezuelan Interior Minister in a 1984 speech in which he called for preference in hiring Venezuelans: "When new workers are hired, we should eliminate the practice of passing over Venezuelan workers in favor of foreigners, especially if they are undocumented" (El Universal, 1984).

Since 1983-1984, there has been a clear bias against Colombian undocumented workers, based on arguments that range from defending national sovereignty and preserving institutional and social order to preventing the further deterioration of the standard of living of wide sectors of the Venezuelan population.

For example, Msgr. Mariano Parrá León, Bishop of Cumaná and a member of the Tourism and Migration Commission, referred to the undocumented problem in this way: "Illegal migration...only contributes to a breakdown in control over the jobs and occupations of Venezuelans...In view of this, there can be no place for charity (toward the Colombians), rather it is a matter of social justice (for the Venezuelan worker)" (El Nacional, 1984).

President Lusinchi warned that his government "would not tolerate Caracas continuing to operate like a ranch, much of which is controlled by foreigners" (La Religion, 1985). The Governor of the Federal District stated that if Venezuelans could get all the undocumented out of Caracas, it would solve all the problems in that city (El Diario, 1984).

Although the migration of Colombians to Venezuela aggravates socio-economic problems that have plagued Venezuela in recent years, the reactions to migration reflect a tendency to exaggerate its negative impact on the country. Likewise, there has been a tendency to discount the role undocumented Colombian workers have played in the process of capital accumulation, by filling labor demand at lower wages than Venezuelans would accept and under conditions clearly advantageous to the Venezuelan entrepreneurial sector.

The reasons that Colombians represent competition in the Venezuelan labor market, particularly at times of growing unemployment and a deteriorating standard of living, are structural. In other words, the capitalist development model followed by Venezuela at this time is at a critical phase that cannot be understood in terms of illegal labor migration alone.

Impact of the Recession on the Principal Urban Sending Areas of Colombian Migrant Workers

This section analyzes the effects of the Venezuelan crisis on the economy and the labor markets of the principal urban sending areas in Colombia. The order of presentation is based upon the degree to which each city has been affected by the economic crisis.

Cúcuta

Cúcuta was the Colombian city most affected by the Venezuelan crisis. The rapid expansion of the Venezuelan economy in the 1970s, insufficient internal demand in Colombia for consumer goods, and different exchange rates between the two countries allowed Cúcuta to become the principal supplier of consumer goods for the Venezuelan market. For example, in 1980, sales of clothing and leather goods to Venezuela represented more than 70 percent of the sales of these articles in Cúcuta (DANE and Cámara de Comercio de Cúcuta, 1983). Since the 1970s, the economic development of the city became more and more dependent upon Venezuela. Cúcuta experienced a strong growth in the commercial and service sectors and a marked stagnation in the industrial sector in terms of capital investment and the generation of employment. In 1982, the commercial sector accounted for 33.2 percent of the employment, the service sector 28.3 percent, and the industrial sector 17.9 percent (Velasco y Asociados, 1983).

While this situation created economic growth in Cúcuta, it also made it vulnerable to changes in Venezuelan economic policies. This vulnerability became clear when the bolívar was devalued in February 1983. The most important economic effects that occurred in the city as a result of the Venezuelan crisis can be summarized as follows:

1) A marked increase in unemployment. While the unemployment rate was 5.9 percent in 1981, it reached 10.4 percent in 1983, 14.6 percent in 1984, and 15.1 percent in 1985 (DANE, 1985a).

2) A reduction in commerce. Expenditures by tourists from Venezuela in Cúcuta fell 76.8 percent in April and 96.2 percent in October 1983, as compared to the same months in 1982. Meanwhile the expenses incurred by Colombians in Venezuela increased by 65 percent between the same two periods (CEFI, 1984).

3) An abrupt fall in commercial activities. The index of retail sales fell 58.8 percent in August 1983 over August 1982. Wholesale purchases declined 51.5 percent (Banco de la República, 1983).

4) Paralysis of external commerce. During the first nine months of 1983, payment for exports to the Bank of the Republic in Cúcuta fell some 90 percent over the previous year. The sectors which were most affected were ready-made clothes and leather goods (Banco de la République, 1983).

5) Closing of commercial establishments. By April of 1984 approximately 600 stores had closed (Escallón Villa, 1984). The informal sector, particularly the street vendors, also felt the effects of the crisis. For each ten existing booths in the city an average of only four continued to operate.

6) Stagnation of tourism. Before 1983, 70 percent of the hotels were occupied by Venezuelans, but in that year the proportion fell to 20 percent, only to recover slightly in 1984 and in the first nine months of 1985 (30 and 40 percent, respectively).

7) Decline of the industrial sector. The impact of the crisis was particularly severe in the shoe, clothing, and food and beverage industries. Approximately 1,000 businesses dedicated to clothing and shoes closed, which resulted in a massive dismissal of workers.

The economic crisis in Cúcuta following the Venezuelan recession and the devaluation of the bolívar produced critical social problems in the city. Unemployment grew rapidly, the level of family income diminished, and the standard of living for wide sectors of the population deteriorated. With the closing of many commercial establishments, 35,000 to 40,000 persons lost their jobs. Employment in the tourist industry declined by approximately 40 percent and this led to temporary workers being hired. The crisis in the industrial sector led to a 45 percent decline in employment while textile and shoe industries practically disappeared (DANE, 1983c).

As a result of this crisis, several migration streams developed. First, many persons from various regions of the country who had traveled to Cúcuta to work during the period of economic expansion were forced to relocate. Second, faced with the deterioration of real wages in Venezuela and the impossibility of maintaining levels of income and savings that could be sent to their families, some workers began to return to Colombia. A segment of these workers remained in Cúcuta because this was their city of origin or they chose to work in border commerce (generally contraband). Other workers only utilized Cúcuta as a point of transit to reach other cities in Colombia.

The Venezuelan crisis did not affect the entire Colombian migrant population in Venezuela. Those who returned had not lived in Venezuela for a long time and had not established strong social, labor, or property ties; others returned because their illegal situation made them more vulnerable to the restrictions imposed by the new economic circumstances. Our interviews with key informants in Cúcuta revealed that increases in unemployment and growth in the informal sector were caused more by the sharp decline in the economic activities of the city than by return migration. When the crisis abated in Venezuela, a new migration flow from Cúcuta emerged. What is noteworthy is that the number of emigrants was somewhat reduced and the laborers were bound for seasonal, rather than full-time, employment.

Cúcuta has not been able to surmount the difficult situation caused by the Venezuelan recession, the devaluation of the bolívar, and the economic recession in Colombia. Therefore, it is not possible to predict with certainty the future characteristics of labor migration between Cúcuta and Venezuela, particularly if we keep in mind that the city is vulnerable to the economic and migration policies which may be adopted by both countries.

Bucaramanga

The city of Bucaramanga was affected by the Venezuelan crisis in two ways. First, it directly felt the impact of the crisis because many of its economic activities had been developed in relation to the neighboring country. For example, in 1982 Venezuela received 56 percent of the exports from the region of Bucaramanga; in 1984, the region's foreign trade with Venezuela had decreased by 63 percent, 52 percent, and 33 percent for the years 1983, 1982, and 1981 respectively (Cámara de Comercio de Bucaramanga, 1983a).

Second, due to its geographical location and its established economic infrastructure, Bucaramanga's industries and small and medium enterprises had become important suppliers for the Cúcuta market. Consequently, the onset of the crisis in Venezuela and in Cúcuta affected the economy of the Bucaramanga region. The impact was felt only when merchandise began to accumulate in Cúcuta and when recovery became very difficult. A number of economic indicators will help to clarify this situation:

1) Between 1983 and 1984 investments in Bucaramanga fell by 7 percent while between 1982 and 1983 they had increased by 2.5 percent.

2) Wholesale and retail sales declined significantly in 1983 after having increased 21.5 percent between 1981 and 1982. During the first three-quarters of 1984 these sales declined by 19.2 percent, 12.5 percent, and 10.2 percent, respectively, over the same periods of the preceding years.

3) In 1984 the value of liquidations reached the highest level for the period 1978 through 1984 and tripled the value of the liquidations occurring in 1983.

4) The close of businesses in 1983 was alarming; 400 shoe and leather businesses and 250 exporting businesses were closed while 350 jewelry manufacturers and 150 jewelry stores reduced their sales by 35 percent on average (FENALCO, 1985).

Other activities were also affected by the crisis. Tourism experienced a 90 percent decline in business from visitors coming from Venezuela during the Holy Week of 1983 over the same period of the previous year (Cámara de Comercio de Bucaramanga, 1983). The agricultural industry was also affected by the loss of sales as a result of the increase in contraband food coming from Venezuela.

This situation produced relatively high rates of unemployment. Bucaramanga, which traditionally had relatively low rates of unemployment compared to the rest of the country (6.4 percent in 1982), attained a rate of 11.5 percent in July of 1985. Between 1981 and 1983 the industrial sector experienced a negative growth rate in employment (-12.9 percent) which left some 675 persons out of work (DANE, 1985b).

The economic crisis in Venezuela led to limited return migration to Bucaramanga. Workers who returned to Bucaramanga had traveled to Venezuela in search of better economic opportunities. These persons were primarily involved in unskilled agricultural activities and domestic services, though some were professionals. While this return flow was relatively large, it did not acquire the intensity of emigration flows to Venezuela in the decade of the 1970s. Furthermore, the returnees were largely recent migrants.

The critical moment of return occurred in 1983. When the economic crisis lessened, migration to Venezuela began once more. The second group of persons who returned to Bucaramanaga had gone to Cúcuta during its period of economic expansion. Many of these people had worked in Cúcuta as street vendors.

Medellín

The economic crisis began in Medellín at the beginning of the 1980s. Especially hard hit by the recession was the industrial sector which represented one-third of the productivity of the city. The increase in the number of unemployed persons in Medellín (31 percent annually between 1981 and 1984) caused a reduction of internal demand for goods. Among the domestic causes which provoked the steep economic downturn were the high cost of credit, scarcity of capital, high prices for raw materials, and the reduction in real wages for a wide sector of the population.

One of the factors which most affected the economy was the downturn in foreign trade. Between 1982 and 1983, net exports from Medellín and Antioquia (the department in which the city is located) fell. Whereas the level of exports to countries outside the Andean region rose by U.S.$27 million, exports within the Andean region (i.e., to Venezuela) fell by U.S.$33 million. This represents a U.S.$6 million net drop in exports.

The devaluation of the bolívar primarily affected the manufacturing sector of Medellín, principally textiles, clothing, and food. Some 58 percent of the enterprises lost Venezuela as their only market. The sales from clothing, food, glass, and metal fell some 86.2 percent between 1982 and 1983, spelling a loss of U.S.$8 million. In addition, enterprises which depended on Venezuela for more than 50 percent of their business saw their sales rates decline by 77.6 percent in the same period, for a loss of U.S.$24.5 million. The textile and clothing sectors, which depended 80 to 95 percent on the Venezuelan market, lost exports of U.S.$7.3 million in 1983.

The small business sector in Medellín also was affected by the Venezuelan crisis. Businesses not only lost sales but also experienced problems in accounts receivable and in the return of merchandise from Venezuela. This merchandise had to be sold in Medellín at prices below the cost of production.

Unemployment rates in Medellín reached 16.5 percent in 1985, 2 points higher than the national average. Between 1981 and 1983 unemployment in the industrial sector of the city rose by an annual rate of 4.6 percent. The 120 largest firms in Medellín eliminated 19,000 positions.

The largest loss occurred in the textile sector (7,000 persons), which all together accounted for 67.7 percent of the total workforce of these firms. Employment fell 9.3 percent in commercial enterprises and 5.7 percent in the commercial service sector (Cámara de Comercio de Medellín, 1984).

The Venezuelan crisis caused the return of workers to the metropolitan areas of Medellín, although in rates substantially lower than the rates of out-migration to Venezuela in the 1970s. Similar to the pattern described for the other migrant-sending cities, those who returned to Medellín had not resided in Venezuela for a long period of time and found it difficult to compete within a labor market where opportunities had become significantly reduced. It is interesting to observe that right after the textile crisis in Antioquia, at the beginning of the 1980s, many workers in this sector chose to emigrate and it was precisely among this group that a relatively large return occurred.

The return of workers to Medellín aggravated the social and labor problems of the city. The economy, particularly the industrial economy, was not capable of absorbing this infusion of labor. The returnees helped to swell the ranks of the unemployed and to increase the informal sector. To a lesser extent, the returnees established small businesses with savings they had accumulated abroad.

Cali

In the early 1970s, the industrial development of the Valle del Cauca and its capital, Cali, began to show the first signs of economic decline. The problem became more serious in the 1980s owing largely to a fall in the international prices for sugar, a decline in exports, and the transfer of some industries to Bogotá, principally chemical and pharmaceutical enterprises.

These regional difficulties generated a series of migratory flows. Some workers chose internal migration to Cali; workers who chose to travel to Venezuela in search of better opportunities found very favorable conditions there. Opportunities were especially good for workers in the sugar industry. In Venezuela they found labor demand high due to the scarcity of local workers. The salaries the migrants earned were significantly greater than those available in Colombia.

In 1981, the unemployment rate in Cali was 6.5 percent; this increased to 9 percent in 1983 and to 12.6 percent in 1984. The average unemployment rate between 1980 and 1985 rose 24 percent annually (DANE, 1985a).

Between 1981 and 1983 the industrial unemployment rate in Cali increased 5.2 percent annually. In the textile and clothing industries, the increase was 8.9 percent a year and in the chemical industries it was 3.1 percent. The paper industry showed an increase in unemployment of 8.8 percent annually; printing experienced a rate of 10.2 percent annually. In other words, these four principal industrial sectors of the city generated 60 percent of the unemployment in the city between 1981 and 1983 (DANE, 1981b and 1983c).

The devaluation of the bolívar and the economic recession in Venezuela aggravated the crisis in this area. Exports to Venezuela declined by 58 percent in 1983 over the previous year; the sectors most affected were textile, clothing, leather, and metal products (DANE).

The decrease in the exchange rate and the increase in unemployment in Venezuela favored the return of Colombians to Cali — particularly those who were working in such vulnerable sectors of the Venezuelan economy as construction. As in previous cases, the period of residency in Venezuela for persons who had returned was relatively short. In addition, most workers returned in the months following the crisis which tends to confirm that the crisis most affected workers who had not obtained stable employment. While return migration did affect the labor market in Cali, its importance was relatively reduced in comparison to the other factors mentioned above. Unemployment and the growth of the informal economy of Cali can be explained more in terms of the internal and external structural conditions in Cali than by return migration.

Cartagena

The economy of Cartagena in recent years has been characterized by the concentration of its economic activities in industry, commerce, and service, each of which contributes to generating the GDP of the city.

Industry has been concentrated primarily in oil refining and in the manufacture of chemical products. These enterprises represent 76.2 percent of the industrial output of the city. The chemical enterprises generate more than one-third of the industrial employment in the city followed by food and beverages (DANE, 1984b). Industry in Cartagena was not affected by the Venezuelan recession because it had depended largely on the national market. Nevertheless, industry did experience some factory closings, slow growth in the levels of production, and consequently a reduction in employment.

For its part, commerce depended fundamentally on domestic markets. Nonetheless, some commercial activity revolved around income derived from tourism at the international level. The decline in persons coming from Venezuela caused an economic contraction in this industry. Moreover, tourism also suffered from a decline in the number of Colombians who could afford to spend tourist dollars in Cartagena. In 1983 the rate of growth in sales from the commercial sector diminished in relation to sales of preceeding years. Of the total number of corporations which dissolved in Cartagena, 47 percent belonged to the commercial sector. Undoubtedly, tourism as a whole was most affected by the Venezuelan crisis.

The problems of unemployment and underemployment in Cartagena seem to be related more directly to the economic crisis in Colombia than to the problems in Venezuela. The labor-market difficulties confronting Cartagena included the dismissal of personnel by many enterprises, the expansion of a temporary workforce, and the continuous arrival of people who were unable to find seasonal work, yet chose to remain in Cartagena.

The return migration from Venezuela cannot be considered a determining factor for the unemployment in Cartagena, nor for the proliferation of employment in informal activities. This does not mean that the Venezuelan crisis has not affected the return of workers who originated from this region. The great part of those who returned were seasonal agricultural workers and domestic servants. What motivated the return of these workers was not so much unemployment, as it was a reduction in income and the inability to save or send remittances to their families. Nonetheless, the return of workers was not massive and never reached the dimensions of earlier migrations. Once the critical period had ended, migration to Venezuela became seasonal. Workers migrated to acquire savings and then returned to Colombia.

CONCLUSIONS

The impact of the Venezuelan crisis on each of the principal urban sending areas of Colombia varied in quantitative and qualitative terms. The differences can be attributed to many factors. These include the economic characteristics and development of each city, the interdependence among the cities, and the relationship of the city to the national economies of Colombia and Venezuela.

Thus, we have seen how Cúcuta most dramatically felt the effects of the crisis which resulted in a sharp decline in the commercial activity in the border area. Bucaramanga, which had structured its commercial and industrial base directly in relation to the Venezuelan market and indirectly through Cúcuta, was doubly affected by the crisis through the loss in demand for its products in these two areas. With respect to Medellín and Cali, the Venezuelan crisis and its impact on the commercial market of Cúcuta added to the economic recession that these cities have suffered since the beginning of the 1980s. Nevertheless, the impact was greater in Medellín. With so much of its economy based on the manufacturing of consumer goods, Medellín was hard hit by the reduction in Venezuelan demand for these products. On the other hand, because of its geographical location, Cali had stronger ties with the Ecuadoran market than with the Venezuelan market. Finally, because Cartagena was so dependent on the internal market, it was only affected by the Venezuelan economic crisis because of the reduction in its tourist activity.

The labor markets in these five principal cities of Colombia experienced the Venezuelan crisis and return migration in different ways. These variations are mainly the result of the overall impact of the Venezuelan recession on the regional economies and, secondarily, as the result of return migration. Generally, return migration occurred among persons who recently migrated to Venezuela but did not have stable and legal working conditions. These workers did not establish economic and social networks in Venezuela and did not consolidate sources of income which could have been competitive with those in Colombia. It would be erroneous to conclude that the returning workers from Venezuela seriously affected the rates of unemployment and underemployment in Colombia. What we can affirm is that the decline in remittances from Venezuela affected the consumer demand in the five cities and it also had a negative impact on the standard of living for many Colombian families. It forced them to search for additional income by undertaking various jobs and extending their workday activities, which contributed to the increase in the informal sector.

It is evident that the structural factors which have determined the migratory flows of Colombian workers to Venezuela have not disappeared. This explains in large part why return migration was not as massive as initially anticipated and why population movements from Colombia to Venezuela have not subsided. The tradition of migration in many Colombian homes has established a complex network of family, social, and economic relations that transcend national boundaries. These relations have been incorporated gradually into a way of life for these families in such a way that it is not feasible for them to abandon this tradition.

The crisis in Venezuela has, nonetheless, caused some changes in Colombian migration patterns. For example, it is clear that the migratory movements are becoming more seasonal and multiple, and it is possible that many persons feel obligated to combine internal migration with international migration to improve their economic situation.

As long as the demand for labor in some sectors or regions of Colombia continues to be inadequate, there will continue to be migratory movements to regions or countries which offer better opportunities. In spite of the crisis, Venezuela still attracts Colombian migrants not only for their comparative advantages economically but also because of the similarities in geography, culture, and language between the two countries. Nevertheless, if the recession in Venezuela continues, it is possible that migration will be redirected to other areas such as the United States or Canada.

REFERENCES

Banco Central de Venezuela
1980   *Informe económico anual.* Caracas.

Banco de la República Federación Nacional de Comerciantes, Norte de Santander
1983   "Situación económica del área fronteriza de Cúcuta". Cúcuta.

Bello, P., C. Cifuentes, M. de Ordóñez and M. Ponce de León
1979   "La migración latinoamericana en Venezuela, en una muestra de trabajo social".

Cámara de Comercio de Bucaramanga
1983a   "Efectos de la situación venezolana en la ciudad de Bucaramanga y su zona de influencia". Parte I. Bucaramanga.

1983b   "Devaluación venezolana y su incidencia económica en Santander". Bucaramanga.

Cámara de Comercio de Medellín
1984   "Cifras coleccionables. No. 3: Indicadores Económicas 1983".

Centro de Estudios de Fronteras e Integración (CEFI)
1984   *Estimaciones del comercio no registrado en la zona fronteriza venezolana-colombiana. (San Antonio-Cúcuta).* San Cristóbal: Universidad de los Andes.

Comisión Económica para América Latina y el Caribe (CEPAL)
1985   "Balance preliminar de la economía latinoamericana en 1984". *Economía Colombiana*, 165:77-980.

1984   *Anuario Estadístico de América Latina.*

DANE y Cámara de Comercio de Cúcuta
1983   "Monografia del Municipio de Cúcuta". Bogotá.

Departamento Administrativo Nacional de Estadística (DANE).
        Anuario de comercio exterior. Bogotá.

1981a   *Anuario de industria manufacturera.* Bogotá.

1982a   *Anuario de industria manufacturera.* Bogotá.

1983a   *Anuario de industria manufacturera.* Bogotá.

1984a   *Anuario de industria manufacturera.* Bogotá.

1983b   *Boletín de avance estadístico.* Bogotá.

1985a   *Boletín de avance estadístico.* Bogotá.

1981b   *Encuesta anual manufacturera.* Bogotá.

1982b   *Encuesta anual manufacturera.* Bogotá.

1983c   *Encuesta anual manufacturera.* Bogotá.

1984b   *Encuesta anual manufacturera.* Bogotá.

1983d   *Encuesta nacional de hogares.* Bogotá.

1985b   *Encuesta nacional de hogares.* Bogotá.

Escallón Villa, A.
1984   "Colombianos con Cúcuta", *El Espectador.* Bogotá.

Federación Nacional de Comerciantes (FENALCO). Sección Santander.
1985   "Decretos No. 2666, Artículo 145. De la Nueva Legislación Aduanera en la Ciudad de Bucaramanga y su Incidencia en Santander".

Gómez A.E. and L.M. Díaz
1983   *La Moderna Esclavitud: Los Indocumentados en Venezuela.* Bogotá: FINES y Oveja Negra.

López Trocelt, M.
1984   "Mediante políticas del ministerio del trabajo, el gobierno trata de frenar el ingreso indiscriminado de Mano de Obra Extranjera". *El Nacional* 17/07, 84, *Acontecer Migratorio* No. 41, p. 19. Caracas.

Mansilla, L.
1979   "Inserción laboral de migrantes indocumentados", *Migraciónes Laborales.* B:85-107 (julio), Bogotá: Ministerio de Trabajo y Seguridad Social-SENALDE, Proyecto PNUD-OTT col/72/027.

Michelena, A. and N. Betancourt
1983   "Características económicas laborales de los inmigrantes durante los años setenta", *Consejo Nacional de Recursos Humanos,* SP 1 2000. Caracas: Universidad Centro Occidental.

Oficina Central de Coordinación y Planificación de la Presidencia de la República (COR-DIPLAN)
1984   *VII Plan de la Nación 1984-1988.* Caracas.

Organization of American States (OAS)
1984   *Boletín Estadístico,* 6(1-4).

Papail, J.
1985   "Casi medio millón de Colombianos había en Venezuela para 1981", *Acontecer Migratorio,* 45:14. Caracas.

Pezzano, S.
1984   "Logros y fracasos de la gestión economica en 1983", *CIFRAS* 2(23):15. enero.

Portes, A. and R. Bach
1985   *Latin Journey: Cuban and Mexican Immigrants in the United States.* Berkeley: University of California Press.

Ruiz, H.
1984   "Algunos interrogantes sobre el futuro la economía colombiana". In *Economía Colombiana.* Bogota: Serie de documentos No. 3, Pp. 152-153. diciembre-enero.

Torrealba, R., Suárez and Schlocter
1985   "Ciento cincuenta años de politicas inmigratorias en Venezuela". In *Democracia y Economía.* Sobretiro del No. 55, Vol. XXIII, Caracas.

Velasco, J. and Asociados, Ltda.
1983   *Plan integral de desarrollo del municipio de Cúcuta.* Bogotá: FONADE-UDRU.

MANPOWER LOSSES AND EMPLOYMENT ADEQUACY AMONG SKILLED WORKERS IN JAMAICA 1976-1985[1]

Patricia Y. Anderson

It is common for manpower analysts to point out that Jamaica, like many developing countries, is characterized by an abundance of un-skilled labor and a shortage of skilled workers. It is also frequently observed that Jamaica shares in the "brain drain" to the developed countries, as professionals migrate to seek their fortunes in the more advanced economies, leaving the country denuded of the skills needed for development. The question of why it is possible for manpower shortages to co-exist with manpower losses tends to be approached as if there is a simple causal relationship, with manpower exports being the antecedent variable which results in the observed shortages of skills, a presumed abundance of "empty places", and the consequent need for "replacement imports" of skills. Far too little attention is paid to the alternative explanation: It is in fact the shortage of adequate jobs which leads to the outflow of skilled workers, and the critical problem which Jamaica faces is the lack of effective demand in retaining its workers.

This chapter looks at the migration of professionals and craftsmen from Jamaica over the ten-year period from 1976 to 1985, and examines evidence for the argument that these groups were being steadily expelled from the labor force through increasing inadequacy of em-

[1] This study was supported by a research grant from the Hemispheric Migration Project, which was funded jointly by the Center for Immigration Policy and Refugee Assistance at Georgetown University and the Intergovernmental Committee for Migration. The study relies on data which was collected through the Population Mobility and Development Project at the Institute of Social and Economic Research, University of the West Indies (Jamaica). This project was funded by the International Development Research Center of Canada. The study also uses material from the 1979 Jamaica Labor Force Survey, which was made available by the Statistical Institute of Jamaica. Special thanks are extended to the staff of the Statistical Institute for Jamaica, to Professor George Roberts of the University of the West Indies, and to Dr. Patricia R. Pessar of Georgetown University.

WHEN BORDERS DON'T DIVIDE

ployment. As the economy started to contract in the mid-1970s, the population experienced increasing economic hardship, and many professionals and craftsmen found that their social position and standard of living became progressively more marginal. While other occupational groups within the country were subject to equally difficult conditions, professionals and craftsmen were among those who were able to take advantage of the "migration alternative" since the policies of the receiving countries were biased towards skilled workers. This was particularly so in the case of the United States and Canada, which were the main destinations during the period.

The 1976-1985 period is of particular interest because it spans two political administrations with widely differing ideological stances and economic policies. The migration outflow in the first half of the period, 1976-1980, has been frequently regarded as political migration since many of the middle classes, in their rejection of the socialist policies of the People's National Party (PNP) administration, sought to distance themselves physically from a possible Communist threat. Adding to their concerns were the economic difficulties occasioned by the prolonged recession resulting from the increase in oil prices, foreign exchange shortages, and currency devaluations. In the second half of the period, 1981-1985, however, under the new Jamaica Labor Party (JLP) leadership, and the friendly support of the United States, there was a considerable influx of financial assistance, a lessening of political violence, and some return migration. Nonetheless, economic conditions continued to be oppressive, particularly for professionals outside of the business class, who did not share in the new prosperity. While manufacturing revived somewhat, production was erratic, and the building industry, under the weight of inflation and spiraling interest rates, remained stagnant. Craftsmen and operatives continued to experience high unemployment and underemployment, many shifting to the informal sector where they found casual work as self-employed artisans or in small-scale activities. Both professionals and craftsmen continued to battle unsuccessfully with the rising cost of living, and out-migration continued.

Since it is also widely acknowledged that the official statistics on migration understate the true extent of manpower losses because they are based only on the reports of persons legally admitted as residents, this study proposes a new methodology — the manpower balance sheet — by which it is possible to obtain a clearer idea of the real dimensions of manpower losses. The manpower balance sheet combines immigration data with national data on labor force and labor mobility to identify unrecorded losses. In this way it demonstrates how the study of labor migration may be integrated with the general analysis of labor market mobility.

PATTERNS OF MOVEMENT 1976-1985
The Background

Any review of Jamaica's experience between 1976 and 1985 encounters the problem of assessing the relative importance which should be attributed to political forces or to economic factors in understanding the considerable changes which this period witnessed. This difficulty is evident in recent analyses of the period and is reflected in some of the issues which these studies raise. These issues involve a series of inter-related questions:

> Was the PNP's socialist declaration in 1984 a greater contributor to economic decline than the rapid increase in the price of oil? (Stephens and Stephens,1986)

> Did the imposition of the bauxite levy offset the increased fuel bill or, by signalling a change in political direction, did it serve to reduce U.S. demand for Jamaican bauxite? (Davis, 1985; Davies, 1986)

> Could the country have survived the higher import burden resulting from increased oil prices had there not been a large-scale capital flight? (Girvan, Bernal and Hughes, 1980)

> Could the Structural Adjustment program have led to renewed growth in the 1980s if there had not been a sharp decline in bauxite demand, or was the program capable only of stimulating uncertain and dependent growth? (Taylor, 1986)

> Was the out-migration of the period a response to changes in political regimes or was it part of a long-established pattern of skill outflows? (Cooper, 1985; Stephens and Stephens, 1986)

If there is any lesson to be learned from the period, it is the close relationship which existed between political and economic decisions, with the result that the analysis of migration flows cannot be understood without reference to the total system of resource flows of which it comprised only one stream. Analyses of the factors which shaped the economy of Jamaica between 1976 and 1985 are provided in the work of several writers (Davies, 1986; Stone, 1985; Jefferson, 1986; Bernal, 1984; Stephens and Stephens, 1986; Brown, 1981; Beckford and Witter, 1980; Girvan, Bernal and Hughes, 1980), and will therefore be only briefly reviewed here. This summary relies primarily on Davies (1986).

The year 1976 with which we begin our analysis of migration flows signalled the end of the first term (1972-76) of the Manley government.

It was a term which had begun with high hopes for social transformation, but which ended with clear evidence of a national economic crisis as well as disaffection on the part of the important business groups in the country. The decade preceding 1972 was the first decade of Jamaica's independence, and it is now generally recognized as one in which there was an impressive growth record, but very little advancement for the mass of the population (Jefferson, 1972). The pattern of dependent capital-intensive growth which was pursued during the 1950s and 1960s in the development of the bauxite/alumina, manufacturing, and tourist sectors entailed a high import content for production, few linkages with domestic sources of raw materials, and a totally inadequate rate of job creation. At the beginning of 1972, therefore, the Manley government saw as its mandate to undertake the task of economic restructuring and to correct the imbalances in social opportunity for the masses.

The government's programs of economic restructuring and social redistribution resulted in large increases in government expenditure which moved from one-quarter of gross domestic product (GDP) in 1973-1974 to 42 percent by 1976-1977, much of this occurring on the basis of deficit financing (Davies, 1986). Whereas the deficit stood at 4.3 percent in 1973-1974, it rose to 15 percent by 1976-1977. A major contributor to the country's problems in this period was the unexpected increase in the price of oil, so that Jamaica's oil-import bill escalated from U.S. $71 million in 1973 to U.S. $195 million in 1974. In an attempt to offset some of this shock to the economy, the government initiated discussions with the multinational aluminum companies operating in the country with the object of increasing bauxite revenues. When these discussions ran into a deadlock, the government imposed a unilateral levy on the bauxite industry which in the first year increased bauxite revenue from U.S. $27 million in 1973 to U.S. $180 million in 1974. Davies concludes that although the bauxite levy did not help to cushion the direct impact of oil-price increases, there still remained several negative consequences of the oil-price hike. Oil-price increases were transmitted to increased prices on a wide range of other goods and services, thus increasing the cost of living. Secondly, the government was forced to use bauxite-levy earnings to finance needed imports, so several development programs which required foreign exchange had to be abandoned or financed through external loans. Lack of economic growth combined with high oil prices to erode the country's balance of payments position, so that by 1976 the government had to resort to borrowing from the International Monetary Fund (IMF).

Stephens and Stephens (1986) point out that the first wave of disaffection of the business classes occurred in years 1973-1974 and was reflected in declining levels of investment. Although the government was returned to office in a landslide victory in 1976, it was primarily because it still held the support of the masses (Stone, 1981). The year 1976 therefore marks the second and last turning point in the support of the business classes with a large increase in capital flight occurring. In this regard, between 1976 and 1980, net private capital outflows amounted to U.S.$412 million (Jefferson, 1986:11). The combination of the current account deficit and capital flight increased the need for official borrowing, so that between 1975 and 1980 the total debt moved from 31.2 percent of GDP to 82.2 percent. This increasing debt burden made inevitable the adoption of austerity programs with severe restrictions on government spending. This program, which was largely put in place by the IMF, served to depress the domestic economy, to reduce growth prospects and employment, and to put the political system under severe pressure (Jefferson, 1986).

The period between 1976 and 1980 was dominated by successive IMF agreements, and the restrictive conditions which they imposed. This was reflected in shortages of basic foods and raw materials, the closure of several businesses, the growth of a black market in foreign exchange and business profiteering — all leading to social discontent and unrest. Finally in March 1980, the Manley government decided to reject the terms of the new IMF agreement which called for public sector layoffs, to curtail negotiations with the Fund, and to call a new election. This October election was preceded by months of political violence, and led to an overwhelming victory for the opposition Jamaica Labor Party (JLP) led by Edward Seaga.

Bernal (1984) has undertaken an assessment of the political impact of the IMF's policies in terms of their economic effect and the social classes which were affected. He demonstrates that the key elements of IMF policy such as wage restraints, reduction in government spending and elimination of subsidies, undermined the standard of living of all workers, especially the poorest groups. Other elements, such as devaluation and increased indirect taxation fell heavily on all groups except large-scale capitalists and self-employed professionals.

Following his analysis, it is not difficult to see why support for the PNP was eroded among those who were subject to unemployment or a reduced standard of living, among those producers who were unable to gain access to the limited foreign exchange or to cope with the higher prices for production inputs, and among those who accepted the anti-Communist propaganda of the JLP and the mass media. It is significant however, as Davies notes, that although the general thrust of the second Manley term (1977-1980) was in direct contrast to that of the first (1972-1976), the macro-economic indicators showed no improvement, and unemployment and growth in GDP actually worsened (Table 1).

The establishment of the Seaga administration in 1980 signalled a change in economic policy, renewed friendly links with the United States, and reestablished the primacy of the private sector. The support of the Reagan administration in the United States also facilitated a high level of concessionary financial support for the country, and both the World Bank and the IMF were lenient in their provision of loans.

These favorable developments, however, were undermined by the decline in bauxite demand, as well as by the IMF-promoted policy of liberalized imports. Between 1980 and 1983, the trade deficit and the current account deficit increased dramatically. and by the end of 1983 the government was forced to institute a formal devaluation and to adopt a policy of tight demand management. The drastic reduction in the value of the Jamaican dollar (from a level of U.S.$1= J. $1.78 in November 1983 to U.S. $1 = J. $5.50 at the end of 1985) had harsh repercussions on the cost of living which were reflected in the movements of the Consumer Price Index (CPI). This index showed an increase of 31.2 percent in 1984, compared with 6.5 percent in 1982.

As Davies points out, the disadvantaged groups in the soceity were seriously affected by price movements on basic foods, as well as on essential items such as cooking gas and electricity. In addition, the IMF pressure to cut government spending had a disastrous effect on the provision of social services, so that hospitals and schools were partially or totally closed, or forced to operate with drastically reduced budgets. These changes were reflected in several socioeconomic indicators of the period which are assembled by Davies, and reproduced here (Table 1).

Size and Composition of Migration 1976-1985

Labor migration has long been a prominent feature of Jamaica's demographic history, contributing to both the size and composition of the population. Roberts (1974) notes that in the intercensal period 1943-1960, net migration was 195,000 or nearly one-third of the natural increase in population size over the period. During the sixties, the net outflow reached a level of 280,000 or 53 percent of natural increase. Within the last intercensal period, 1970-1982, net migration estimates at 210,000 or 38 percent of natural increase.

In analyzing migration from Jamaica during the 1970s, Cooper (1985) makes a strong argument for the use of a longer time perspective, showing that the seventies outflow was part of a much larger and well-established process. It is therefore useful to compare out-migration levels between 1976 and 1985 with those experienced during the previous decade when the change in U.S. and Canadian immigration law had stimulated a large outflow to North America. Jamaica participated actively in this movement, often referred to as the "new immigration"

(Massey, 1981; Bryce-LaPorte, 1983), and the peak flow occurred in 1968 when the amendments to the U.S. Immigration Act took effect. In that year net migration was estimated at 20,000 but out-migration to the U.S., Canada, and the U.K. reached 25,000, with the U.S. accounting for 17,470 migrants. Four years later, in 1972, when the People's National Party assumed control of the government out-migration was still heavy (18,139), but appeared to be partially offset by a fairly significant inward flow so that net migration was on the order of 11,200 (Table 2). In the first four years of the Manley administration, net migration ranged between ten and thirteen thousand, while out-migration moved from 18,139 in 1972 to a high of 25,091 in 1974, falling back to 20,681 in 1975. During this period, the main increase was in the expansion of the Canadian migrant stream which tripled between 1972 and 1973. This increase was part of the general expansion which took place in Canadian immigration which grew by 51 percent between 1982 and 1983, in response to their perceived manpower shortages (Passaris, 1983).

If levels of out-migration are compared with net migration over the period since 1970, it becomes apparent that the closest correspondence between these two sets of figures occurs between 1976 and 1980 (Table 2). There is, of course, no reason why these figures should inevitably

TABLE 1

Socio-Economic Indicators for Jamaica
Selected Years 1972 - 1985

Socio-Economic Indicator	1972	1976	1978	1980	1982	1984	1985
% Unemployed	23.6	20.5	23.0	27.9	27.0	25.6	25.0
Youth Unemployment (persons 14-24 years; April)	40.3	38.2	43.5	50.6	50.7	47.7	44.9
Rate of Growth of GDP Compared to Previous Year	2.3	-6.5	0.4	-5.8	1.0	-0.4	-3.7
Inflation % (CPI Dec. to Dec. Jan. 1975 = 100)	–	8.1	49.4	29.0	6.5	31.2	23.1
Trade Balance (US $mill.) (-)	(251.3)	(280.3)	(126.6)	(213.4)	(607.4)	(459.0)	(575.0)

Source: Davies, 1986. Economic and Social Survey, 1980, 1985.

coincide, since net migration estimates take account of the inward flow of immigrants or return migrants. Accordingly, it is only in periods when in-migration is low, that one may expect the two sets of figures to converge. It is not possible to say whether the increase in official estimates of net migration in the second half of the 1970s was the result of improved data-management practices, or whether it reflected lower levels of in-migration at that time. There are no national data on return migration which would serve to support this second explanation. However, what is clear is that out-migration did remain at high levels between 1976 and 1980, reaching a total 106,660 or an average of 21,332 annually. This was very close to the annual average of 21,068 in the first half of the 1970s (1971-1975), and the level of 21,183 annually between 1966 and 1970 (Table 3). Over the five-year period 1976-1980, the highest level of out-migration was recorded in 1978 when the total reached 23,889 as a result of the rapid increase in U.S. migration from 11,500 in 1977 to 19,265 in 1978.

During the first five years of the Seaga government, out-migration continued at roughly the same level, except for the year 1981 when it peaked at 26,543. Since it may be reasonably argued that the 1981 migrants had initiated their relocation process from the previous year, preceding the October elections, an alternative approach is to include the 1981 out-flow with the earlier period in calculating annual averages. This produces an annual average out-migration level of 22,200 for the Manley period and an almost identical level of 22,240 for the Seaga period 1982-1985.

The migration statistics assembled in Tables 2 and 3 reveal both continuity and change. It is clear that out-migration has been a continuously high process since the mid-1960s, but at times it is also possible to discern accelerated rates which are explained in terms of the economic and socio-political changes of the period. Thus, average annual out-migration rates were very similar under the Manley and Seaga administrations, being 10.2 per thousand during 1976-80 and 10.3 per thousand for 1981-1985. Alternatively, the rates were 10.6 per thousand for 1976-1981, and 9.9 per thousand for 1982-1985. However, for individual years such as 1978 and 1981, the out-migration rate was 11.4 and 12.3 per thousand, respectively, indicative of the social turmoil in the preceding years.

From Table 2 it is also possible to gain an appreciation of the importance of out-migration relative to the natural increase in the population over the period and for each year. For the decade 1976-1985, out-migration reduced the population by an amount equivalent to half of the natural increase over the period. The reduction in population growth caused by net migration was estimated to be about one-third.

TABLE 2

Out-Migration Flows
Net Migration Estimates and Population Changes for Jamaica
in 1972 and 1975 - 1985

Year	Mean Population	Natural Increase	Net Migration	Out-Migration[a]	Annual Rate Out-Migra. (per 1000)	Out-Migra. as Percent of Natural Incr.
			(-)			
1972	1,907,900	50,400	(11,200)	18,139	9.5	36.0
1975	2,012,800	45,700	(12,100)	20,681	10.3	45.3
1976	2,040,500	44,200	(22,200)	17,506	8.6	39.6
1977	2,063,100	44,300	(21,100)	18,821	9.1	42.5
1978	2,087,700	43,900	(17,800)	23,889	11.4	54.4
1979	2,112,000	44,000	(21,400)	23,664	11.2	53.8
1980	2,133,200	44,100	(24,300)	22,780	10.7	51.7
1981	2,162,300	44,200	(5,900)	26,543	12.3	60.0
1982	2,200,100	47,000	(9,800)	21,745	9.9	46.3
1983	2,240,800	48,800	(4,300)	22,394	10.0	45.9
1984	2,279,800	44,100	(10,500)	22,650	9.9	51.4
1985	2,311,100	42,300	(13,400)	22,165	9.6	52.4
1976-80	2,087,300	220,500	(106,800)	106,660	10.2	48.4
1981-85	2,238,800	226,400	(43,900)	115,497	10.3	51.0
1976-85	2,163,100	446,900	(150,700)	222,157	10.3	49.7

Note: [a] Based on migration to the U.S., Canada and the U.K.

Since 1981 the fairly close correspondence between net migration figures and total out-migration observed between 1976 and 1980 has disappeared. Net migration dropped to 5,900 in 1981 from a level of 24,300 in 1980, and this decrease was acclaimed by the Seaga administration as evidence of massive return migration by Jamaicans who had fled the country during the 1970s. An even lower figure of 4,300 was reported in 1983, despite the fact that total out-migration was more than 22,000. This net migration figure proved more difficult to explain in terms of return migration, in view of the recognized economic difficulties which the country was experiencing. Net migration has since showed an increase in 1984 and 1985, but still remains considerably below the out-migration totals. While official sources still argue for the reliability of

TABLE 3

Main Streams of Out-Migration from Jamaica 1966 - 1985
Out-Migration to U.S., Canada and U.K.

Years	Total	Annual Average
1966-70	105,913	21,183
1971-75	105,342	21,068
1976-80	106,660	21,332
1981-85	115,497	23,099
1976-81	133,203	22,201
1982-85	88,954	22,239
1976-85	222,157	22,216

the net migration data, it appears that the accuracy of migration statistics in Jamaica has become severely undermined by the pattern of
short-term circular migration in which many of the Jamaican business
and professional classes now engage. Many of these individuals acquired U.S. permanent resident status during the 1970s, but instead of
embarking on a permanent long-term move, they have developed a
dual base of economic activity, traveling regularly between both countries. Since it is possible for such individuals to be counted as returning
residents when they enter Jamaica, but to be excluded from the departure count when they leave, a false inflation can occur in return migration estimates, thus leading to undercounts of net migation. In this
regard, it is of interest to note Bilderback's conclusion that "emigration
from Jamaica is not a flight, but a massive coming and going on a scale
larger than even the gross figures, or the generally held conception
suggests" (Bilderback, 1983:4).

The changes in U.S. immigration policy since 1965, and in Canadian
immigration law in 1967, have served not only to facilitate increased
migration levels, but have also encouraged a greater outflow of skilled
workers. Unlike the earlier movements to the United Kingdom in which
blue-collar workers predominated, the new immigration to the U.S. has
drawn on professional and managerial workers as well as lower skill
levels (Keely, 1975; Thomas-Hope, 1983), with the result that there has
been considerable concern at the official level about the effects of this
loss on national development. The impact of this "brain drain" has been

examined by several writers (Girling, 1974; Palmer, 1983; Murray, 1982) and is summarized by Cooper's statement: "The brain drain therefore forms a chronic feature of the Jamaican economy, a permanent sapping process of much needed labor" (Cooper, 1985:739). In her review of Caribbean migration research, Chaney (1985) notes that the loss of skilled workers is universally deplored because of its adverse development effects, and only occasionally has the question been raised as to whether there is a real scarcity or surplus of skilled workers (Reubens 1980; Anderson,1985).

Between 1976 and 1985 there have also been significant changes in the direction and composition of out-migration from Jamaica. With the 1962 curtailing of U.K. immigration, this country has come to have little importance as a destination for new migrants, while the United States has become the main recipient. In 1973 and 1974, Canada greatly increased its share of Jamaican migrants, but since that time there has been a steady decline. Tables 4 and 5 show the numbers of migrants to the U.S. and to Canada in the 1976-1985 decade as well as the distribution of those who were expected to join the workforce and of those who fell into two occupational groups: 1) professional, technical, managerial and administrative and, 2) craftsmen and operatives.[2] For brevity, these groups will be referred to as "professionals and managers" and "craftsmen". The importance of these two groups may be appreciated by examining their representation over the period. Professionals and managers accounted for 9.7 percent of all Jamaican migrants to North America between 1976 and 1985, and were 22.2 percent of those who were classified as the experienced work force. Craftsmen and operatives represented 12.0 percent of all North American migrants from Jamaica, and 27.6 percent of the experienced migrant work force.

Analysis of the trends in occupational composition over the period are complicated by the fact that the data on occupational composition of migrants to the U.S. in 1980 and for 1981 are not available, and also by a change in the U.S. classification system so that operatives have been grouped with laborers since 1983. These difficulties may be surmounted by different methods of estimation, and in our analysis we have simply chosen to apply the 1979 work and occupational distribu-

---

[2] The study recognizes that some of the occupations which are grouped together under the title of operatives may have a fairly low level of skill, differing significantly from the craftsmen occupations. However, the combined group is used in this analysis in order to maintain comparability with the statistics published by the Statistical Institute of Jamaica in the series on Labor Force Surveys. Until 1982, the migration statistics for North America provide separate information for craftsmen and operatives. The Planning Institute of Jamaica reported that between 1970 and 1980, the numbers of craftsmen, foremen, and kindred workers who migrated to North America were 13,990, while operatives and kindred workers numbered 18,001 (Murray, 1982).

TABLE 4

Representation of Professionals and Craftsmen Among Migrants to the United States, 1972 and 1976 - 1985

Year	Total Migrants	Total Work Force Migrants	Professional and Managerial Workers		Craftsmen and Operatives	
			Numbers	Percent of Work Force	Numbers	Percent of Work Force
1972	13,427	6,311	1,004	33.5	2,117	33.5
1976	9,026	3,806	715	18.8	1,242	32.6
1977	11,501	5,175	1,725	33.0	1,211	23.4
1978	19,265	9,112	2,418	26.5	2,310	25.4
1979	19,714	9,255	2,472	26.0	2,453	26.5
1980[a]	18,970	8,906	2,316	26.0	2,360	26.5
1981[a]	23,569	10,271	2,239	21.8	3,061	29.8
1982	18,711	8,154	1,775	21.8	2,427	29.8
1983	19,582	9,725	1,749	18.0	2,456	25.3
1984	19,822	10,618	1,852	17.4	2,702	25.4
1985	18,923	8,772	1,649	18.8	2,630	30.0
Total 1976-80	78,476	36,254	9,646	26.6	9,576	26.4
Total 1981-85	100,607	47,540	9,264	19.5	13,276	27.9
Total 1976-85	179,083	83,794	18,910	22.6	22,852	27.3

Note: [a] The occupational composition for the years 1980 and 1981 is based on estimates.

tion to the available total for 1980, and to use the 1982 distribution to estimate the 1981 composition. This approach may serve slightly to underestimate the numbers of professionals who migrated in 1981 since the 1982 distribution has a significantly smaller proportion of professionals (21.8 percent of the work force in 1982 as compared with 26.0 percent in 1979), but it has the advantage of preserving a peak in the 1980 distribution which is probably consonant with expectations based on the period trends. In any case, the differences are not dramatic between the results from different estimation methods. In order to maintain comparability with our grouping of craftsmen and operatives and the classification since 1983, we have decided to assume that the relative proportions of laborers between 1983 and 1985 remained at the 1982 level, which was 18.2 percent of the combined group of operatives and

TABLE 5

Representation of Professionals and Craftsmen Among Migrants to Canada, 1972 and 1976 - 1985

Year	Total Migrants	Total Work Force Migrants	Professional and Managerial Workers		Craftsmen and Operatives	
			Numbers	Percent of Work Force	Numbers	Percent of Work Force
1972	3,092	1,619	199	12.3	545	33.7
1976	7,282	1,893	391	20.7	700	37.0
1977	6,291	1,880	490	26.1	545	29.0
1978	3,858	1,169	287	24.6	322	27.5
1979	3,213	883	174	19.7	273	30.9
1980	3,161	798	170	21.3	252	31.6
1981	2,553	594	115	19.4	158	26.6
1982	2,593	535	111	20.7	154	28.8
1983	2,423	529	64	12.1	163	30.8
1984	2,479	717	51	7.1	176	24.5
1985	2,911	1,020	94	9.2	310	30.4
Total 1976-80	23,805	6,623	1,512	22.8	2,092	31.6
Total 1981-85	12,959	3,395	435	12.8	961	28.3
Total 1976-85	36,764	10,018	1,947	19.4	3,053	30.5

Note: [a] New entrants without occupations are excluded from this total.

laborers. This seems to be a safe procedure since the numbers of laborers involved are small. The migration figures for the U.S. and Canada are presented separately since there are trends in the Canadian data which are the independent result of changes in that country's immigration practices, as they relate to their assessments of their manpower needs, and which are not explainable in terms of "push forces" from Jamaican society.

Given these fairly minor reservations about the quality of the occupational data for the United States, it is of interest to observe from Table 4 the rapid increase in the numbers and proportions of professional and managerial workers who migrated to the United States between 1976 and 1977. This group jumped from 715 in 1976 to 1,725 in 1977, and peaked at 2,472 in 1979. The 1977 outflow of professional and administrative workers represented a third of the experienced migrant labor force, as compared with 18.8 percent in 1976, and this proportion remained in the region of 26 percent for the following two years. Cooper (1985) points out that the numbers of professionals and managers who were lost to the United States and Canada in 1977, 1978, and 1979 (2,215, 2,705, and 2,646) were similar to the numbers who departed in 1968 and 1969 (2,236 and 2,271, respectively). He therefore contends that since the base population was smaller in the sixties, the effects of the "brain drain" must have been more severe at that time.

With the change in political direction in 1980, there was some slight abatement of the professional and managerial outflow. The numbers of U.S. migrants in these high-skill categories decreased from 2,472 in 1979 to 1,775 in 1982, but, nonetheless, did not fall far below this level for the next three years. The 1982 decrease, therefore, did not initiate any prolonged decline in the emigration of high-level manpower. Whereas professional and managerial workers averaged 26.6 percent of the migrant work force going to the U.S. between 1976 and 1980, they averaged 19.5 percent between 1981 and 1985. If the combined outflow to the U.S. and Canada is considered, for the second half of the 1970s the outflow of professionals and managers was 11,158 or 26.0 percent of the classifiable workforce, while between 1981-1985 it totalled 9,699 or 19.0 percent of migrant workers.

Although it seems clear that the first five years of the Seaga administration did witness some slackening in professional out-migration, the exact opposite appears to be the case in regard to the migration of craftsmen and operatives. Like the professional and managerial group, craftsmen and operatives had participated actively in the "new immigration" to the U.S. in the 1960s, and their flow peaked at a level of 3,600 in 1970. The first half of the 1970s showed a decline in the numbers migrating, with the lowest level of 1,211 migrant craftsmen being recorded in 1977. In 1978, however, the outflow nearly doubled reaching a level of 2,310. The outflow stabilized around 2,400 between 1979 and 1983, but since then it has continued to increase. While the level of 2,630 estimated for 1985 is slightly lower than the 1984 estimate of 2,702, in percentage terms it was 30 percent of the experienced migrant work force, similar to the proportion in 1982: Therefore, whatever the factors were that allowed a slackening of professional out-migration under the new Seaga administration, it is clear that they did not have much impact on the migration of mid-level skilled workers.

Motives for Migration

The extent to which Jamaican migration in the 1970s represented a new movement, differing in kind or in quantity from previous outflows is still a matter of some debate. Cooper (1985) shows that if the 1970s migration is examined within a larger time perspective, it becomes apparent that high and mid-level skilled workers have been leaving the country in large numbers since the 1960s, and that if anything, during the 1970s, they left in somewhat reduced numbers. Cooper rejects the claim that the 1970s migration should be interpreted primarily in political terms, arguing that Manley's democratic socialist policies must be seen"as merely one moment in a much larger and well-established process of out-migration from the country" (1985:743). While acknowledging that migration had become the subject of sharp political debate during this period, he attaches greater weight to the policies of the receiving countries as determinants of actual levels of out-migration. Although Cooper is correct in insisting on the chronic nature of manpower exports, his explanation in terms of external quota levels remains incomplete. To demonstrate that a ceiling exists is not the same as to explain why at certain times that ceiling should be reached, while at other times there is a clear shortfall.

Furthermore, the considerable discretion which U.S. consular officers exercise in the granting of visitor visas introduces some flexibility into the system, since as Cooper notes, this was one of the means of indirect migration used by prospective migrants from Jamaica. This route was more available to the middle classes who were able to provide evidence of economic and financial resources, which were considered by visa officers as constituting "ties to the country", and thus, a lower probability of visa violation. By attributing primary importance to external determinants in shaping migration flows, Cooper's study fails to acknowledge sufficiently the ways in which the changing political context affected both the composition and the character of migration. In particular, we would argue that because the 1970s movement had clear relationships to social class formations, it was accompanied by greater outflows of other resources, such as capital and skill. It also appears to have introduced important changes into the circular pattern of migration, replacing long-term flows with short-term circularity among particular groups.

In their review of this period, Stephens and Stephens (1986) argue that the first wave of disaffection which the business classes experienced towards the Manley government occurred in 1973 and 1974, and was reflected in a cutback of investment and increased out-migration to Canada. In the second wave, between 1975 and 1976, all but the most liberal capitalists swung to a position of extreme hostility towards the government. They are careful to point out that both the first wave of migration and the fall in investment occurred before the 1974 declaration of democratic socialism, the rise of the PNP Left, and the heightened ideological debate that ensued.

However, they argue that the withdrawal cannot be simply explained as a rational economic reaction to the PNP's austerity policies, which did impact on the commercial bourgeoisie, but must also be explained in terms of the elite's rejection of the government's egalitarian and social inclusionary policies. Specifically, this was exhibited in opposition to the property tax and to the National Youth Service, both of which were part of a larger program aimed at introducing egalitarian change into a very elitist society. In this regard, Stephens and Stephens comment, "When those who had been privileged...began to feel their social position threatened, some of them began to abandon the society...It cannot be denied that the socio-cultural process as indicated by the emphasis on African heritage and black identity, which the PNP under Manley promoted, was feared and resented by many whites, 'socially white' upper-class browns, and other ethnic minorities" (1986:99). The second wave of disaffection identified by the writers is related both to the introduction of the austerity package of 1975, which severely curtailed imports and restricted foreign exchange availability, and to the government's increasing linkages with Cuba and the anti-capitalist and anti-U.S. rhetoric of PNP spokesmen. This was reflected in the sharp increases in migration to the U.S. from 1977.

Since the focus of the Stephens' study is on the role of the capitalist class, their concern is with explaining the reactions and behavior of those migrants who are classified in the official statistics as managers and administrators. Indeed, this group does merit special study both because of the disinvestment and capital export which their alienation and migration induced and because of their role as employers in the society, and thus the multiplier effect of their withdrawal from economic activity within Jamaica. Nonetheless, while acknowledging this, it is important to recognize that even in 1977 the managerial and administrative class constituted only 7.2 percent of total U.S. migrants, and 16.0 percent of workforce migrants. Although they increased their size relative to professional and technical workers during the period, they remainded heavily outnumbered. Therefore, attention must also be paid to the motives of professional and technical workers as well as of other white-collar and skilled workers who constituted the bulk of the migrant flow.

Stephens and Stephens acknowledge that their information on the causes of the alienation of the upper middle class is sketchy, but they relate it to the deterioration of the economy and of opportunity. Other studies, such as Stone's (1981), relate the out-migration of the middle class to the political hysteria about impending Communism, created by the orchestrated accusations of the opposition JLP, the local and the North American mass media, the local business class, and a vocal minority among the professional middle class. Stone notes that as business interests entered a state of panic, there was a massive out-flow of capital and foreign exchange. The PNP's response of increasing mass mobilization only served to accelerate the capital flight, and the out-migration of local capitalists and the middle class.

In his May 1977 poll, Stone (1982) reported that there was wide support for migration across class and party lines, with 60 percent of the sample saying that if they had the opportunity, they would also migrate to the United States. Noting this, Maingot (1985) suggests that the error of the Manley government may have been to allow migration to become a political issue, since migration to the U.S. has always been "poly-class", stemming from a variety of motivations. Some of this debate may be summarized by reference to Henry and Johnson's comment on Guyana (1985) where they observe that education and training have always been viewed as a passport to geographic and social mobility. To the extent that avenues of domestic mobility appear to be blocked, or downward mobility appears imminent, the migration alternative is likely to become more attractive, or may even seem to be the only viable path. In the following section we review some aggregate data to examine the question of whether the changing balance between manpower demand and supply was not in itself a factor which precipitated migration, as many skilled workers found that their mobility chances and standard of living were severely constricted by increasing under-utilization of their labor within Jamaica.

EFFECTIVE DEMAND AND SOCIAL NEED

Low levels of living in countries such as Jamaica and the persistence of malnutrition and functional illiteracy seem to present incontrovertible evidence that the country needs skilled manpower. In fact, Jamaica's development planning since the 1970s has been built around the general acceptance of a basic needs philosophy, with human resource development being accorded particular importance. However, as we have argued elsewhere (1985), social need is not easily translated into effective demand, and the retention of trained workers is extremely problematic. It is the lack of effective demand in terms of the country's ability to employ skilled workers at levels of remuneration that repay their own investment in their training which creates intractable problems in attempting to reconcile projected manpower demand with training requirements. In discussing the impact of out-migration on the supply of skills, the 1985 Economic and Social Survey of Jamaica reported that over the five-year period, 1985-1990, the output of professional, technical, and managerial manpower from the training institutions was expected to be approximately 2,800 annually, but that the annual emigration of this group was expected to be in excess of 2,000. The failure of effective demand to match social need is most clearly demonstrated in the case of the health services as shown below.

Mobility and Scarcity in the Health Sector

In 1985 the Government of Jamaica reported that malnutrition among children under five years was as high as 40.8 percent (Economic and Social Survey 1985). At the same time they acceded to IMF pressures by instituting a 12.5 percent reduction in health personnel and by restricting the access of the poor to the public hospitals by reinstating fees for services. The severe strain on health services in Jamaica is evident from the statistics on the ratio of health personnel to the population. In 1985, there was one dentist to 20,000 people, in contrast to the PAHO recommendation of 1:2,857; there was one doctor to 5,240 persons, compared with the international recommendation of 1:910; and there was one registered nurse to every 1,172 persons, as against the ideal level of 1:769. These disparities can be attributed only in part to inadequacies in training provisions, since in the case of doctors and nurses considerable resources have been allocated to this area. The significant and continuous attrition which takes place in the stock of health personnel may be demonstrated not only on a directbasis of migration data, but also through indirect estimates based on labor market data. This is illustrated here through a simple hypothetical exercise, based on comparisons of the stock of health personnel in 1978 and 1985, and the locally trained output over the period.

Table 6 shows that in the case of doctors, the 1978 ratio of 1:5,900 persons was roughly equivalent to a stock of 354 physicians with a mean population of 2,087,800. The training output for the years 1978 to 1985, inclusive, totalled 393 doctors, and if we assume a totally closed situation in which none of the doctors migrated, and none were lost through death or retirement, the total stock should have been 747 in 1985, producing a doctor/population ratio of 1:3,094. In fact, with a 1985 mean population of 2,311,000, the reported ratio of 1:5,240 is equivalent to a stock of approximately 441 doctors. This indicates a net loss of 306 doctors over the 1978-1985 period, equivalent to 78 percent of the training output. It is worthwhile noting that even the hypothetical stock of 747 physicians would have resulted in a service ratio that was still much larger than the international recommendation of 1:910.

If similar calculations are made for registered nurses, it may be seen that the estimated 1978 stock of registered nurses of 1,884 should have been augmented by a local training output of 1,822 nurses between 1978 and 1985, bringing the new stock to 3,706 in 1985. This would

TABLE 6

Hypothetical Estimates of Changes in the Stock
of Health Personnel, 1978 - 1985

	Doctors	Nurses
1978 Ratio of Staff to Population	1:5,900	1:1,108
1978 Mean Population	2,087,800	2,087,800
1978 Estimated Stock	354	1,884
Local Training Output 1978 - 1985	393	1,822
Expected Stock in 1985 (Assuming no Loss)	747	3,706
1985 Ration of Staff to Population	1:5,240	1:1,172
1985 Mean Population	2,311,100	2,311,100
1985 Estimated Stock	441	1,972
Difference Between Expected Stock and Estimated Stock in 1985	306	1,734
Deficit as a Percent of Training Output	78%	95%

Source: Economic and Social Survey of Jamaica, 1978, 1981, 1985.

have surpassed the international recommendation, being equivalent to one nurse for every 624 persons. However, the estimated available stock in 1985 stood at 1,972 nurses, indicating a net loss of 1,734 nurses, equivalent to 95 percent of the new output.

In reality, the country would have lost some of its health personnel through retirement and mortality, but in the relatively short period of seven years, these sources of loss should not have been significant. Changes in occupation also represent a source of decrement in the occupational stock, and this is more likely to have occurred in the case of nurses who were faced with low salary levels and the rapid increase in the cost of living. Migration and occupation changes are both likely to have been responsible for the failure of the nursing stock to have expanded in any way consistent with the increases from the training system. For doctors, however, the main source of attrition is likely to have been out-migration. What this illustration serves to show is the extent to which the Jamaican manpower system is constantly replacing old workers with new, more experienced with less experienced. The situation

becomes particularly acute in the social services where there is a high
level of social need but a severe contraction in the government's ability
to employ or retain professional workers.

Surplus and Mobility in the Jamaican Labor Force

Lack of effective demand is apparent in open unemployment, in low
income levels relative to the training investment, and in the country's
inability to provide the complementary factors of production needed
for effective utilization of skilled labor. In this section, we review some
of the data on employment, unemployment, and job vacancies
in order to arrive at an assessment of whether the migration outflow
was in part an "overflow", as a result of inadequate demand.

In attempting to assess the relative demand for different categories of
labor, it is important to examine not only unemployment rates but also
the stock of jobs available at different times, as indicated by levels of
employment and vacant positions. One of the most striking features of
the Jamaican labor market is the high degree of mobility and turnover
as workers move between industries and sectors, in and out of the labor
force, and across national boundaries. Because of this mobility, a contraction in employment in one sector may not be reflected completely
or for very long, in the industry's unemployment rate since workers
may shift to other industries or resort to self-employment, often
changing occupations in the process. This is clearly illustrated in the
case studies of the urban informal sector conducted by Anderson in
1985, where it was found that many workers, currently employed as
drivers and conductors in the urban minibus service, had been employed as craftsmen in manufacturing and the building industry in
1982. The corresponding national survey data from this project, the
Population Mobility and Development Project, showed that in 1984,
among self-employed craftsmen in construction and manufacturing,
nearly 40 percent had been in wage employment in the secondary
sector five years previously.[3] This intersectoral mobility underlines the
need to examine actual employment levels in order to gain some understanding of patterns of labor demand over time.

The mobility observed in the Jamaican labor force is a direct result of
the instability of the employment structure, induced by the high degree
of openness in the economy. Under the conditions of dependent capi-

---

[3] In the Population Mobility and Development Project, the urban labor market is divided into three sectors: the primary-formal, the secondary-formal and the informal. The
secondary-formal included large-scale manufacturing, construction, large-scale transport,
wholesale and retail trade, personal services, and hotels, restaurants, and recreational services.

talist production, the balance between demand and supply is constantly shifting, and this instability is aggravated by low levels of worker protection. In periods of economic and political crises, as in the 1970s, a shortage of skilled workers in a particular occupation may be quickly converted into a surplus, as managers cut back on production and delay further investment. Even in periods when the investment climate is considered hospitable and capital inflows occur, as between 1981 and 1985, it may still be difficult for the government to stimulate or to maintain adequate employment under the burden of debt servicing and public expenditure restrictions. The rapid increase in the cost of living which has been imposed on the population also serves to restrict the size of the domestic market and to undermine jobs in those industries which had previously relied on domestic demand.

Finally, it should also be acknowledged that only very general assessments may be made on the basis of examining broad occupational groups since it is quite possible for skill shortages to exist with regard to particular categories of professionals, although the wider grouping of "professional, technical, administrative, and managerial workers" may show persistent unemployment. This has consistently been the position with regard to engineers and accountants, while managers have been in short supply at different points in time. The need to rely on aggregate data from sample surveys to obtain estimates of employment and unemployment necessitates the use of these broad categories in order to avoid problems of unreliability in estimation.

Table 7 charts changes in employment and unemployment for the total labor force, for professional/managerial workers, and for craftsmen and operatives for selected years between 1972 and 1985. The data in this table reveal several important patterns which may be summarized briefly.

(1) The country has clear difficulty in absorbing new entrants into the labor force as may be inferred from the differences between total unemployment rates and unemployment among the experienced labor force.

(2) The series of employment levels show the expansion of jobs in the first six years of the Manley administration (1972-1978), followed by a two-year period of absolute decline between 1979 and 1980. The period since 1980 has shown a significant though uneven expansion of employment.

(3) Professional unemployment emerged as a problem after 1976 and still remains high despite the large expansion in the numbers of these jobs in the seventies.

TABLE 7

Levels of Employment and Unemployment for the Experienced Labor Force, Professionals and Craftsman, Selected Years April 1972-85

Year	Total Labor Force	Total Experienced Labor Force			Professional and Managerial			Craftsman and Operatives		
	Percent Un-employed	Employed	Unemployed	Percent Un-employed	Employed	Unemployed	Percent Un-employed	Employed	Unemployed	Percent Un-employed
1972	23.6	598,200	102,300	14.6	43,300	1,200	2.7	101,000	23,400	18.8
1975	20.0	663,000	112,400	14.5	59,700	2,900	4.6	99,900	20,900	17.3
1976	20.5	678,500	125,700	15.6	57,200	2,900	4.8	95,000	26,100	21.6
1978	22.9	695,700	145,300	17.3	62,500	6,100	8.9	83,100	26,200	24.0
1980	27.9	680,200	164,800	19.5	61,300	5,900	8.8	77,900	31,500	28.8
1982	27.0	732,300	160,700	18.0	65,100	5,900	8.3	85,900	24,600	22.3
1984	25.5	778,400	156,800	16.8	67,900	7,900	10.4	102,400	31,600	23.6
1985	24.4	782,300	148,300	15.9	63,700	6,200	8.9	95,000	31,600	25.0

Source: Labour Force Survey of Jamaica, 1973, 1985.

(4) Unemployment among craftsmen and operatives has been extremely high over the entire period both in terms of absolute numbers and unemployment rates.

(5) The general lack of correspondence between net changes in employment and unemployment reveals considerable mobility in and out of occupations or across labor force boundaries.

This review of employment and unemployment levels over the period shows that regardless of the political motives for out-migration during the 1970s, economic factors, as they related to the adequacy of employment, must also have been major determinants. These same factors undoubtedly contribute to the continuing out-migration. The imbalance between occupational demand and supply is evident from the fact that even in some periods when employment has expanded, unemployment has also increased, indicative partly of shifts into self-employment, movement in and out of the labor force, and the continuing supply from the training system. This is illustrated among the professional and managerial class by the increased employment and unemployment that was recorded between 1976 and 1978 as well as between 1982 and 1984. Unlike Buffenmeyer's (1970) conclusion based on his analysis of professional out-migration in the 1960s, we would argue, that effective demand for professional manpower became a significant problem during the 1970s.

The labor force mobility of craftsmen and operatives provides an interesting contrast to that of professionals and managers since they exhibit much lower occupational attachment. Contraction in the supply of jobs for craftsmen and operatives is reflected in movements in and out of the occupation, out of the labor force, or out of the country. An expansion of jobs seems to stimulate their re-entry into the occupational supply, even though this may be to a position of unemployment. This flexibility in occupational supply may be illustrated by calculating hypothetical unemployment rates under the assumption that there is a completely closed situation with no movements in and out of that occupational group in the labor force. With these assumptions, it is possible to see that between 1976 and 1978, the loss of 11,900 craftsman jobs should have increased the numbers of unemployed craftsmen from 26,100 in 1976 to 38,000 in 1978, and the unemployment rate should have moved up from 21.6 percent to 31.4 percent. In fact, 1978 recorded an apparently stable level of 26,000 unemployed craftsmen and an unemployment rate of 24.0 percent, indicating that most of the net increase in unemployment had shifted out of this job sector. Conversely, the expansion of 16,500 jobs for craftsmen and operatives between 1982 and 1984 should have led to a significant reduction in unemployment for this group (to a hypothetical level of 7.3 percent), if there had been no "slack" in the system. Instead of this occurring, the increased employment of craftsmen has been paralleled by increased numbers of unemployed; thus, the numbers of unemployed grew from 24,600 in 1982 to 31,600 in 1984, and the unemployment rate increased from 22.3 percent to 23.6 percent.

Similar illustrations may be made for professionals and managers to show that if occupational outflows were not taking place, the contraction in employment between 1975 and 1976 should have led to a hypothetical unemployment rate of 8.6 percent in 1976 instead of to the recorded rate of 4.8 percent unemployment among professionals. In the same way, the loss of 4,200 jobs between 1984 and 1985 should have led to an unemployed professional labor force of 12,100, and increased the unemployment rate from 10.4 percent to 16 percent, instead of the recorded decline to 8.9 percent in 1985.

These illustrations cannot determine whether the explanations for expansions and contractions in occupational supply are to be found in occupational changes, labor force withdrawal and re-entry, or in out-migration and in-migration. What they do demonstrate is the considerable degree of "slack" which now exists in regard to the supply of craftsmen and operatives, thus raising serious doubts about claims of skill shortages at least at this level. This may also be increasingly the case with some categories of professional manpower. For professionals and managers, there is less evidence of a continuing surplus although there is indication of mobility. For this group, it is more likely that their mobility involves international movements than that it entails a shift out of professional work or out of the labor force. In the following section, we suggest a methodological approach by which the net changes in occupational supply may be disaggregated through the use of a manpower balance sheet, in order to provide estimates of the loss due to unrecorded out-migration.

In addition to the information which we can obtain from labor force data, establishment surveys are generally useful in identifying scarce skills and vacant positions. Since 1979, the Government of Jamaica has conducted two large-scale establishment surveys in order to identify training needs and manpower requirements. While these surveys provide a wealth of valuable data, neither the 1980 nor the 1985 survey has been able to provide much evidence of a large stock of vacant positions. The totals which they report in different occupational categories represent only a small fraction of the recorded out-flow due to migration.

It must be acknowledged that the relatively small numbers of job vacancies may be partly explained by the fact that some of the empty slots created by out-migration may have been filled by replacement mobility within the labor markets including promotions, job changes, and new entrants. In addition, some of the managerial and related support service jobs may have ceased to exist once the managers and proprietors had migrated. Nonetheless, the impression which is gained from an examination of vacancy data is that there does not exist any extensive unutilized capacity. This is not to deny that the economic need exists for increased production, and that there is a critical need for additional teachers and health personnel. However, it is clear that the other factors of production are not lying idle in the country, waiting for skilled manpower to become available. Moreover, even where there is a formal recognition of the need for selected personnel in the public sector, budgetary constraints prevent the filling of these posts. In this situation, the inevitable outcome of the manpower system must be training for export.

MANPOWER BALANCE SHEET FOR JAMAICA

Methodology and Data

The question of changes in occupational supply may be explored in greater depth by the development of a manpower balance sheet for the period 1979 to 1984 (Anderson, 1986). The manpower balance sheet is an exploratory technique based on a comparison of recorded supply at two points in time and estimates of increment and decrement to the supply over the period. This technique serves to show that there is a significant outflow of skilled manpower which is not recorded in the immigration data currently available from the receiving countries, although that data is now the primary source for manpower analyses of migration losses. It is already widely recognized that this recorded outflow is occurring, for two reasons: one, because many people migrate indirectly through the use of a visitor's visa to North America, and therefore are not included in figures such as those provided by the U.S. Immigration and Naturalization Service on persons admitted; and two, because many women who were economically active in Jamaica are reported in the immigration statistics as housewives. In addition, the occupational composition of migrants to countries outside of North America is not available.

The estimation of unrecorded manpower losses is made possible because a series of retrospective questions on population mobility were introduced into a large-scale national survey undertaken by the University of the West Indies, known as the National Mobility Survey. These questions looked into former residence, labor force status, and occupation. The balance sheet for occupations proceeds by comparing the occupational stock in two time periods and attempts to determine whether the known sources of increment and decrement are sufficient to account for the observed change between the beginning and the end points. This is expressed schematically as follows:

Original Stock in   New Stock in
Occupation X   + Increments − Decrements =   Occupation X

The sources of increment in labor supply are identified as: (1) the output from training institutions, (2) intra-occupational mobility, (3) return migration, and (4) foreign workers admitted under work permits and work-permit exemptions. The sources of decrement are: (1) outmigration, (2) intra-occupational mobility, (3) death, (4) retirement, and (5) labor-force withdrawal. Since the study looked at the total stock of occupations and not only at those in the labor force, this approach had the advantage of making it unnecessary to estimate labor force withdrawal, reentry and retirement since all occupational incumbents are counted, regardless of their labor force status.

The balancing equation for manpower supply was estimated for professionals and craftsmen between the ages of 20 and 49, by individual five-year age groups within this range. The application of this technique entailed tracing the population over the five-year period, in the same manner that life-table survival ratios are used to estimate age-structures at a later period. Accordingly, persons who were between 20 and 49 years in 1979 were expected to be five years older in 1984, and if they survived and remained in the country, would be numbered among the 25 to 54 age group.

Estimates of occupational stock at the beginning of the period were obtained from the 1979 Labor Force Survey, while estimates of occupational stock for the end of the period were obtained from the National Mobility Survey.[4] The Mobility Survey also provided the estimates of return migration, new labor market entrants, and intra-occupational mobility through the retrospective data. The design of the National Mobility Survey and the methodological issues which it raises are discussed in greater detail in Gordon (1985). The other components of change, namely, death and migration, were estimated from independent sources. Deaths among each age-group were estimated by the application of sur-

---

[4] The 1979 Labor Force Survey is part of the continuous household survey of the Statistical Institute of Jamaica (STATIN), based on a one-percent sample of dwellings. The April 1979 survey had a sample size of 26,052 persons 14 years or older. The National Mobility Survey (NMS) was conducted for the Institute for Social and Economic Research (ISER) by STATIN using the same sample frame as the labor force surveys. The NMS was based on a sample size of 11,994 persons in 4,604 households.

vival ratios from the life-tables developed by George Roberts for Jamaican males and females for 1970. Out-migration of professionals and craftsmen was estimated on the basis of U.S. and Canadian immigration data.

Findings from the Manpower Balance Sheet

Between 1979 and 1984, the stock of professionals aged 20-49 years in 1979 grew by 3.6 percent from 58,000 in 1979 to 60,100 in 1984. The analysis showed that this net growth of 2,100 actually concealed a loss of approximately 6,300 professionals from the expected stock in 1984 (Table 8). The results were even more striking in the case of craftsmen and operatives. Although the total stock of craftsmen in all age groups grew by 16.6 percent between 1979 and 1984, the age-stock 20-49 years, as shown in Table 8, suffered a net decline from 137,700 in 1979 to 125,700 in 1984. This net loss of 12,000 persons is shown by the balance sheet to reflect a true loss of 24,000. To rephrase this, when all known increments and decrements are taken into account, the stock of craftsmen who were aged 20-49 in 1979, and who were expected to be 25-54 in 1984, had shown an unexpected loss of 24,000 persons, or 16 percent of the expected stock. These unrecorded losses are attributed to out-migration.

The manpower balance sheet is still an exploratory technique, and its results are critically dependent on the quality of the data which are used to estimate the components. However, it has the major advantage of being able to disaggregate the components of net change in occupational supply and of providing some estimate of the rough orders of magnitude of unrecorded migration. From this study it appeared that unrecorded out-migration among professional workers stood at 6,300, equivalent to about 71 percent of the recorded outflow of 8,900 migrants between 1979 and 1984. Among craftsmen, the unrecorded loss of 24,000 was more than twice the recorded migrant out-flow of 11,000 workers over the five-year period.

CONCLUSION

This paper has sought to examine labor migration from Jamaica within the wider context of labor market mobility and has suggested a methodology, the manpower balance sheet, for the analytic integration of both sets of movements. The need for such a technique is evident from examining the failure of the stock of particular occupations to expand in pace with development needs, despite the continuous supply of new graduates from the training system. This slow growth, and at times ab-

TABLE 8

Balance Sheet of Changes in Stock of Professionals and Craftsmen, 1979-84

| | Professionals | | | Craftsmen | | |
	Male	Female	Both Sexes	Male	Female	Both Sexes
Persons Aged 20-49 Years in 1979	23,900	34,100	58,000	102,900	34,800	137,700
Components of Change 1979-84						
a) Persons Admitted to North America	-3,900	-4,900	-8,900	-8,200	-2,900	-11,100
b) Deaths	-300	-400	-700	-1,500	-500	-2,000
c) Return Migration	+1,400	+1,300	+2,700	+1,000	+300	+1,300
d) Occupational Changers and New Entrants	+6,800	+8,500	+15,300	+14,500	+9,300	+23,800
Expected Population Aged 25-54 Years in 1984	27,900	38,600	66,400	108,700	41,000	149,700
Recorded Population in 1984	24,300	35,800	60,100	91,000	34,700	125,700
Difference Between Recorded and Expected	-3,600	-2,800	-6,300	-17,700	-6,300	-24,000
Difference as % of Expected Stock	12.9%	7.3%	9.5%	16.3%	15.4%	16.0%

solute decline, of workers in occupations that are accorded high social and economic priority is the result both of movements within the labor force, as well as across labor-force and national boundaries.

The logic behind the manpower balance sheet is that there is a commonality between all movements of labor, and that it is only at the spatial level that migration differs from other labor-market movements within a national boundary. For this reason, it is desirable to relate migration flows to the general pattern of labor-market movements which includes labor force entry, reentry, and withdrawal as well as occupational changes and mortality. A comparison of the differences in the stock of occupations at two points in time produces an estimate of net change, and this net change may be appropriately allocated to different sources of increment and decrement, assuming that these can be estimated fairly accurately. Since in the case of Jamaica it is widely accepted that migration is the source of out-flow in which occupational losses are most severely under-estimated, it is reasonable to attribute these unrecorded losses to unrecorded out-migration.

Our application of this technique to labor force movements between 1979 and 1984 showed that unrecorded losses among professionals were equivalent to more than two-thirds of the recorded migration outflow, while among craftsmen the unrecorded loss was twice the recorded migration in North America. While the findings from the balance sheet must still be regarded as suggestive data, the technique is of value both in identifying the rough dimensions and the composition of unrecorded migration outflows as well as in disaggregating the components of net change in a particular period. Its usefulness is contingent on the availability of relatively accurate data on the other components of change, and, in order to increase the accuracy of recall, the time-span may be shortened to two or three years for the retrospective questions. These questions can be included very easily in continuous social and demographic surveys of the type that are usually used for labor-force assessments.

By comparing out-migration patterns under two very different political regimes between 1976 and 1985, it has been possible to point to both the differences in outward flow as well as the continuities in the movement. While political changes are not discounted as factors which precipitate changes in the composition or the rate of particular flows, this chapter has sought to emphasize that the analysis of Jamaica's labor migration must be related to the changing balance of demand and supply within the domestic labor market as well as to the deterioration in the standard of living over the period. The 1970s has brought to the fore both the failure of the economic system to keep pace with the expanding labor supply, and also the country's lack of effective demand in retaining workers whose skills are desperately needed for development and who may even have been trained at public expense.

The similar experiences of two different political regimes have helped to demonstrate that the radical increases in the cost of living which undermine effective demand for labor cannot simply be dismissed as "mismanagement". The common scenario is created by the country's internationally weak bargaining position as a small, debt-ridden country with an extremely open economy.

In raising the questions of whether there is currently a shortage or an over-supply of different categories of skilled workers, and whether the manpower outflow is in part an overflow, we have sought to show that analysis must be directed towards the changing balance of demand and supply in different periods, and we argue that it is the instability of this balance which represents one of Jamaica's greatest development problems.

Changes in product demand which may represent minor ripples within the U.S. economy can create major shocks to Jamaica's economic structures, and this problem is likely to become more pronounced under the present pattern of export-propelled growth. In summary, therefore, the instability of labor demand and the continuous deterioration in the standard of living since the mid-1970s are both expressions of the inadequacy of employment and the results of Jamaica's dependent position within the international capitalist economy.

While this constitutes the wider context of manpower losses, the migration of the 1970s may have changed in character by increasing the frequency of short-term circular moves relative to long-term movements. The pattern of short-term and repetitive circular movements is evident primarily among the business classes and appears to be accompanied by the movement of capital. These groups may officially reside overseas but engage in economic activity within Jamaica. Whereas the 1977-1980 exodus induced a sudden and large-scale capital flight, it is possible that these outflows continue to occur, but in a more gradual and "orthodox" manner. To the extent therefore, that the 1970s migration served to integrate the Jamaican business class into the overseas business community, it is likely that the country may experience less of the benefits traditionally associated with long-term circular flows, such as the return of remittances and skills. If this is so, the 1970s migration may prove to be more of a "hemorrhagic flow" than a process of population transfer with off-setting costs and benefits (Guengant, 1985).

For the majority of migrants, however, the move overseas was an attempt to arrest the decline in their standard of living and to improve their social-mobility chances. So strong were the sociocultural and political linkages between Jamaica and its metropolitan partners that international borders did not present a mental barrier in the search for legitimate self-improvement. And so, thousands migrated. From their perspective, to do less may have been "lacking in ambition".

REFERENCES

Anderson, P.Y.
1986   "Migration off the Record: A Balance Sheet of Manpower Losses from Jamaica, 1979-1984". Report presented to Hemispheric Migration Project, Center for Immigration Policy and Refugee Assistance, Georgetown University.

1985   "Migration and Development in Jamaica". *Migration and Development in the Caribbean: The Unexplored Connection*. Edited by R. Pastor. Boulder, CO: Westview Press.

Beckford, G. and M. Witter
1980   *Small Garden, Bitter Weed: The Political Economy of Struggle and Change in Jamaica*. Morant Bay, Jamaica: Maroon Publishing House.

Bernal, R.
1984 "The IMF and Class Struggle in Jamaica, 1977-1980", *Latin American Perspectives*, 11(3):53-82.

Bilderback, L.
1983 "The Jamaican Experience: Population and Labor Migration 1950-2000", *OAS Report*. International Migration Project. Washington, D.C.: Organization of American States.

Brown, A.
1981 "Economic Policy and the IMF in Jamaica", *Social and Economic Studies*, 30(4):1-51.

Bryce-LaPorte, R.
1983 "The United States' Role in Caribbean Migration: Background to the Problem". *Caribbean Migration to the United States*. Edited by R. Bryce-LaPorte and D. Mortimer. Washington, D.C.: Smithsonian Institution, Research Institute on Immigration and Ethnic Studies.

Buffenmeyer, J.R.
1970 "Emigration of High-Level Manpower and National Development: A Case-Study of Jamaica". Unpublished Ph.D. dissertation, University of Pittsburgh.

Chaney, E.
1985 *Migration from the Caribbean Region: Determinants and Effects of Current Movements*, Hemispheric Migration Project Occasional Paper Series. Washington, D.C.: Georgetown University and the Intergovernmental Committee for Migration.

Cooper, D.
1985 "Migration from Jamaica in the 1970s: Political Protest or Economic Pull?", *International Migration Review*, 19(4):728-748.

Davies, O.
1986 "An Analysis of the Management of the Jamaican Economy: 1972-85", *Social and Economic Studies*, 35(1):73-108.

Davis, C.
1985 "The Jamaican Bauxite Industry: Present Situation and Prospects", *Occasional Paper Series* No. 4. Kingston, Jamaica: Department of Economics, University of the West Indies.

Girling, R.K.
1974 "The Migration of Human Capital from the Third World: The Implications and Some Data on the Jamaican Case", *Social and Economic Studies*, 23(1):84-96.

Girvan, N., R. Bernal and W. Hughes
1980 "The IMF and the Third World: The Case of Jamaica", *Development Dialogue*, 2:113-115.

Gordon, D.
1985 "Methodological Issues in the Analysis of the National Mobility Survey", *Working Paper* 1, Population Mobility and Development Project, Institute for Social and Economic Research (ISER), University of the West Indies.

Guengant, P., with D. Marshall
1985 *Caribbean Population Dynamics: Emigration and Fertility Challenges*. Barbados: Conference of Caribbean Parliamentarians on Population and Development.

Henry, R. and K. Johnson
1985 "Migration, Manpower and Underdevelopment of the Commonwealth Caribbean", *Migration and Development in the Caribbean: The Unexplored Connection*. Edited by R. Pastor, Boulder: Westview Press.

Jamaica. Planning Institute.
1985 *Economic and Social Survey of Jamaica*. Kingston.

1981 *Economic and Social Survey of Jamaica*. Kingston.

1980   *Economic and Social Survey of Jamaica*. Kingston.

1978   *Economic and Social Survey of Jamaica*. Kingston.

Jamaica Statistical Institute
1985   *Labor Force Survey*. Kingston.

1979   *Labor Force Survey*. Kingston.

1973   *Labor Force Survey*. Kingston.

Jefferson, O.
1972   *The Post-War Economic Development of Jamaica*. Kingston, Jamaica: Institute for Social and Economic Research (ISER), University of the West Indies.

1986   "Jamaica's External Debt: Size, Growth, Composition and Consequences". In *The Debt Problem in Jamaica: Situation and Solutions*. Edited by O. D. Kingston. Jamaica: Economics Department, University of the West Indies.

Keely, C.
1975   "Effects of U.S. Immigration Law on Manpower Characteristics of Immigrants", *Demography*, 12:179-92.

Maingot, A.
1985   "Political Implications of Migration in a Socio-Cultural Area". In *Migration and Development in the Caribbean: The Unexplored Connection*. Edited by R. Pastor, Boulder: Westview Press.

Massey, D.
1981   "Dimensions of the New Immigration to the United States and the Prospects for Assimilation", *Annual Review of Sociology*, 7:57-85.

Murray, L.
1985   *Emigration to North America from Jamaica, 1970-80*, Special Report of the National Planning Agency. Kingston, Jamaica: National Planning Agency.

Palmer, R.
1983   "Emigration and the Economic Decline of Jamaica". In *White-Collar Migrants in the Americas and the Caribbean*. Edited by A. Marks and H. Vessuri. Netherlands: Royal Institute of Linguistics and Anthropology.

Passaris, C.
1983   "Immigration to Canada in the Post Second World War Period: Manpower Flows from the Caribbean", *White-Collar Migrants in the Americas and the Caribbean*. Edited by A. Marks and H. Vessuri. Netherlands: Royal Institute of Linguistics and Anthropology.

Reubens, E.
1980   Review Article of William Glaser's "The Brain Drain", *International Migration Review*, 14(3):434-435.

Roberts, G.
1974   *Recent Population Movements in Jamaica*. Paris: Comité International de Coopération dans les Recherches Nationales en Démographie (CICRED).

Stephens, E. and J. Stephens
1986   *Democratic Socialism in Jamaica*. Princeton: Princeton University Press.

Stone, C.
1985   *Class, State and Democracy in Jamaica*. Kingston, Jamaica: Blackett Publishers.

1982   *The Political Opinions of the Jamaican People 1976 — 1981*. Kingston, Jamaica: Blackett Publishers.

1981   Decolonization and the Caribbean State System—the Case of Jamaica", *Perspectives on Jamaica in the Seventies*. Edited by C. Stone and A. Brown. Kingston, Jamaica: Jamaica Publishing House.

Taylor, L.
1986   "Sovereign-Debtor Dilemmas in Negotiating Debt Relief". In *The Debt Problem in Jamaica: Situation and Solutions*. Edited by O. Davies. Kingston, Jamaica: University of the West Indies.

Thomas-Hope, E.
1983   "Off the Island: Population Mobility Among the Caribbean Middle Class". In *White-Collar Migrants in the Americas and the Caribbean*. Edited by A. Marks and H. Vessuri. Netherlands: Royal Institute of Linguistics and Anthropology.

EMIGRATION OF ARGENTINES TO THE UNITED STATES[1]

Adriana Marshall

Since the late nineteenth century Argentina has received more immigrants than any other country in Latin America. However, since the late 1950s, if not earlier, the country has experienced a significant outflow of emigrants as well. This emigrating population differs distinctly from the immigrating population, whose presence and features are better documented.

The existing studies on Argentine emigration tend to underscore the high level of skills of the emigrants. Nevertheless, the Argentine migration stream is heterogeneous; in addition to professional and technical personnel, it includes other occupations. To cite just one example, in 1965, 31 percent of Argentine immigrants admitted into the United States were professionals and technical personnel, while 50 percent were manual workers (U.S. Immigration and Naturalization Service,1965). In point of fact, no one has made a comprehensive study of migratory flows from Argentina, in terms of such features as educational levels and occupational characteristics. This chapter represents an attempt to fill this gap.

In recent years the phenomenon of Argentine emigration has gained some notoriety among the public both in Argentina and abroad. Although some estimates disseminated by the news media on the number of Argentines living abroad are exaggerated, there is no doubt that from the first days of the military regime in the mid 1970s emigration has accelerated for both political and economic factors. Available statistical information is fragmentary, but revealing: The annual statistics on migration, for example, indicate that by 1976 there was an annum e-migration loss of almost 44,000 people; and in 1983 the loss surpassed 75,000. A new strata of the population was joining the flow abroad.

In this chapter we first examine changes in the Argentine labor market that could have encouraged emigration. Then, we compare the

[1] This paper is based on research carried out with the financial support of the Intergovernmental Committee for Migration and Georgetown University. The complete results are presented in Marshall (1985b).

educational and occupational characteristics of the Argentines emigrating to the United States with the same characteristics of the population residing in Argentina. Some of the changes in the composition of
flows of Argentines abroad after 1976 will be analyzed. Finally, we examine the educational characteristics of the Argentine immigrants in
the United States and analyze their insertion into the U.S. labor market
in comparison with other Latin American immigrants in the United
States.

We have chosen the case of Argentines residing in the United States
for two reasons: First, this country offers rich statistical information on
Argentine immigrants. Second, the United States has become the main
destination of Argentine immigrants since the 1970s. By 1980, 22 percent
of the Argentines living abroad resided in the United States; almost 39
percent resided in all of the countries bordering Argentina together; and
only 11 percent lived in a group of eight Western European countries.
Canada and Australia, countries that seem to be emerging as new alternatives
for Argentines, together received only 4 percent of Argentine emigrants.[2]

THE CAUSES OF EMIGRATION

Argentina is not a net labor-exporting country. It still attracts the population of neighboring countries, even under the adverse conditions that
have characterized the Argentine economy in recent years. Even in
1983, the year of the greatest emigration by Argentines, there were still
more foreigners immigrating to Argentina than Argentines emigrating.[3] Thus, Argentina is not typical of labor-sending countries, although it shares with the peripheral economies the factors that give rise
to systemic emigration of highly-skilled individuals.

Although Argentina does not generate a massive and chronic emigration of workers, for several decades there has been, alongside the emigration of scientists, professionals, and technical personnel, an outward
flow of manual and less skilled non-manual workers. The loss of these
workers is due not to serious labor-expelling conditions, but simply to
the fact that wage levels in Argentina have declined relative to wage
levels in the receiving countries to which they migrate, and to the fact
that the demand for labor in Argentina has hardly increased, given the
slow pace of economic growth.

---

[2] My own estimates, based on data cited in Bertoncello, *et al.* (1985:33).

[3] Information from annual migration statistics (Dirección Nacional de Migraciones),
cited in Raspanti and Lujan (1984:3): influx of foreigners, 95,056; out-flow of Argentines, -75,714; total net influx, 19,342.

Argentine emigration reached one of its highest points in 1976. This is not surprising as it coincides with the harsh and generalized repression carried out by the military which took power in early 1976. One of the effects of the military takeover was the forced exile of broad sectors of the population. This sudden and high rate of emigration was due to political causes. The influence of economic factors, such as the clear decline in the purchasing power of wage-earners and the decline in employment opportunities, had not had such an immediate impact by 1976. From 1977 to 1982 emigration continued to increase regularly.[4] This phenomenon began to draw the attention of the news media and consequently, the public at large. The Argentine public began to echo journalistic accounts which referred to some two million Argentines residing abroad. In 1983, with the economic crisis full blown, the emigration of Argentines peaked at approximately 75,000; in 1984, it fell off only slightly.

This phenomenon of relatively high and continuous emigration can be easily explained in terms of prevailing real-wage levels in Argentina during this period as well as in terms of changes in the structure of employment and the labor market.[5] In the first place, real wages declined sharply after 1976, and in 1982 real wages were less than they had been ten years earlier. This decline affected the vast majority of wage earners, with the exception of a small elite sector. In addition, the purchase power of self-employed workers also declined, though less than that of formal wage-earners.

Second, reduced employment in manufacturing, and later in construction, resulted in a loss of over 300,000 jobs from 1976 to 1982. During the same period, moreover, public sector employment diminished markedly, above all in state-owned companies. Employment in some sectors of the economy, such as finance and other services, experienced some growth, which nonetheless was too limited to compensate for the decline in employment in the other sectors. In any event, the activities in which employment expanded offered job opportunities for workers with educational characteristics and occupational training not generally found among manufacturing wage-earners and others who had been left jobless.

Before 1981 the open unemployment rates did not reflect this decline in employment. However, in 1981 unemployment rose visibly. Several

[4] There are no annual migration statistics for 1977 to 1981, but there is a certain consensus that emigration was relatively high.

[5] The following paragraphs are based on several studies published in recent years on the evolution of wages and employment in Argentina. These include: Cortés; 1985, Marshall, 1985a; Beccaria and Orsatti, 1979; Ministerio de Trabajo, Argentina, 1983, 1984, and 1985; Sánchez and Ferrero, 1979.

factors contributed to this delayed response in the unemployment rate. Many workers who became unemployed opted for self-employment while others withdrew, "discouraged", from the labor market. Withdrawal from the labor market occurred both among adult male heads of household and among young people who were not in school, but also failed to enter the labor force, *i.e.*, those who usually would have made up the new generation of workers who enter the labor market each year. Furthermore, underemployment increased. The movement of the low-income households from Greater Buenos Aires to areas surrounding it, a process that was linked to the project of slum eradication taken on by the military, also affected the unemployment rate as many unemployed workers moved to an area not covered by the unemployment surveys. Furthermore, the greater retention of population within the provinces that traditionally dispatched workers to the industrial centers, and the slowdown in immigration of workers from bordering countries, were also among the factors that kept unemployment rates down.

In light of the bleak economic conditions described above, one would expect that many of those who emigrated abroad were blue-collar and low-paid white-collar workers, the groups hardest hit by the deteriorating economic conditions. Nevertheless, the emigration of professionals and scientists may also have increased as a result of general political conditions and because of policy regarding science and culture. Likewise, there was probably heightened emigration among privileged social groups. Such individuals left with capital to invest abroad. These emigrants were beneficiaries of the military's economic policies which helped to redistribute income "upward" and to overvalue the Argentine currency. The final result of all these economic and political changes was not necessarily a recomposition of the emigrant flow in terms of occupational characteristics and educational levels. Let us then examine in greater detail the educational and occupational profile of the Argentine flows to determine whether there was a change after 1976.

THE MIGRATORY FLOWS TO THE UNITED STATES

For the reasons set out in the introduction we have limited our investigation at this time to the information on Argentine migrants who have gone to or resided in the United States. A comparison (*circa* 1980) of characteristics of Argentines in the United States with those of the Argentine population as a whole reveal the following differences: Argentines in the United States stand out for their higher educational levels, their higher rate of labor-force participation, above all among women, and the inclusion of many more professionals and managers than are found in the Argentine population in general.

TABLE 1

Educational and Labor Characteristics of the Argentine Population and the Argentine Emigrants to the United States, c. 1980

	Argentine Population %	Argentine Emigrants %
Educational Level[1]		
Percentage with:		
— Secondary Studies		
Men	23.6	45.3
Women	23.9	40.1
— University Studies		
Men	7.5	38.6
Women	9.3	46.9
Labor Force Participation Rate	35.9	44.2[2]
Occupational Distribution[3]		
Percentage of:		
— Professionals and Technical Personnel	11.5	25.4
— Managers	0.6	15.5
— Sales and Clerical Workers	32.5	12.4
— Blue-Collar Workers	39.1	33.0
— Service Workers	13.6	13.3

Notes: [1] Population 20 years of age and older.

[2] Average for 1975-1979.

[3] Occupational distribution of the working population for the Argentine population is for the urban population.

Sources: Censo de Población de la Argentina, 1980; annual migration statistics from the U.S. Immigration and Naturalization Service; unpublished data from the 1980 U.S. Population Census.

The educational characteristics of the population of Argentine residents in the United States is very different from the general population in Argentina[6]: There are many more people who completed secondary

[6] This refers to the population 20 years of age or older. This lower age limit was chosen to exclude the population of children and adolescents who at the time of the census were attending educational institutions, although those persons enrolled in higher levels of education were included. The purpose is to approximate as best as possible the educational characteristics at the moment of emigration.

school and also who have studied at universities among Argentines in the United States. This is either because they left Argentina already having carried out such studies, or because they completed these studies in the United States (*See,* Table 1).

Furthermore, the proportion of people who work (*i.e.,* the labor force participation rate) among Argentines who emigrate, and especially among those residing in the United States, is greater than that found in the population in Argentina (*See,* Table 1). The fact that emigrants have a greater rate of participation in the labor market is consistent with the findings of other studies on international migration. It is linked, above all, to the very cause of migration: the search for new employment opportunities. In particular, this finding is consistent with the results of research that has shown how migration leads to a substantial change in the status of women and in their incorporation into the labor market.[7] In the Argentine case too, we find that the most radical change was experienced by women, who in the United States practically doubled their labor force participation rate with respect to that of the urban female population in Argentina.

There are clear differences between the pre-emigration occupations of the U.S.-bound Argentines and those of the overall Argentine population. Among the emigrants there is a greater proportion of professionals and technical personnel than among the population working in Argentina (which was to be expected), and also more managers and entrepreneurs.[8] On the other hand, there are fewer blue-collar workers than among the population residing in Argentina. Even more noteworthy is the relative absence among the emigrants of the most "intermediate" occupational sectors, such as sales and clerical employees. Curiously, the "service workers" (who are a subset of blue-collar workers and who include household service workers) are represented in the flow to the United States in a similar proportion as among the population of Argentine cities (*See,* Table 1). The low proportion of sales and clerical workers among the emigrants may be associated with the fact that job opportunities for this group tended to increase in the last three decades, while those for manual workers stagnated.

A striking fact, largely neglected in the literature on Argentine emigration, is that the most important grouping within the flow to the United States has almost invariably been manual workers. This grouping encompasses skilled blue-collar workers, foremen, operatives, laborers, and service workers, including household workers. Their par-

---

[7] *See,* Pessar on Dominican women.

[8] There is practically no Argentine emigration to the United States originating from rural areas.

ticipation in Argentine migration to the United States varied from a minimum of 41 percent in 1967 to a maximum of 81 percent in 1970. Certainly, this does not rule out another important group among the emigrants, "professionals and technical personnel", who from 1965 to 1983 almost always accounted for more than 20 percent of the flow. The rest of the flow is made up of managers, sales, and clerical workers.[9]

An analysis of the employment trends among Argentines in the United States reflects the effects of conditions in Argentina to a greater extent than it does conditions in the United States. Beginning in 1978, the presence of white-collar (sales and clerical) workers tended to increase, which is consistent with the dramatic deterioration in these sectors' incomes, especially those of sales workers, whose wages were more affected than any other occupational category. In addition, operatives within the general category of blue-collar workers increased while the proportion of more skilled workers within that category decreased. Finally, the participation of managers and entrepreneurs increased, among the emigrants, possibly resulting from the movement of investors abroad promoted by the availability of foreign currency, as mentioned above.[10] Other changes, nonetheless, are linked to characteristics of U.S. immigration policy, and are shared by migration flows from other countries (*e.g.*, the increase of operatives at the expense of skilled workers).[11]

Let us now turn to the employment situation of Argentines residing in the United States.

ARGENTINE EMIGRANTS IN THE UNITED STATES

The 1980 United States census recorded almost 69,000 Argentines.[12] In the following pages the educational characteristics and labor force participation of Argentines residing in U.S. metropolitan areas are examined, along with aspects of their socioeconomic status: What is their type of employment (wage or self-employed)? In which economic sectors are they employed? And what occupations do they hold? Their situation is

---

[9] My own estimates on the basis of INS data, both unpublished and from *Annual Reports*. The complete tables are presented in Marshall (1985b).

[10] *Ibid.*

[11] *Ibid.*

[12] U.S Bureau of the Census, 1984. The analysis that follows was carried out on the basis of data from the 1980 U.S. Population Census (unpublished data from the 1980 Census of Population and Housing: Sample of microdata for public use; sample B; prepared by the Bureau of the Census, Washington: the Bureau, producer and distributor, 1983). The sample corresponds to metropolitan areas with 500,000 or more inhabitants. For more details *See,* Marshall (1985b).

viewed in a comparative light with other Latin American immigrants (except Mexicans),[13] to identify the characteristics most typical of the labor force insertion of Argentines.

Argentine immigrants stand out among Latin American immigrants for their educational levels. Although the differences are not spectacular, both Argentine women and men[14] possess a greater level of education than other Latin Americans in the United States. More have secondary and university education (*See,* Table 2). At the other end of the educational spectrum, we find a lesser proportion of Argentines than other Latin Americans have had only primary education or none at all (16 percent compared to 30 percent among women, and 13 percent compared to 26 percent among men). These differences are due in part to the fact that the average educational level is higher in Argentina than in Latin America as a whole, but also, as we saw, to the fact that Argentine emigrants have greater educational levels than the Argentine population itself. It is worth noting that among Argentine immigrants who came to the United States from 1975 to 1980, and especially among women, there is a greater share of persons who have completed secondary education than among the Argentines residing in the United States. However, a greater portion of this latter group has finished its university education, supporting the hypothesis that after 1976 emigration of the more "intermediate" social groups, such as white-collar workers, increased.

The rate of labor force participation of Argentines of both sexes in the United States which, as we saw, was higher than that of the Argentine population, is nonetheless lower than that for the rest of Latin American immigrants (*See,* Table 2). This fact can be related to the growing weight among Argentines of professionals and managers, which does not occur to a comparable degree among other Latin American immigrants. In homes headed by professsionals and managers, whose incomes are generally high, the wives do not need to become incorporated into the labor market to complement the family income. This is in contrast to the situation in households of other Latin American immigrants in the United States which are commonly headed by operatives or service workers.[15] This argument is in keeping with the fact that the difference between the rates of labor force participation of Argentines and other Latin Americans is accentuated among women.

---

[13] Mexicans were analyzed as a separate group due to their numerical importance and specific characteristics. In this chapter we do not include Mexicans in the analysis. The category 'Latin Americans' excludes Argentines as well.

[14] *See,* note 7.

[15] This fact has often been analyzed in studies on Latin Americans in New York.

TABLE 2

Educational and Labor Characteristics of Argentine and Other Latin American Immigrants in the United States, 1980[1] (Metropolitan Areas)

Argentine	Men		Women [2]	
	Argentine	Latin Amer.	Argentine	Latin Amer.
Percentage with:				
— Secondary Studies	40.1	36.9	45.3	39.7
— University Studies	46.9	37.1	38.6	30.2
Labor Force Participation Rate (%) [3]	84.1	86.3	54.8	84.1
Occupational Distribution[4]				
Percentage of:				
— Professionals and Technical Personnel	15.8	10.0	16.1	9.4
— Managers	11.2	9.8	9.7	5.0
— Sales and Clerical Workers	15.8	16.6	39.5	33.6
— Skilled Blue-Collar Workers	30.3	19.4	3.2	4.1
— Operatives and Laborers	18.4	30.1	14.5	28.4
— Service Workers	8.5	14.5	16.9	19.2

Notes: [1] "Latin Americans" excludes Mexicans and Argentines.

[2] Population 20 years and older.

[3] Population 16 years and older.

[4] Of the working population.

Source: Unpublished data from the 1980 Population Census.

Also the children of these economically privileged families can pursue their studies instead of entering the labor force.

Argentine immigrants residing in U.S. metropolitan areas are generally wage-earners in the private sector. Nonetheless, the proportion of self-employed workers and employers among Argentine men is greater than among other Latin American men (22.3 percent as compared to 9.2 percent of the working men), as is the proportion of unpaid family workers (2.4 percent as compared to 0.5 percent of employed women). This pattern may result from the fact that groups that emigrated with some capital make up a greater proportion among Argentines, making it possible for them to set up enterprises in the United States. If the enterprise is small, it is probable that other family members also work in it, but without direct pay. In recent years this difference between Argentines and other Latin Americans appears to have become more accentuated, as the migration to the United States of Latin American blue-collar workers with limited means has been increasing.

The Argentines and the other Latin Americans also differ in the economic activities in which they tend to find employment. In the first place, Argentine women work less than other Latin American women in manufacturing (27 percent as compared to 34 percent), an activity that in recent years has become among the most common for immigrant female labor in the United States. Argentine women tend to work instead in retail trade activities (22 percent of Argentine women as compared to 15 percent of other Latin American women). Secondly, what most distinguishes Argentine men from the rest of Latin Americans is their greater access to construction (12 percent as compared to 6 percent) and to business and repair services (13 percent as compared to 7 percent). A greater proportion of Argentine men are also employed in restaurants and similar activities (9 percent and 6 percent, respectively), a very typical area of insertion among immigrants in the United States.[16] Many self-employed Argentine immigrants who had capital for setting up a business have probably established themselves in the sectors cited above.

Finally, Argentines are better situated than other Latin Americans in the U.S. urban labor market from the standpoint of their occupations. A greater proportion of Argentine women who are employed are professionals and managers, as well as sales and clerical workers. Conversely, Argentine women are employed less than other Latin American women in manual work, such as machine operation. Argentine men differ from the rest of Latin American men insofar as they work more frequently as professionals. A second distinguishing characteristic is that many are skilled manual workers, suggesting that their employment in manufacturing (which employs 27 percent of Argentine men), construction, and repair services often takes the form of skilled manual work, since there are relatively few non-skilled operatives among them (See, Table 2). The occupational differences between Argentines and the rest of Latin Americans are certainly related to the difference, already mentioned, between their educational levels.

[16] See, Bailey and Freedman (1981).

In sum, Argentine immigrants differ from other Latin American immigrants both in their characteristics when they arrive in the United States and in their employment characteristics once they are settled. Argentine immigrants have somewhat higher educational levels, are characterized by a significant proportion of professionals, managers, and skilled blue-collar workers who continue to work as such in their new place of residence, and they are often favored by the fact that they have capital for setting up their own enterprises. It would seem that the social experience of Argentines contrasts with those of other nationalities studied.[17] Among other Latin American immigrant groups, it is common to find individuals employed as factory operatives and service workers despite having worked in their home country in non-manual, often skilled positions. Among Argentines this form of downward social mobility as a survival mechanism is less common. The occupational mobility of Argentine migrants and the ways in which women are incorporated within the labor market are subjects that require special attention in future studies of Argentines abroad.

FINAL OBSERVATIONS

Due to both political and economic causes, Argentine emigration accelerated in the second half of the 1970s, and continued throughout the period of military government (1976-1983). At present, despite the constitutional government now in power, there are indications that Argentine emigration may turn upward once again.

The barriers to entry imposed by the principal host countries limit the actual magnitude of Argentine emigration. Nonetheless, the growth in the number of "potential" emigrants is evinced, for example, in the growth in the number of people who seek information from the diplomatic offices of countries which, like Australia, are becoming new options for Argentines interested in emigrating. According to consular sources in Buenos Aires, the number of people who sought information on conditions for emigrating to Australia in 1984-85 more than doubled from 1983-84, and was comparable to 1981-82. In the present recessionary context of few employment alternatives and low wages, Argentines continue to pursue better-paying job opportunities abroad. Within a few years, it will be possible to determine whether the increase in the number of potential and actual emigrants is merely a passing, short-term phenomenon, or if stepped-up Argentine emigration will endure into the next decade.

[17] *See,* for example, Foner (1983) and Urrea (1982) on Jamaicans and Colombians in New York, respectively.

The volume and destination of Argentine emigration will be strongly influenced, on the one hand by immigration policies of the traditional receiving countries, in which employment opportunities have also declined dramatically, and on the other hand, by the demand for labor and wage levels in Argentina. Naturally, whether employment and wages in Argentina become favorable depends on whether the Argentine economy is able to recover positive growth and emerge from its long-term stagnation.

The occupational profile of Argentine emigration, specifically to the United States, has not changed significantly over the last 20 years. Its composition differs from that of the Argentine population as a whole: There are more professionals and managers among the emigrants than in the general population, and emigrants also have higher levels of education. Nonetheless, in the flows of Argentines to the United States, the presence of manual workers, and above all of skilled blue-collar workers, has also been significant. The occupational structure of the Argentine immigrant population is more polarized than that found in Argentina; this has not been altered by the recent trend toward increased emigration of more "intermediate" occupational groups, such as sales and clerical workers. After 1976, spectacular changes in the occupational composition of the emigrant flows did not occur. While on the one hand emigration of blue-collar and less-skilled white-collar workers has apppeared to increase in line with the labor-market situation in Argentina, on the other hand emigration of professionals, managers, and entrepreneurs interested in investing abroad has also showed an upward trend.

Further research on the occupations of Argentine migrants to both traditional and new destinations will contribute greater knowledge about recent occupational changes. Such research will allow us to develop new forecasts concerning the trends to be witnessed in coming years.

REFERENCES

Argentina. Ministerio de Trabajo (Argentina)
1985   "La terciarización del empleo en la economía argentina". Bueno Aires: *Anexo Estadístico*, ARG84029.

1984   "Salarios e inflación, Argentina, 1970-1983". Buenos Aires: ARG81008.

1983   "Ocupación y producto en la industria manufacturera argentina, 1976-1983". Buenos Aires: ARG81008.

Bailey, T. and M. Freedman
1981 "Immigrant and Native-born Workers in the Restaurant Industry", *Conservation of Human Resources*. New York: Columbia University.

Beccaria, L. and A. Orsatti
1979 "Sobre el tamaño del desempleo oculto en el mercado de trabajo urbano en la Argentina", *Desarrollo Económico*, 19(74): 251-267.

Bertoncello, R., A. Lattes, D. Moyano and S. Schkolnik
1985 "Los argentinos en el exterior". Buenos Aires: Centro de Estudio de Población and United Nations Research Institute for Social Development.

Cortes, R.
1985 "Cambios en el mercado de trabajo urbano argentino, 1974-1983", *Documentos e Informes de Investigación*, 13. Buenos Aires: Facultad Latinoamericana de Ciencias Sociales (FLASCO).

Foner, N.
1983 "Jamaican Migrants: A Comparative Analysis of the New York and London Experience", *Occasional Papers*, 36.420. New York: New York University for Latin American and Caribbean Studies.

Marshall, A.
1985a "La estructura de los salarios en la Argentina, 1976-1982", *Documentos e Informes de Investigación* 14. Buenos Aires: Facultad Latinoamericana de Ciencias Sociales (FLACSO).

1985b "La migración argentina", Unpublished manuscript.

Pessar, P.
1985 "The Role of Gender in Dominican Settlement in the United States". In *Women and Change in Latin America*. Edited by J. Nash and H. Safa. South Hadley, MA: J.F. Bergin, Publishers.

Raspanti, M. and C. Luján
1984 "República Argentina: Movimiento de ingreso y egreso de personas correspondiente al año 1982 y al año 1983". Buenos Aires: Internal documents of the Dirección Nacional de Migraciones (Argentina).

Sánchez, C., F. Ferrero, and W. Schulthess
1979 "Tamaño de la fuerza laboral y desempleo oculto en la Argentina", *Desarrollo Económico* 19(74): 269-274.

U.S. Bureau of the Census
1984 *1980 Census of Population*. Vol. I. Characteristics of the Population. Chapter D. Detailed Population Characteristics. Part I. United States Summary — Section A. Washington, D.C.: U.S. Government Printing Office.

U.S. Immigration and Naturalization Service.
    Annual Reports. 1965-1983, inclusive.

Urrea Giraldo, F.
1982 "Life Struggles and the Labor Market: Colombians in New York in the 1970s", *Occasional Papers*, 34. New York: New York University, Center for Latin American and Caribbean Studies.

SOCIAL INTEGRATION AND EMPLOYMENT OF CENTRAL AMERICAN REFUGEES

Lelio Mármora

Migration between Central American countries is not new. The migration history of these countries has been shaped primarily by economic factors such as wage differentials, employment opportunities, and the rural settlement of unoccupied areas. Since 1980, however, the migration flows between these countries have doubled and have been composed mainly of refugees. Today, there are some 175,000 refugees in Central America; and as many as 350,000 if we include those Central Americans also in Mexico and Panama (Torres-Rivas, 1985).

TABLE 1

Estimates of Central American Refugees in the Region
(1980 - 1984)

Receiving Countries	EL Salvador	Guatemala	Nicaragua	Others	Total	Percentages
Mexico	120,000	55,000	—	—	175,000	50.1
Guatemala	70,000	—	—	—	70,000	20.0
Nicaragua	17,500	500	—	500	18,500	5.3
Honduras	19,000	1,000	19,200	—	39,200	11.2
Costa Rica	10,000	1,000	25,000	2,700	38,700	11.0
Belize/ Panama	3,000	5,500	—	—	8,500	2.4
Total	239,000 (68.4%)	63,000 (18%)	44,200 (12.6%)	3,200 (1.0%)	349,900 —	— 100.0%

Source: Torres-Rivas, 1985.

The political conflicts that gave rise to these involuntary movements of refugees have become long and drawn out. Thus, one of the main challenges faced by the host countries is what to do with the refugees whose stays have become prolonged. There is no doubt that durable solutions to the crisis of the hundreds of thousands of refugees and displaced persons in Central America can only be found in long-term political and economic solutions to the problems that generate these forced population movements. Until such time as these problems are resolved, however, other avenues must be pursued to alleviate the refugee crisis.

Traditional relief programs have proved to be an inadequate response to the refugee crisis in Central America because of the high human and financial costs over time for all concerned. As these same countries are currently facing the most serious economic crises in their history, we are left with the following dilemma: How can the receiving countries effectively integrate the refugees into their society and economy so that the refugees no longer pose such a great burden?

In the search for a durable solution for the refugees, many refugee-receiving countries in the region, in concert with international relief agencies, have established productive projects to help bring refugees to self-sufficiency. The results of their efforts have varied, depending on the characteristics of these flows and the external factors affecting such migration.

Based on my first-hand experience with refugee resettlement and my review of the literature on refugee programs in the region, I will highlight those factors that condition the relative success or failure of programs designed to integrate refugees in Central America.

ECONOMIC CONTEXT

Any study of durable solutions in Central America must begin with a consideration of the economic crisis in the region. We use the term "crisis" to refer to economies strangled by exorbitant foreign debts, a steady process of income accumulation in the hands of a small elite, a gradual deterioration in the terms of trade, an even more dramatic reduction in production, and a gradual impoverishment of the overall population. This crisis both worsens the conditions leading to migration and sets up obstacles to the creation of durable solutions for refugees in the receiving countries.

Taken together, the foreign debt of the Central American countries and Panama amounts to U.S.$21 billion, and the debt per capita, U.S.$750. Meanwhile, GDP per inhabitant has declined in all Central American countries in the last five years (*See*, Table 2).

TABLE 2

GDP per Inhabitant 1981-1984 in Central American Countries

| | GDP per Inhabitant 1970 U.S. Dollars | | | |
	1981	1982	1983	1984
Panama	1197	1236	1214	1173
Nicaragua	344	329	333	317
Costa Rica	926	836	834	861
Guatemala	577	541	512	498
El Salvador	394	369	364	367
Honduras	348	331	318	316

Source: ECLA, 1984a-e.

This crisis has brought on growing unemployment and underemployment. A relative decrease in the formal sector's share in the economy as a generator of employment has resulted in an increase in self-employment and has aggravated pre-existing job shortages in most of the Central American countries. Furthermore, with almost no exceptions, unemployment rates have increased between 1980 and 1984 between 20 and 90 percent (*See,* Table 3). For example, in Costa Rica, unemployment rose from 5.3 percent to 6.4 percent (ECLA, 1984b), while in El Salvador, unemployment rose from 16.1 percent to an estimated 30 percent (ECLA, 1984c). Only in Nicaragua was there a slight drop in unemployment from 22.4 percent in 1980 to 19.9 percent in 1984 (ECLA, 1984e). This contraction of labor markets, for which no improvement is in sight for the next few years, will have a negative impact both on the real capacity to absorb labor and on observable trends in the immigration policies of the various Central American countries.

In effect, the problems that arise as Central American governments plan to meet employment needs will give rise to a trend of ever more restrictive immigration policies. There are some indications that these restrictions are beginning already. For example, Central Americans entering Costa Rica are now required to present a visa upon entering the country; previously, they had had free entry (Torres-Rivas, 1985). Fear that large numbers of Central Americans would settle and eventually compete for jobs raised the new barrier. In recognition of the numbers of undocumented persons in Costa Rica in 1984, that country declared a mass amnesty in an attempt to gain control over its existing population. Also, Mexico proposed a special temporary residence status for

TABLE 3
Unemployment in Central America and Panama

	1980	1984
Costa Rica	5.3	6.4
El Salvador	16.1	30.0[a]
Guatemala	n.a.	n.a.
Honduras	15.2	23.9
Nicaragua	22.4	19.9
Panama	8.2	9.4

Note: [a] Estimated.
Source: ECLA, 1984a-e.

Guatemalans so as not to set a precedent in declaring them refugees (Torres-Rivas, 1985). Such a precedent might have forced the Mexicans to regularize the status of large numbers of undocumented Salvadorans also residing there.

MIGRATION FACTORS

Another factor that influences the integration of refugees is the history of international labor flows into the refugee-receiving country.

We hypothesize that the existence of prior migration flows in general establishes a pattern that in many cases helps refugees successfully integrate themselves into the new community. This would be the case for some flows, such as of Salvadorans to Costa Rica, Nicaragua and Guatemala — those countries into which there already had already been Salvadoran labor migration (ILO-UNHCR, 1984a; ILO-UNHCR, 1984b).[1] Elsewhere in South America it has also been found that prior migration experience has helped later refugees assimilate, for example, Chileans into Argentina (ILO-UNHCR, 1984c) and South Americans into Venezuela (ILO-UNHCR, 1984d).

[1] Emigration from El Salvador to the northern coast of Honduras started in the first decade of this century during the increase in banana production on the Honduran Atlantic coast. A migration flow was thus established which was interrupted only during the 1969 conflict between the two countries, when around 250,000 persons returned to El Salvador. It was at this time that Salvadoran emigration to Guatemala increased. In 1973, a total of 14,000 persons were recorded as legal migrants in Guatemala. The figure would, of course, be several times larger if migrants entering by illegal means were included. Salvadoran emigration to Nicaragua was much lower and could be estimated at 2,000 permanent migrants and 5,000 temporary ones in 1978 (Mármora, 1978).

Conversely, migration flows that have been associated with border conflicts may be a negative antecedent to forced migrations, such as the case of Salvadorans to Honduras. Honduras had been unreceptive to Salvadoran refugees in 1980 and 1981, until the weight of international opinion forced it to allow the United Nations High Commissioner for Refugees (UNHCR) to coordinate refugee assistance (Torres-Rivas, 1985).

There are, of course, other cases in which the refugee population does not have a "historic cushion" of earlier movements, such as the presence of Salvadorans in Panama or Belize. In Panama, Salvadoran refugees settled in relatively isolated forest areas, farming colonies, and, with the direct assistance of UNHCR, in Panama City. In Belize, about 2,000 Salvadorans have been officially recognized as refugees. The assistance strategy pursued by Belize favored their integration by granting land in the Valley of Peace to Salvadoran and Belizean farmers, and by allowing Salvadorans to settle temporarily near the capital (Palacio, 1985).

It should be noted that even if there has been a prior history of labor migration, forced migrants are likely to require new forms of socio-economic integration. This is because the numbers and characteristics of the new movements will differ from the old. And now, the new group is likely to encounter restrictive migration policies and saturated labor markets.

The changed characteristics of new migration can be observed in the case of Salvadoran and Nicaraguan refugees in Costa Rica, where their current social and labor integration is quite distinct from the traditional labor migration from those countries. The change has been due to the fact that their refugee status implies restrictions on their paid labor — limits that are not imposed on the ordinary immigrant (ILO-UNHCR, 1984a).

REFUGEE TRAITS AND RECEIVING SOCIETY FACTORS

Still another set of factors exists that directly influences the success or failure of projects for the social integration and employment of refugees. These factors include the traits of the refugees, the characteristics of the receiving society, the characteristics of the institutional support structure for refugees, and the very nature of the durable solutions developed to assist the refugees.

Clearly, with respect to refugee traits, age and educational level are direct factors conditioning the chances for successful integration — especially if we take into account the low educational level observed for some refugee flows. The diverse characteristics of different refugee flows have been documented (Torres-Rivas, 1985). Refugees are not homogeneous even within nationality groups. For example, it has been documented that uneducated Salvadorans of rural origin tend to be found in the refugee camps along the Honduran border, while more educated, mostly male Salvadorans of urban origin are found in cities such as Mexico City. It is imperative, then, that the background and qualifications of the specific refugee population are taken into consideration in planning durable solutions. In too many cases, projects requiring heavy labor, for example, were doomed because planners had not counted on the high proportion of women and children among the particular refugee group.

The cultural distance between the refugee and the receiving society also influences social integration. This distance is often one of the causes for failure of small firms in the urban informal sector. Refugee businesses have foundered due to the newcomers' lack of familiarity with the new cultural standards encountered — even more important in the informal sector. Different forms of association in the workplace unfamiliar to the refugee also lead to difficulties. For example, some projects involving cooperative enterprises have suffered when the collective nature of such associations is not understood; researchers found that these refugees' notions of labor relations were based only on the "owner" and the "employee" model, which is not applicable to cooperatives.

Other factors directly affecting the resettlement process are the characteristics of the community into which the refugee is placed. As is the case with all refugees, migration is spontaneous and provoked by fear. The Central American case is no different. Therefore, refugees generally end up in a place they have not chosen, in a foreign country, and in a community with characteristics different from those of their place of origin.

In the cases in which the move and settlement is from and to rural areas, the changes in social and work habits are not so great. Yet, even when this happens, there may be other factors to consider. Refugees often resist relocation away from border areas. Border settlements provide refugees with the sense that they may return to their own country easily and as conditions warrant; such settlements reinforce the temporary nature of the refugees' dilemma. When they are moved from the border, refugees must come to terms with potentially long-term exile. To cite one example, many thousands of Guatemalan refugees on the Mexican border have refused to relocate to new settlements in the Yucatan for fear that such a move may not allow them to return home when they wish (Torres-Rivas, 1985).

Furthermore, whether refugee settlement takes place in an isolated area or in an area integrated into a larger rural society can make or break a refugee project. As this is a key point, we will cite some examples of rather large refugee settlements in Central America.

One such settlement is the "Los Angeles" farm in northern Costa Rica, made up of Salvadoran families and located along the border with Nicaragua. This settlement was established in such a fashion that it is isolated from the rural community that surrounds it. It was privileged in terms of housing and service infrastructure, and in the financial and technical support it has received. Nonetheless, the "enclave" phenomenon that resulted gradually gave rise to hostility in the surrounding community which, when the settlement's internal problems worsened, played a determinant role in the failure of this initiative (ILO-UNHCR, 1986).

A similar situation developed in the settlement of Salvadorans in Belize. Some 150 Salvadoran families along with 50 Belizean families were officially resettled in the Valley of Peace, seven miles from Belize City. One of the problems that arose was that although it was a mixed settlement, it was located in a remote area and appeared "divorced" from the socioeconomic structure of Belizean cities (Mebtouche, 1985). In terms of the settlement's internal dynamics, bringing nationals into cooperatives with Salvadorans presented problems due to cultural, racial, and linguistic differences between the two groups. In some cases the problems proved impossible to resolve.

The "Ciudad Romero" settlement of Salvadorans on the left bank of the Caño river in the province of Colon, Panama had a different experience. This settlement, in an isolated area, unfolded without competitive relations with surrounding communities; but difficult access led to serious problems in transportation, logistical support, and marketing of products (Coch Castro, 1985).

Finally, there is the case of Salvadoran refugee families who were integrated successfully into rural cooperatives in Nicaragua. The fact that the cooperatives were experiencing operational problems made their members especially receptive to the arrival of Salvadorans who came with capital and machinery. In addition, the social integration and employment of the refugees was aided by other factors such as ideological affinities with the Nicaraguan members of the cooperatives (ILO-UNHCR, 1986).

INSTITUTIONAL SUPPORT

The characteristics of the institutional support structure for refugees also play an important role in the viability of durable solutions for refugees. Governmental, private, national, and international institutions continue to support refugee projects and have been the moving force for the integration of refugees.

The UNHCR is the international body that has played the greatest role in developing productive projects for refugees in Central America. To this end, it has harnessed an enormous amount of technical and material resources; furthermore, it has increased the technical level of its work, either directly or by working together with other institutional agencies such as the International Labor Organization (ILO) and the Organization of American States (OAS). In an endeavor to shift from solely assistential or emergency relief to the provision of durable solutions for refugees, UNHCR and ILO have collaborated on a study of the economic and institutional dimensions of the refugee situation in Central America. The study, whose findings are reflected in the conclusion here, examines national labor markets and migrant working conditions as these relate to recent refugee flows. For the purpose of improving the social and economic integration of refugees, the institutional responses taken by the governments of Costa Rica, Honduras, and Nicaragua to the refugee problem were also reviewed in that study (ILO-UNHCR, 1986). Moreover, the UNHCR has undertaken jointly with the OAS a research project that compares the protection of refugees and the displaced offered by the covenants on asylum, extradition, and human rights as ratified by the United Nations and the OAS (UNHCR/OAS, 1983). Likewise, intergovernmental agencies such as the Intergovernmental Committee for Migration (ICM) have supported these efforts to achieve durable solutions for refugees in some countries of the region, even though their main task in relation to Central American refugees continues to be their resettlement inside and outside the region.

In the case of government institutions, there is ever greater inter-institutional coordination, more specific refugee-related legislation (UNHCR/OAS, 1983), and greater participation in planning and administering resources for refugees.

The positive aspects of this growing interest are manifested in greater protection for refugees, higher coordination among governments, the UNHCR and voluntary organizations, and ever-more rational planning for social integration and employment of refugees.

Yet, the negative aspects of this greater governmental involvement are sometimes manifested in excessive bureaucratization in the implementation of programs. At times, there is a lack of planning and unified criteria in program management on the part of some governmental bodies. In an evaluation carried out several years ago of the Costa Rican institutions providing services for refugees, a 50 percent reduction in

personnel was recommended, as was the employment of more techni-
cally qualified individuals. The researchers found a tremendous dupli-
cation of efforts among agencies that tended to pull resources away
from the primary objective of assisting the refugees (Mármora and
Vargas, 1984).

Private voluntary agencies have carried out much of the direct support. They have progressed from a posture exclusively of providing relief to identifying and promoting durable solutions. However, their aid
approach has often been a hindrance to the effective promotion of durable solutions. This is because private voluntary agencies too often
have adopted a paternalistic orientation toward durable-solution
projects. Furthermore, the projects of these agencies have commonly
suffered from insufficient feasibility and management planning (CON-
APARE, 1983).

The success or failure of durable-solution projects is many times contingent on careful planning before start-up. Analyses of profitability,
productivity, and marketing opportunities are often absent from proposals for specific durable-solution projects, as was demonstrated in the
project examples given in the previous section. The lack of feasibility
studies may be due to the immediacy with which refugees' problems
need to be addressed. Another contributing factor may be the lack of
experience of support institutions, whose past functions have been
more to provide social assistance and protection than to promote economically profitable activities. For example, mistakes are often made
when new projects are found to compete with local businesses in
markets for which there is limited demand. Ultimately, these projects
have no chance for the successful integration of refugees.

The social organization of production is an important element to consider in assessing the opportunities for successful durable-solution
projects. Lack of knowledge of objective variables, such as productivity,
the refugees' employment background, and the size of the enterprise,
frequently characterizes the "planning" of these productive projects.
Each organizational form to be developed — whether it be a "cooperative", "self-employment", or an "associative firm" — carries with it its
own set of requirements. When other objective variables, such as the
characteristics of the refugees, do not match the economic and social
requirements for establishing the specific organization, a project may be
jeopardized. A review of numerous productive projects created for refugees in Costa Rica and Nicaragua indicated repeated problems with
reaching self-sufficiency. The number of active cooperative members is
quite low in many projects, for example. Whether members drop out
due to the inappropriateness of their skills, background, or lack of
training has yet to be explored.

STRATEGIES FOR PROVIDING EMPLOYMENT
FOR REFUGEES

Now, let us take a closer look at the durable solutions themselves. The objective of all the projects referred to above is to employ refugees productively, and thereby, offer them a durable solution to their present crisis. Strategies for providing employment for refugees can take on different forms and be developed in many different settings. Two types of strategies can be described: obtaining work within the labor market and generating new employment.

In the first instance, employment is found when a given agency plays the role of broker and places the refugees where there is an unsatisfied demand for labor. In Costa Rica, for example, the Instituto Mixto de Acción Social has set up a job exchange program for placing Nicaraguan and Salvadoran refugees in jobs in agriculture, industry, and the service sector (ILO/UNHCR, 1985). Similarly, Costa Rica's experience employing Nicaraguan refugees in cotton and coffee harvests is noteworthy.

This strategy has the advantage of more or less immediate integration, with minimal cost, when appropriate vacancies are found. Nonetheless, neither the region's labor markets nor the governments' immigration policies make it possible to place much hope for this mechanism in the future.

Generating productive employment would be the surest way to achieve a durable solution for refugees, without at the same time provoking competition with the local labor suply. But taking into account the economic and political factors and prior migration history mentioned earlier, one must also ensure that indirect competition with local production is avoided.

Employment may be found at various levels: self-employment and work in small, medium, and large firms. Self-employment among refugees tends to be limited to one-person operations and these tend to be situated in the receiving countries' urban informal markets.

The strategy of creating small firms as a means of seeking durable solutions has generated a great deal of discussion in Central America in terms of the results to date. In all the countries of the region, this strategy has been the most widely used, yet the results have hardly been satisfactory. The problems have included the weak position of such firms in the highly competitive markets in which they are found. In most cases, Central American refugees are not familiar with these markets, which are often more complex than those in the refugees' places of origin. Another problem that small firms have faced in integrating refugees productively is posed by the accelerated and increasingly more competitive growth of the informal sector in Central American economies. Finally, the low profitability of such firms has made economic self-sufficiency practically impossible in most cases.

Neither self-employment nor small firm strategies have proved to be totally effective for integrating refugees. The failure of such strategies in all the Latin American countries in which these strategies have been studied leads us to take a closer look at medium-sized and large enterprises to see why they ought to be more likely to succeed.

The larger size of the enterprise allows for the preparation of feasibility studies that narrow the margin of risk and forecast productivity, marketing channels, and the time factor in the return on the investment of capital. Such enterprises permit economies of scale that facilitate greater productivity, and, therefore, better quality and prices. As a result, the better competitive stand of the enterprise in the market allows for the export of the final products of these enterprises (which is harder for small firms), thus preventing competition within the receiving country and increasing that country's acquisition of foreign currency.

Unlike the small firm, the larger enterprise provides the flexibility to vary the social organization of production so that the refugee can keep a wage-earning status, as far as the functional aspects of production are concerned, but at the same time, share in the profits of the enterprise. In such cases, technical and administrative monitoring could ensure the enterprise's efficiency. Without such supervision, the refugees' lack of experience and training in the operation of particular collective enterprises has resulted in earlier failures.

The larger firm allows for simultaneous employment of nationals in different administrative and productive areas, inasmuch as the greatest possible integration of refugees with the local population is recommended. This mixed configuration of the personnel would play an important role not only in terms of the refugees' social integration, but also with regard to the general social approval of the refugees in the receiving country.

Lastly, all of the arguments cited for larger enterprises also show that they can be effectively integrated into government development plans and programs of the receiving countries.

Yet, we have seen a number of examples of the failure of medium and large-scale enterprises for which refugee labor was specifically contemplated. While such enterprises should be economically viable, they do present some challenges. For example, in order to conduct the necessary feasibility and market studies, greater planning and lead time are required. These studies were not always conducted in the cited examples. Also, significant financial and technological investments are required for larger enterprises that must become integrated into the formal sector of the economy. As with the small-firm strategy, however, the medium and large enterprises find their success or failure determined by the mix of economic, social, historical, and cultural factors at play. To the extent that investment in durable solutions for refugees can be matched with national and regional development plans, however, the results may be more successful and palatable to both the local population and the refugees.

CONCLUSIONS AND PROSPECTS

The search for durable solutions in the region is becoming ever more pressing. Population movements between Central American countries have changed both quantitatively and qualitatively in the last years. The number of persons born in a country other than the one in which they currently reside has tripled. The new migration carries the distinction of having been forced, with consequently far greater implications for the refugees' subsistence and assimilation. Moreover, when we consider the causes for this forced migration, we find no evidence that it will end in the short run.

The context in which projects for the durable solution to the refugee crisis are attempted determines the projects' success or failure. Resettlement of refugees within Central America is ever more complex due to the pressure on already saturated labor markets and the diminished capacity of the different societies to absorb growing populations. Despite the great effort made by public and private, national and international agencies to facilitate this integration, results to date have not been encouraging. Attempts to employ refugees often engender hostility toward the refugees on the part of the local population — whether those jobs are found in the existing market or newly created. The population strain is reflected in the restrictive policies of the region's governments, which, having institutionalized the process of receiving refugees, show no growing receptivity to new refugee flows.

Hence, any proposal for the integration of new refugees should not be viewed in humanitarian terms alone. Refugees must be seen for their contribution of labor and capital to the future socioeconomic development of Central American nations. In this way, durable solutions proposed for the region's countries may have greater chances of success, insofar as they are planned not only in terms of the refugees' subsistence, but also with regard to the benefits that the refugees will bring to regional and national development programs in the receiving countries. As noted in the Nicaraguan case, the resources that refugees brought with them to existing cooperatives were well received by the local population and helped rejuvenate otherwise declining enterprises.

Finally, those concerned about the refugee crisis in Central America should consider extending the context for durable solution projects to the rest of Latin America. Especially in South America, there are countries that still have open-door policies toward immigrants as part of their population and development policies.

There is precedent for such resettlement in South America. Among the previous cases are the resettlement by the UNHCR of Guatemalan refugees to rural areas of Bolivia and the resettlement of displaced Salvadorans in the Argentine provinces of Salta and Jujuy undertaken by the ILO and ICM (1985). While still new projects, these efforts represent a viable alternative for the social integration and employment of select numbers of refugees outside Central America. Such resettlement projects contribute to development in the host country, and at the same time, avoid additional pressures on the Central American countries that have been receiving refugees to date.

In conclusion, the interest shown by Bolivia and Argentina in third-country resettlement of Central American refugees is further demonstration of the truly international concern for the plight of these refugees and of the willingness of countries in the Hemisphere to share responsibility with Central America for finding durable solutions to the refugee crisis.

REFERENCES

Coch Castro, C.
1985   *Asentamiento rural Ciudad Romero, Panamá: Informe de progreso.* Geneva: UNHCR.

Consejo Nacional para Refugiados (CONAPARE)
1983   *Situación de los proyectos para refugiados en Costa Rica.* San José, Costa Rica.

Economic Commission for Latin America (ECLA)
1984a   *Estudio económico de América Latina y el Caribe, Panamá.* LC/L.330/add.15.

1984b   *Estudio económico de América Latina y el Caribe, Costa Rica.* LC./L.330/add.4.

1984c   *Estudio económico de América Latina y el Caribe, El Salvador.* LC./L.330/add.2.

1984d   *Estudio económico de América Latina y el Caribe, Honduras.* LC./L.330/add.3.

1984e   *Estudio económico de América Latina y el Caribe, Nicaragua.* LC./L.330/add.17.

Herrera Balharry, E. and N. Zamora Chacon
1985   *Los proyectos productivos para refugiados: Casos de Costa Rica y Nicaragua.* Genebra: Proyecto de Migración Hemisférica, CIM-CIPRA, Georgetown University.

International Labor Office (ILO) and the UNHCR
1984a   *Migraciones laborales e integración del refugiado en Costa Rica.* Proyecto RLA/83/VAROV. mimeo.

1984b   *Migraciones laborales e integración del refugiado en Nicaragua.* Proyecto RLA/83/
        VAROV. mimeo.

1984c   *Migraciones laborales e integración del refugiado en Argentina.* Proyecto RLA/83/
        VAROV. mimeo.

1984d   *Migraciones laborales e integración del refugiado en Venezuela.* Proyecto RLA/83/
        VAROV. mimeo.

1985   *Proyecto integración socioeconómica de refugiados urbanos y semi-urbanos en Costa Rica:
        Diagnóstico preliminar del programa de atención para refugiados en Costa Rica.* San José,
        Costa Rica.

1986   *Labour Migration and Integration of Refugees in Latin America. Final Report.* Geneva:
        Project RLA/83/VAROV.

ILO and the Intergovernmental Committee for Migration (ILO)
1985   *Resettlement Programme for Salvadorean and Argentine Farmers in Salta and Jujuy Prov-
        inces, Argentina.* Geneva.

Mármora, L.
1978   *Bases para una política nacional de migraciones laborales en El Salvador.* San Salvador:
        Fondo de las Naciones Unidas para Actividades en Materia de Población. FNUAP/
        ELS/P01.

Mármora, L. and V. Vargas
1984   *Análisis de los aspectos de coordinación y ejecución de los programas de acción sobre los
        refugiados en Costa Rica.* San Jose: Ministerio de Justicia y Gracia de Costa Rica.

Mebtouche, L.
1985   *Evaluation du projet de la Vallé de la Paix.* Geneva: UNHCR.

Palacio, J.O.
1985   *A Rural Environment for Central American Immigrants in Belize.* Washington, D.C.:
        Hemispheric Migration Project, ICM-CIPRA, Georgetown University.

Torres-Rivas, E.
1985   *Report on the Condition of Central American Refugees and Migrants.* Hemispheric Mi-
        gration Project, Occasional Paper Series. Washington, D.C.: Georgetown University
        and the Intergovernmental Committee for Migration.

United Nations High Commissioner for Refugees (UNHCR) and the Organization of
American States (OAS)
1983   *Estudio comparativo entre los instrumentos internacionales de las Naciones Unidas sobre re-
        fugiados, asilados y desplazados y los instrumentos interamericanos sobre asilo, extradición y
        derechos humanos.* Washington, D.C.: OAS.

ILLEGAL ALIENS IN BELIZE: FINDINGS FROM THE 1984 AMNESTY[1]

Joseph O. Palacio

In mid-1984 the government of Belize announced an amnesty period for "illegal aliens" in Belize to register with the police. The main target group was Central American refugee/migrants who had been fleeing into the country since the late 1970s in response to the political violence and economic dislocation spreading throughout the region.[2] This chapter reviews the information collected during the amnesty and presents demographic and socioeconomic profiles of the four main refugee/migrant populations in Belize — Guatemalans, Salvadorans, Hondurans, and Mexicans.

This study also provides the most realistic estimate available of the number of Central American refugee/migrants residing in Belize as of September 1984.

Belize — Haven for Central American Refugee/Migrants

For whatever reason they came, the Central Americans found in Belize a secure haven. As we shall see, most came without any travel documents across the heavily forested border with Guatemala. There were

[1] This study was done under the auspices of a grant from the Hemispheric Migration Project coordinated by the Intergovernmental Committee for Migration (ICM) and the Center for Immigration Policy and Refugee Assistance (CIPRA) of Georgetown University. Additional funding came from the Inter-American Foundation (IAF). I wish to record gratitude to ICM, CIPRA, and IAF.

[2] The use of the term "refugee/migrant" for those coming to Belize is an attempt to include within one broad category, persons who may be coming as refugees as well as economic migrants.

no holding stations for those claiming refugee status.[3] They were free to
travel to any part of the country and settle. They made use of the public
educational and medical services. Employers hired them openly, notwithstanding the regulations against hiring aliens.

Gradually, Belize acquired an international reputation as being a
country that welcomed all arrivals — legal or illegal. The Valley of Peace
resettlement project added to the reputation. It was a scheme sponsored
by the United Nations High Commissioner for Refugees (UNHCR) and
the Belize government to resettle 100 families divided equally between
Belizeans and Salvadorans, each receiving on lease 50 acres of land for
farming. Five years after it started and despite severe administrative
problems, the scheme remains an unusual attempt at integrating non-
Belizeans into the national fabric.

Separating Belize from its neighbors are land and sea borders that
can be easily traversed at innumerable points, notwithstanding the
border-guard patrols. Belize has a population of about 160,000 and a
land area of 8,756 square miles (or 22,680 square kilometers), resulting
in one of the lowest population-to-land ratios in the region (18 per
square mile or 7 per square kilometer). There are large tracts of unoccupied land in the countryside that appear attractive to persons coming
from countries with acute land shortages. Belize's systems of parliamen-
tary democracy and justice, inherited from Britain, enshrine a deep-
seated regard for human rights that is noteworthy in Latin America.
Although English is the official language of the country, about 35 percent of its population speak Spanish as their first language, while many
are fluent in English and Spanish. Finally, for decades multinational
corporations have dominated the fragile economies of Central American countries moving their work sites and laborers with ease from one
country to the other. Belize has been drawn into this process as both an
exporter and importer of labor.

The study of Central American migrants cannot keep pace with their
ever increasing numbers. Torres-Rivas (1985) recently presented an
overview of the causes of Central American refugee migration, its direc-
tions, and implications for policy formation. He observed that the bulk
of recent migration from El Salvador and Guatemala took place between 1980 and 1984, as the regimes in these countries increased their
use of violence to quell mass protests and liquidate counterinsurgency
among select segments of the population. Torres-Rivas estimates that

[3] Belize acquired political independence in 1981. So far it has not signed the United
Nations Convention on Refugees. The present immigration regulations allow for the
claim of refugee status. Such persons receive assistance through a joint Belize govern-
ment/UNHCR program.

during this period about 350,000 Salvadorans, Guatemalans, and Nicaraguans fled their countries. Mexico was the country in the region that received the majority — 175,000 (50 percent), while Belize and Panama together received the least, 8,500 (2.4 percent).[4]

In appreciating the place of Belize within the current refugee/migrant scenario in Central America and Mexico, it is necessary to establish three main points at the outset. First, the proportion coming to Belize is insignificant compared to that going to other countries. However, with Belize's minuscule population and correspondingly limited absorptive capacity, the small numbers do in fact create a major problem.

Second, there is selectivity among those leaving their countries that predetermines the population directed to Belize. Some come because Belize is the closest country — a fact applicable to the Guatemalans and Mexicans, especially those originating in nearby departments. Others come after learning about Belize from relatives and friends who are already residents there. While this applies to all nationalities, it is especially true of those coming to Belize from places further away, such as El Salvador. A few may also come on work invitations by agro-industries requiring large numbers of contract laborers.

Third, there is a wide range of reasons for ending up in Belize. Some individuals come searching for long-disappeared relatives; others look for work; and others flee for their lives due to political violence. Using a broad definition, Guatemalans and Salvadorans would most probably be classified as political refugees — persons forced to leave their habitual homes and work place due to "political violence" (Torres-Rivas, 1985:13) The Hondurans and Mexicans would be mostly economic migrants. Nonetheless, the terms "political refugee" and "economic migrant" are often used arbitrarily. There could be political refugees fleeing from Honduras as well as economic migrants from Guatemala. Indeed, some argue that the use of these terms for the Central American migrants is currently a conceptual block for members of both the academic and policy communities (*See,* Jamail and Stolph, 1985).

Declaration of Amnesty

In late April, 1984, the Minister of Home Affairs declared an amnesty for all "illegal aliens" in Belize. The declaration marked the beginning

---

[4] Further observations of the movements of refugee/migrants in Belize will help in arriving at estimates of their total number. There are indications that whereas several are remaining in the country permanently, there are others who may be staying for shorter periods and are in transit to Mexico, the United States, and Canada; or who may return to their country of origin. Those in this "in transit" category would include younger unattached men and women, who could more easily travel and who have been more affected by cutbacks in the sugar agro-industry.

of a new policy of enforcing the law against non-Belizeans who were in the country illegally. The main targets of the amnesty were refugee/migrants fleeing from the neighboring republics. The government had been caught off-guard by the overflow of this population into the country that started in the late 1970s. Belize was experiencing the largest immigration in memory with thousands coming through its land and sea borders and settling in its towns and countryside. An initial step was taken to measure the extent of the problem with the ultimate goal of stemming the movement. The step was to allow those already in the country to legitimize their status.

In his speech introducing the amnesty, the Minister of Home Affairs pinpointed some grave social problems associated with the refugee/migrants. Belizeans were shocked at the increase in crimes — especially murder, armed robbery, and drug cultivation and trafficking. There was fear of the spread of communicable diseases, such as malaria, from persons who had not received medical screening. The large number of foreigners was alleged to be undermining the cultural identity of Belizeans while disturbing the current "ethnic balance" that exists among the different groups.

At one extreme, members of the local press incited national hysteria against the "aliens". Generally, most people felt that it was a problem that had gotten beyond the control of the government. It was incumbent on the government to be seen as implementing solutions to this intractable problem. However, the amnesty was more than that. It was a humanitarian act toward persons — thousands of whom had lived and maintained families in Belize — who would face uncertain futures should they be deported. For our immediate purposes it was a massive information-gathering effort on immigrants that included a great deal of baseline data.

The amnesty allowed those who were in the country illegally to register with the police with impunity. Originally, the Minister had designated a period of 90 days for the registration from May 1 to July 31, 1984. The period was extended, although there was no consensus on how much additional time was allowed.

The immigration section of the Police Department took responsibility for the registration procedure. The "illegal alien" went to the nearest district police station to give information about himself or herself and his or her dependents as required by the registration card. The police prepared a registration booklet and gave it to the registrant after a delay of a few days. It served as the identification document for the registrant and his or her dependents.

Having registered, the "alien" could then apply for one of the several kinds of legal permits that are available. There is the refugee resident permit for those who show genuine fear for loss of life for themselves and family, but retain an intention to return home after the conflict. There is the provisional resident permit for those who want to remain permanently in the country; and there is the work permit for those who are in the country specifically for work purposes.

The reality in the implementation of the registration fell short of the ideal. The police were not prepared for the large numbers of persons who wanted to register. The lack of preparation meant protracted delays in queues and, no doubt, a loss of interest among many potential registrants. There was insufficient publicity generated throughout the country about the program, especially within the distant rural communities where several immigrant groups live. Closely related is the fact that there was no public education program to inform persons — either foreign or Belizean — about the implications of the amnesty. The police were not adequately trained to fill in the cards in a standardized manner. And they were not careful to include all the data required for each person. As a result, important pieces of information were sometimes overlooked, and it was often difficult to interpret nonstandard terms that were used. In conclusion, more adequate preparation by the police would have ensured more comprehensive coverage.

Research Methods

The objectives of the research were to extract specific data from the registration cards, in order to construct profiles of the main migrant/refugee populations.

The fieldwork took place between October 1985 and March 1986. It was done by specially trained men and women from all the districts working in their district police stations. The pre-selected data were transcribed from registration cards onto prepared schedule forms. Then the variables were coded in our office and entered into a microcomputer for processing.[5]

The Illegal Alien Population

This section presents a statistical overview of the total illegal alien population which was registered during the amnesty period. Among the characteristics considered are gender, age, nationality, arrival, and settlement patterns, and occupation.

[5] There were 6,305 cases with 25 data fields. The microcomputer application used was the Survey Mate by Henry Elkins and Associates of New York. The data specification program allowed the programmer to specify long and short labels as well as value ranges and acceptable values outside of these ranges. This served as a debugging device.

Biographical Data

Out of the total sample of 6,305 registrants, 3,833 (60.8 percent) were male and 2,472 (39.2 percent) female. Persons over the age of 16 registered. The median age for the sample was 30. Those between the ages of 16 and 39 represented 71 percent of the total.

The percentage breakdown of the four main nationalities is presented in Table 1. The other three nationalities were included to show the relative predominance of the first four.

TABLE 1

Distribution of Seven Main Nationalities

Nationalities	No.	Percentage
Guatemala	3,204	50.8
El Salvador	1,725	27.4
Honduras	903	14.3
Mexico	314	5.0
U.S.A.	70	1.1
West Indies	13	0.2
Nicaragua	11	0.2
Other	65	1.0
Total	6,305	100.0

The respondents were asked to indicate whether they had a spouse or children. A total 6,250 responded to the question and of these, 74 percent said that they did not have one. A little more than 10 percent said that they had children. The total number of these minors were 2,223, subdivided into the following age groups — 837 under 5; 793 between 6 and 10; and 593 between 11 and 16.

The information available on spouses and children is probably not accurate. First, it is not certain whether the information was obtained only for those with spouses and children who were not Belizeans. Second, there could have been a misunderstanding about whether having a spouse meant being legally married only. Third, usually women answered the question about minors, although there were no doubt men who registered who also had children in their families.

Arrival and Settlement Patterns

Almost all registrants came from their home countries directly to Belize. Table 2 has the percentages for the four most frequently reported countries which are almost identical to those on nationality in Table 1. This is especially significant for Salvadorans, most of whom travelled by road through Guatemala on their way to Belize.

TABLE 2

Last Residence Outside Belize

Country	No.	Percentage
Guatemala	3,187	52.3
Salvador	1,726	28.3
Honduras	877	14.4
Mexico	306	5.0
Total	6,096	100.0

Although the earliest arrival took place in 1910, half of the registrants came during the three and three-quarter year period between 1981 and September 30, 1984, the cutoff date for our sample.

Table 3 shows the numbers of arrivals by year from 1973 to 1984, the percentage and cumulative percentage starting from 1910. The inflow increased each year reaching its peak in 1983. The number that arrived between January 1 and September 30, 1984 was only slightly smaller than the whole of 1983.

There were seven ports of entry listed on the registration card. The percentages of the respective arrivals are presented in Table 4. Benque Viejo del Carmen, a station on the western border, was the most frequently used place of arrival (59.6 percent), especially among Guatemalans and Salvadorans, whereas Belize City Harbor was the least used port of entry (1.9 percent).

The police accepted three types of identification during the registration — passport, *cédula*, and birth certificate.

Table 5 presents a breakdown in the percentage of forms of identification. One-quarter had met the normal prerequisite of international travel, namely acquiring a passport. An additional 73 percent had *cédulas* and birth certificates, both of which were suited for use only within their home countries. A *cédula* is mandatory identification used in most of the neighboring republics.

TABLE 3

Arrivals Between 1973 and 1984

Year	No.	Percentage	Cummulative %
Pre-1973	1,167	18.5	18.5
1973	58	.9	19.4
1974	115	1.8	21.3
1975	137	2.2	23.4
1976	141	2.2	25.7
1977	110	1.7	27.4
1978	232	3.7	31.1
1979	344	5.5	36.5
1980	615	9.8	46.3
1981	589	9.3	55.6
1982	715	11.3	67.0
1983	1,111	17.6	84.6
1984	971	15.3	100.0
Total	6,305	99.9	

TABLE 4

Place of Arrival

Place	No.	Percentage
Benque Viejo del Carmen	3,517	59.7
Punta Gorda	876	14.9
Dangriga	555	9.4
Santa Elena	374	6.3
Mango Creek	235	4.0
Belize International Airport	225	3.8
Belize City Harbor	111	1.9
Total	5,893[a]	99.8

Note: [a] 412 from the sample of 6,305 did not mention where they arrived.

TABLE 5
Types of Documentation

Type	No.	Percentage
Cédula	2,431	42.6
Birth Certificate	1,756	30.8
Passport	1,486	26.0
Other	33	0.6
Total	5,706[a]	100.0

Note: [a] 599 persons from the sample of 6,305 did not show an identification.

TABLE 6
Address in Belize

Districts	Urban #	%	Rural #	%
Orange Walk	548	8.8	735	11.8
Corazal	221	3.5	847	13.6
Belize	574	9.2	277	4.4
Cayo	101	1.6	1,419	22.7
Stann Creek	24	0.4	759	12.2
Toledo	63	1.0	673	10.8
Sub-Total	1,531	24.5	4,710	75.5
Total			6,241[a]	100.0%

Note: [a] Out of the total sample of 6,305, 64 did not answer this questionnaire.

Table 6 contains a breakdown of the places of residence of the respondants by district and urban/rural area. Belize has six districts each having urban and rural communities. The urban communities are the commercial center of Belize City, the capital city, Belmopan, and the district towns. The rural communities are villages scattered throughout the countryside. With a population of 40,000, Belize City is by far the largest urban community. The others range in population between 2,000 and 9,000. The villages have fewer inhabitants, most ranging between 100 and 500.

The districts with the majority of the registrants were Cayo, Orange Walk, and Corozal. In all the districts, except Belize, there were more registrants in the rural than urban areas. Throughout the country there were 4,710 refugee/migrants found in the rural areas or 75 percent of the total number of registrants. The general population of the country however, is divided almost equally between urban and rural areas.

Occupation

From a list containing 77 categories, the occupations of 6,296 (99 percent) of the registrants were coded. It is necessary to highlight some basic issues surrounding the occupation variable to appreciate the extent of its usefulness. First, the answers that the police recorded, no doubt, referred to the normal means by which the respondent maintained his or her livelihood — not whether the individual was currently employed.

Second, there were no set definitions used to distinguish among occupations resulting in a lack of clarity about what was meant. For example, it was not clear what the difference was between "housewife" and "domestic", as both are often used interchangeably in Belize for women who take care of their home as well as those employed as maids. Since several officers participated in the recording of information on the registration cards, it is virtually impossible to arrive at a consensus about occupations. The frequency and percentage distribution for the eight most frequently reported occupations are placed in Table 7.

TABLE 7
Eight Most Frequently Reported Occupations

Name	No.	Percentage
Farmer	1,692	26.9
Domestic	1,630	25.9
Laborer	1,370	21.8
Housewife	749	11.9
Cane Cutter	89	1.4
Fisherman	81	1.3
Mason	74	1.2
Mechanic	60	1.0
Unknown	551	8.6
Total	6,296	100.0

The best that can be done with the information in Table 7 is to isolate gross categories of the occupations represented. The domestics and housewives together made up 47 percent of the total. They are women's activities. The two most frequent occupations (48.7 percent) for men were farmer and laborer. Whereas farming is a rural activity, the laborers could be based in either rural or urban areas. There were relatively small proportions of masons and mechanics — which are skilled trades that men would more easily perform in the urban than rural areas.

In conclusion, most of the registrants were engaged in low-skilled or unskilled manual labor based in the rural areas. At least one-quarter were farmers. Several others were no doubt argicultural wage laborers doing clearing, taking care of farms, and harvesting sugar cane and other crops. The proportion of self-employed tradesmen was minimal and representation in white-collar occupations was negligible.

Nationality Profiles

In the following section we construct profiles of four nationalities — Guatemalans, Salvadorans, Hondurans, and Mexicans — in terms of gender, date of arrival, place of arrival, documentation, place of residence, and occupation.

In Figure I, the proportion of men to women is closest among the Guatemalans. This is a reflection of two factors, both of which influence each other. First, it indicates the relative ease with which Guatemalans can come to Belize. Second, it underscores the fact that both men and women from Guatemala had a greater need to come to Belize than did the Mexicans, for example. The early 1980s was a period of heightened political and economic dislocation in Guatemala, and these were the years in which most of the Guatemalans relocated to Belize.

The fact that proportionately more Guatemalan women were coming also meant that there would be a greater tendency for Guatemalan families to become established in Belize.[6] In earlier studies we carried out under the auspices of the Hemispheric Migration Project, we observed that the refugee/migrants came as family units either together or in quick succession (Palacio, 1986). Futhermore, those that were without spouses formed unions most often with their compatriots.

The fact that proportionately fewer women registered among Salvadorans and Mexicans suggests that probably fewer of them were heads

---

[6] Guatemala has long claimed Belize as part of its national territory. The dispute reached the point of threatened invasion by Guatemala within the past ten years. The resettlement of thousands of Guatemalans is regarded suspiciously by some Belizeans who see behind it a sinister plan by Guatemala to take over the country through its people, if not its arms.

FIGURE 1

Diagram Showing Percentage Distribution of Nationalities by Gender

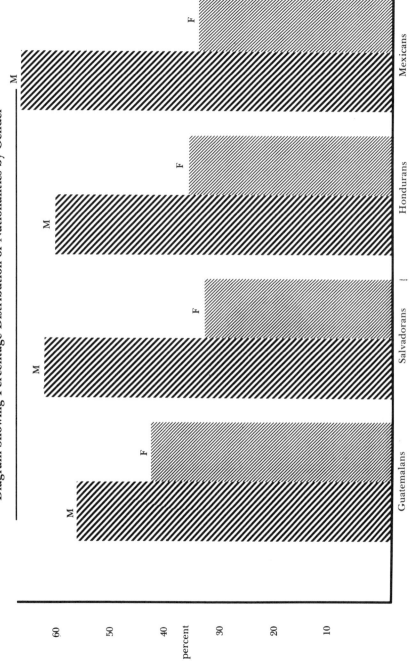

of household — as spouses, they were most likely registered as dependents by their husbands. The other possibility is that there were in fact proportionately more men among them than among other nationalities. If this is the case, it would mean that the men were coming in larger numbers to avoid the military draft in El Salvador or as migrant wage laborers from Mexico originally with intentions to return.

The period of arrival amplifies the picture on the types of movements into Belize. The graph in Figure 2 shows the sequence of arrivals since 1978. In Table 3 we saw that half of the total number of registrants came after 1980. The exception were the Mexicans, three-fourths of whom came before 1978. Several of them were Mennonites who started coming to Belize in the late 1950s.[7]

Since 1978, there has been an increase in arrivals among Guatemalans, Salvadorans, and Hondurans. The increase remained fairly steady and gradual for the Guatemalans, with the exception of a decline in 1984. The pattern was similar for the Hondurans, except for the dramatic increases in 1983 and 1984. Compared to the others, the inflow of Mexicans during this seven year period has been minimal.

The relatively steady pattern in the movements from Guatemala, Honduras, and Mexico reflects a tradition of travel, which Belizeans also share in their trips to these countries.[8] Over the course of generations, extensive kin and friendship ties were formed, as individuals followed wage-labor opportunities from one side of the border to the other. The unusual increase among these nationalities coming to Belize within the past few years is a testament to the fact that their economic situation had worsened compared to that of Belize. In other words, what originally had been a "see-saw" pattern of movements across the borders has greatly increased in dimensions with more profound effects on Belize than the previous migrations.

The greatest fluctuation in arrivals was among the Salvadorans. This together with the fact that the distance they had to traverse was the furthest, and that they had to cross a third country, indicate that their sojourn responded to severe push factors. The first great wave came in 1980, the year after the start of the current civil war. Four times as many people came in 1980 as had arrived the previous year. In 1981 and 1982, arrivals stabilized. However, in 1983 and 1984, large numbers of Salvadorans came again probably as a result of increased

---

[7] Mennonites from Mexico and Canada came to Belize through a special arrangement with the government.

[8] During the first half of this century, Belizeans went to work for the United Fruit Company in neighboring departments of Guatemala and Honduras. With the recent decline in the sugar industry in the Orange Walk and Corozal Districts, it is reported that scores of Belizeans have crossed to Mexico in search for work.

FIGURE 2

Percentage Arrival of Nationalities by Year

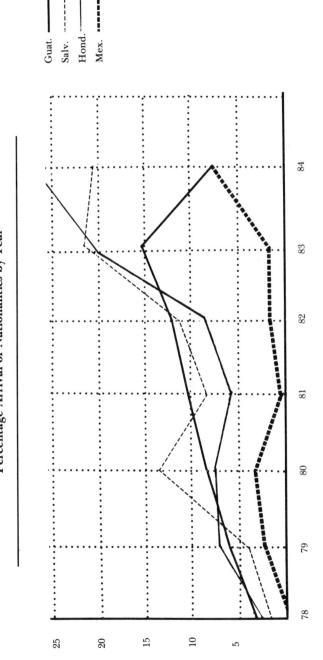

civil strife. No doubt more Salvadorans and Guatemalans will arrive in Belize if the conflicts in these countries continue.

The registrants came primarily over land and sea. The Guatemalans, Hondurans, and Mexicans arrived at ports of entry closest to Belize (Table 4). For Guatemalans, the most-favored ports were Benque Viejo del Carmen and Punta Gorda. Benque Viejo del Carmen is the town bordering Guatemala in the West and Punta Gorda is the nearest seaport in the southern part of the country. The Guatemalans who arrived at Benque Viejo del Carmen were most probably ladino campesinos originating from El Petén or 'adjoining departments. Another large group came further south through El Petén, crossing at numerous bush paths into the Toledo District. Based on the names of these registrants, we believe that they are Kekchi travelling to settle among their fellow Mayans in scores of villages in the southwestern Toledo District.

The vast majority of Salvadorans also entered at Benque Viejo del Carmen, having passed through Guatemala on their way. Over the years as a well known transit route has developed through the highways of El Salvador and Guatemala to Benque Viejo del Carmen (McElroy, 1986).

A little more than 70 percent of the Hondurans arrived in the Stann Creek District either at Dangriga or Mango Creek. They came on motor boats or sailing dories through a course long charted by the Garifuna who migrated from Honduras early in the last century. The Garifuna are the predominant inhabitants of the Stann Creek District. Several of the registrants in the district were themselves Garifuna. They came driven by economic need, but expecting to capitalize on kinship ties. In this way they reinforced the traditionally strong loyalty of the Garifuna kinship ties.

By law, persons coming to Belize from any of the four countries should have a passport with a visa. Through bilateral arrangements

TABLE 8
Percentage Distribution of Nationality by Documentation[a]

Nationality	Passport	Cédula	B. Cert.	Other Documentation	None	Unknown	Total Number
Guatemalan	10.2	44.0	28.3	0.3	1.3	13.4	3,204
Salvadoran	37.5	42.2	18.4	0.3	0.6	1.0	1725
Honduran	36.3	20.3	39.5	1.0	1.8	1.2	902
Mexican	17.5	7.3	51.9	1.0	11.5	10.8	314

Note: [a] Due to rounding, not all percentage totals in this table and others may add up to 100.

between Belize and Guatemala and Mexico, visitors who limit their stay in Belize to border towns and for seventy-two hours can use special travel permits. The vast majority of the Guatamalans and Mexicans, however, came without their travel documents. Table 8 on the types of documents confirms the relative ease with which Mexicans and Guatemalans cross the border. Proportionately, they had fewer passports than Salvadorans and Hondurans.

Figure 3 shows patterns in the geographical distribution of the four nationalities in the districts and urban/rural areas. There is a tendency for persons to remain in the districts where they first arrived. Most of the Guatemalans arrived at the Cayo and Toledo Districts and a little over half of them continued to reside in these districts. Similarly, almost half of the Hondurans were concentrated in Stann Creek, the district of their arrival. The same applies for the Mexicans with respect to the Corozal District.

Slightly more than one-quarter of the Salvadorans remained in the Cayo District, the point of their arrival. More than half, however, lived in the rural and urban parts of the Orange Walk and Corozal Districts. There they do farming or work as agricultural laborers. During the 1970s and early 1980s, these two districts were the hub of the sugar industry which is labor intensive throughout the production cycle. As a result, large proportions of the registrants, save the Hondurans, settled there. Next to the Stann Creek rural area, the Hondurans were most concentrated (26 percent) in Belize City.

Figure 3 indicates that the urban areas of the Cayo, Stann Creek, and Toledo Districts have the lowest proportion of registrants. These are areas of low economic activity which offer few wage labor opportunities. The 25 percent who live in urban areas are concentrated in Belize City where manual wage labor was most available.

Table 9 provides additional information on the association between nationality and occupation. Earlier we had discussed the broad parameters within which we could use the information on occupation (given the difficulties created by the imprecise definitions of certain occupations). There are two significant observations forthcoming from this table. One is the rather low proportion of domestics *vis-à-vis* housewives for the Mexicans. It is difficult to explain this, unless it arises from an idiosyncrasy of the registering officer.

The other observation is the low proportion of Honduran farmers to laborers compared to this ratio among the other nationalities. In Figure 3 we saw that Hondurans were concentrated in the rural Stann Creek District and Belize City. In both of these areas they were not greatly involved in farming. Rather they were laborers, most probably workers

FIGURE 3

Percentage of the Four Nationalities in Districts by Urban/Rural Area

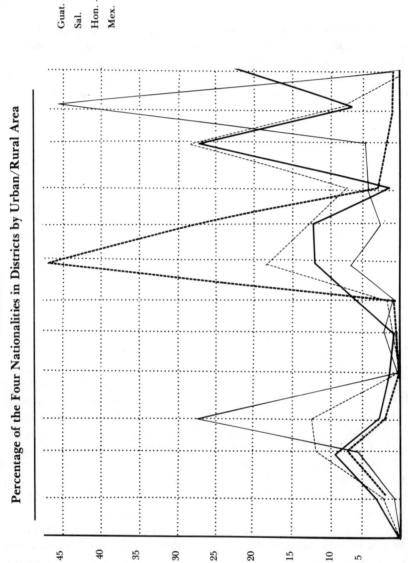

Note: [a] Dangriga is the principal town in Stann Creek district.

TABLE 9

Percentage Distribution of Nationality by Six Occupations

Nationality	Housewife	Domestic	Farmer	Laborer	Mechanic	Mason	Total Number
Guatemal.	16.1	29.1	35.9	21.8	1.0	0.2	3,026
Salvadoran	7.4	27.9	27.8	29.3	1.8	0.2	1,585
Honduran	4.3	35.2	5.2	47.4	1.8	0.6	772
Mexican	28.3	7.2	39.9	21.8	1.0	0	293

in the banana plantations and in processing plants in the Stann Creek District. In Belize City they also remained laborers in unskilled occupations. Thus, the indications are that the Guatemalans, Salvadorans, and Mexicans were more involved in rural-based land cultivation than were the Hondurans. The former worked as farmers or as field laborers in the rural areas of the Cayo, Orange Walk, and Corozal Districts.

Amnesty as a Process

We can explore further the significance of the amnesty as a means of legitimizing the status of non-Belizeans and as an exercise that enables an appreciation of the scope of immigration into Belize.

Police records show that 8,680 persons registered during the amnesty. Discussions with some officers revealed that several hundred registrants had proceeded to the next step of applying for residence permits. The police mentioned that there remained confusion among some persons about what they needed to do after registering. However, the procedure has not been altogether clear-cut. Six months after the beginning of the amnesty period another political party was elected to form the government. It has appointed a committee to make an overall review of the immigration problem, which will become the framework for a policy. Decisions, such as those affecting the amnesty registrants, are being temporarily postponed.

As the first attempt in the modern history of the country to amass information on so many immigrants, the amnesty figures are an invaluable resource. The total number of those registering with the police — 8,680 — is broken down into nationalities in Table 10. The figure 8,680 is 2,375 greater than the sample in our study, although we had hoped to include all the police registrants in our sample. The reason for the dis-

TABLE 10

**Distribution of Nationalities Among Registrants
(Police Sample)**

Nationality	No.	Percentage
Guatemalan	4848	55.9
Salvadoran	2351	27.1
Honduran	999	11.5
Mexican	320	3.7
Other[a]	162	1.8
Total	8680	100.0

Note: The category "other" includes countries such as the United States, Costa Rica, Chile, Belgium and Iran. The figures were obtained from the Ministry of Home Affairs, Belmopan.

crepancy is that the police in some districts continued registration beyond the September 30, 1984 deadline that we had placed for our sample. The relative proportion of the four nationalities in the police sample is similar to that in our study sample (Tables 1 and 10).

One of the thorny issues within the study of immigration is the number of immigrants in the country. Sources, such as census figures and police registers on immigrants, are not helpful because of their methods of data collection. The census asks persons about their place of birth. However, if such a person is in the country illegally, he may not admit to his correct country of origin. The 1980 census indicates that there were 573 foreign-born persons in Belize. In 1984 there were 11,893 aliens registered with the police. Some leave the country at the end of their stay and their names may not be deleted from the list. Furthermore, several do not bother to register with the police. The UNHCR estimates the number of arrivals after 1979 at 15,000 (GIS/ PAHO, 1985:5).

Using the amnesty figures we can attempt to arrive at an estimate of the number of non-Belizean heads of household who were in the country illegally up to September, 1984. In carrying out such an exercise, we bear in mind the hypothetical nature of the results given the fluidity in the numbers of those arriving, staying in the country, and then leaving. We can assume that for every person who registered there was one who did not. This assumption is based on the non-appearance of some persons for registration as well as on the possibility that some who had registered may have already left the country. Using the police sample we arrive at an approximate figure of 17,360.

Some of these persons had been in the country from early in this century. Our studies show that half of the arrivals took place during 1981 and afterwards. Using the police sample, the estimate for heads of household who came during this period (*i.e.*, the recent arrivals) is 8,180. The fact that some of these men and women had spouses and children increases the number considerably. If we assume that for every household head, there were three other persons, then the approximate number of recent illegal arrivals was 24,540.[9] By 1986 this number would have increased, as indications are that the population flow continued into Belize.

How does this situation in Belize compare with that in other countries that receive refugee/migrants? Using a figure of 7,000 collected in the late 1970s, the Ford Foundation in a 1983 publication placed Belize as the fifth country in the world in the ratio of refugee to native population. But since the late 1970s, the number of refugee/migrants has increased at least three-fold, so the country may now have the world's highest proportion of refugee/migrant to native population.

The intrusion of so many persons into a country with an approximate 1984 population of 162,000 affects all aspects of daily life. In demographic terms, the newcomers comprise thousands of younger men and women (average age 30) at the peak of their child bearing years. They may contribute to the already high birth rate of the country. Culturally they are rural/semi-urban people with cultural traits that are not similar to those of the Belizeans, even to the Spanish-speaking Belizean Mestizos. They swell the pool of surplus, cheap labor in the towns and exert pressure on available agricultural land among the villagers. Furthermore, they represent the forces of "Latinization", a process that is not compatible with the defintion of modernization to most Belizeans.

The effects of the immigration are more dramatic in rural than urban communities. There is a great concentration of migrants in the rural areas and by virtue of their traditionally close-knit social organization, rural communities are less tolerant of outsiders. The resettlement of the foreigners has not always brought a harmonious blending within the host communities. There would seem to be a prevailing atmosphere of dominance by one group over the other with occasional feuding between them. There are reports of foreigners settling in the outskirts of villages from which they have easier access to the land and crops of the

---

[9] In our study of refugee/migrants in four urban communities (1985) we found that the ratio of household head to household members was 1:4.7. For this sample I reduce the ratio to 1:3 because it may include large numbers of males stationed in rural agro-industries without dependents.

villagers. They squat on land that is not theirs and steal its produce.[10] There are also reports of foreigners establishing their own village over which they maintain control, forbidding access to Belizeans. What is most feared is that as hired hands, the foreigners engage in illicit activities, including drug cultivation and related criminal activities.

SUMMARY AND CONCLUSIONS

This study grows out of research done on records compiled by the police during the 1984 amnesty. It discusses characteristics of the registrants and presents profiles of the four most numerous nationalities. The analysis leads to an appreciation of the scope of the refugee/migrant situation in Belize. Using the amnesty figures, we calculate the approximate number of household heads who came illegally between 1981 and September 1984 as 8,180; when including household members the figure climbs to about 24,540 persons.

Time is absolutely crucial in forcing the hand of the Belize authorities to formulate and implement policies to deal with the immigration situation. The amnesty itself has been fairly successful in assisting thousands to legitimize their status. The question remains what to do about those who did not make use of the amnesty and those illegal entrants who came subsequently. Moreover, what measures need to be enacted to stem the continued flow into Belize?

Along with planning restrictive immigration measures, it is also incumbent on government and non-government agencies to initiate ameliorative projects for the social well-being of the refugee/migrants. We need to keep abreast of the human component of the immigrant experience.

The cultural presence of so many Central Americans and Mexicans in the country has catapulted Belize closer into the Latin American sphere of influence. There is a need, now more than ever, to retain close diplomatic, economic, and cultural exchanges with our neighbors. In this way Belize can learn more about what happens in these countries and plan its actions in concert with developments her neighbors undergo.

---

[10] In a study of Salvadoran refugees in Belize, Wouters (1983) found that among those working land on their own, 10 percent had their own land, 40 percent were renting, and 50 percent were squatting.

REFERENCES

Belize. Government Information Service (GIS) and Pan American Health Organization (PAHO).
1985 *Priority Health Needs/Belize.*

Ford Foundation
1983 *Refugees and Immigrants — Problems and Program Responses — A Working Paper.* New York.

Jamail, M.H. and C. Stolph
1985 "Central Americans on the Run: Political Refugees or Economic Migrants?" *Public Affairs Comments,* 1(3):1-7. Lyndon B. Johnson School of Public Affairs, The University of Texas at Austin.

McElroy, C.
1986 "The El Salvadoran Refugee Move to Belize: A Geographic Study of Refugee Migration". Masters thesis presented at Texas A & M University.

Palacio, J.O.
1985 "A Survey of Central American Immigrants in Four Urban Communities in Belize". Manuscript submitted to the Hemispheric Migration Project, Center for Immigration Policy and Refugee Assistance, Georgetown University.

Torres-Rivas, E.
1985 *Report on the Condition of Central American Refugees and Migrants.* Occasional Paper Series, Hemispheric Migration Project. Washington, D.C.: Center for Immigration Policy and Refugee Assistance (CIPRA), Georgetown University and the Intergovernmental Committee for Migration (ICM).

Wouters, M.
1983 *Report on the Socio-Economic Survey of the Dispersed Salvadoran Refugees Living in Belize.* Unpublished report submitted to the UNHCR, San José, Costa Rica.

BACK HOME: PSYCHOSOCIAL ASPECTS OF THE EXILES' RETURN TO ARGENTINA

Hector Maletta
Frida Szwarcberg
Rosalia Schneider

Much of the literature on return migration focuses on the material aspects of resettlement and reintegration (Kubat, 1984; Rogers and Pessar, 1987). In this study of repatriation to Argentina, we explore another, inadequately treated, dimension of return migration: the psychosocial readjustment of the repatriate. Drawing on our case studies of Argentines who have returned from political exile, we present a series of hypothetical propositions about exile and return. These propositions are informed by psychoanalytical and psychosocial thinking on exile, identity, and stigma.

Before presenting these propositions, we will provide some background material on the estimated numbers of Argentine emigrants and returnees. We will also briefly review the political and economic conditions that promoted these population movements. Finally, we will present some background material on the returnees who were included in our study.

In the middle of the 1980s, almost one-half million Argentines were residing outside of the country in different parts of the world. More than half had emigrated after 1970 (Bertoncello *et al.*, 1985). A part of this population was comprised of political exiles pushed out by the violence and repression that ruled the country in the 1970s.

The socioeconomic composition of the emigrant population includes a high proportion of technical and professional persons (*See*, Oteiza, 1971; Houssay, 1966; and Marshall, 1987). The majority of the emigrants travel in search of better economic and professional opportunities. A high proportion lives in the United States whose 1970 census registered 70,000 Argentines. Argentine consulates registered more than 500,000 persons living abroad in 1982; this figure probably involves a degree of exaggeration, since some who returned to Argentina or moved to another country remain registered at the consulates. This may explain why, for example, the consulates' figures show more Argentines in the United States than were registered by the U.S. census (Gurrieri, *et al.*, 1983). This, however, is partially balanced by emigrants not caring to register at Argentine consulates. The true figure was probably a little below 500,000 in the early 1980s.

There are no reliable statistics on the return rate of migrants to Argentina, but some estimates can be inferred from the 1980 Argentine census. Data on those persons who were living abroad five years before the census show that between 1975 and 1980 approximately 4,000 per year returned to Argentina.[1] This represents an annual rate of return of 1.5 percent relative to the Argentine population residing abroad in those years. The normal rate of return, over the period 1970-1983, is probably greater, as return was discouraged by the political situation in the country from 1975-1980.

The number of persons who emigrated for political reasons is difficult to estimate, but it is probably a small part of the total. This figure can be deduced from the increase of the Argentine population since 1975 in places where exiles most frequently resided (Latin America, Spain, France, and Scandinavia), which leads us to estimate that the number of political exiles was about 30,000-50,000. Apart from the lack

[1] The estimate is based on the census taken on October 22, 1980. The data used herein refer exclusively to the resident population in the country at the time, excluding persons who habitually resided abroad. The data were taken from census data, especially from tables which present migration statistics. The following data and calculations are essential:

A. Persons residing five years or more in the country, who, five years earlier (*i.e.*, Oct. 22, 1975) were residing abroad — 128,375.

B. Persons born abroad, residing in the country, who arrived after January 1, 1976 and before the census of October 22, 1980 — 114,659.

C. Persons born abroad, residing in the country, who are between 0-4 years of age — 11,119.

D. Persons born abroad, 5 years of age or more, residing in the country and arrived between Jan. 1, 1976 and Oct. 10,1980 (D = B-C) — 103,540.

E. Persons born abroad, 5 years of age or more, residing in the country and arrived between Oct. 10, 1975 and Oct. 22, 1980 (estimate) — 109,787.

F. Persons born in Argentina who resided in the country in 1980, 5 years of age or more, who, on Oct. 22, 1975 were residing abroad (F = A-E) — 18,588.

G. Persons born in Argentina who on Oct. 22, 1975 were residing abroad and returned to Argentina before the census (includes an estimate of those who died after returning but before the census) — 19,255.

The last figure does not include Argentines residing in the country on Oct. 22, 1975 who emigrated after that date and returned before the 1980 census. Nor does it include the census error (approximately 3 percent). Therefore, the result should be considered as a conservative estimate. It represents about 1.5 percent per year relative to total Argentine population living abroad (average 1975-80, estimated from data in Bertoncello *et al.*, 1985).

of statistical data, the uncertainty of the estimates stems from the fact that most of the exiles did not formally assume the status of refugee.

The flow of political emigrants began in 1974. At this time, left-wing militants suffered serious persecution at the hands of death squads formed with the support of the extreme right wing of the government of Isabel Perón. The majority of the political exiles, however, emigrated after the March 1976 coup which developed an extremely repressive regime. The full force of repression was felt between 1976-1978; the characteristics of this period will be analyzed in the next section.

The crisis of the military regime, which began in mid-1982 after the unfortunate war in the South Atlantic, saw a slow opening of the political system. This process culminated in the 1983 election of the democratic government of Raúl Alfonsín. The continual process of democratization promoted the return of political exiles which reached a peak in the first half of 1984.

At that time, a program established at the request of the Argentine government and financed by the United Nations High Commissioner for Refugees (UNHCR) and the Intergovernmental Committee for Migration (ICM) provided for the return of thousands of political exiles from different parts of the world. Many of these returnees did not even have the formal status of refugees. There are no available quantitative data on the exiles since many returned of their own accord without resorting to international assistance. A prudent estimate is that the total number of returning exiles and their families could have reached 20,000-30,000 around the end of 1984. As there are no realistic figures on the total number of exiles from 1974-1983, it is not easy to authenticate this return estimate, but there are various indications that a high proportion of the exiles chose to return, probably one-half to two-thirds.

This chapter is based on a 1985 survey of 134 exiled families who returned to Argentina and 86 families who returned, but did not originally emigrate for political reasons. The principal objective of the survey was to determine the problems encountered by the migrants after they returned. The problems were envisioned as both material (job, housing, etc.) and psychosocial (adaptation and social integration into the national environment).[2]

The results of the survey showed that economic motivations did not play a relevant part in the decision to return. This was true not only for the exiles, but also, surprisingly, for those who emigrated for apolitical

[2] The survey questionnaire was quite extensive with some 90 questions — most of which were open-ended. Moreover, twelve families with exiles were studied with greater depth through even more extensive interviews. *See*, the methodologies and quantitative results in Maletta and Szwarcberg (1985).

reasons. The basic reasons for returning to Argentina involved the need of émigrés to rediscover the country and their own identities. At the same time, expectations of economic difficulties after return did not seem to have been a disturbing influence. The repatriates were affected by the problems of reentering the national environment — for example, their perception of indifferent attitudes or hostility on the part of their compatriots, or their own rejection of authoritarian elements in daily life. Economic hardship at home only mattered in cases of prolonged unemployment, which in some cases brought about plans to emigrate again.

Therefore, this chapter concentrates on psychosocial aspects of return migration more than on the pragmatic problems of employment or income. In spite of the serious economic difficulties that affect Argentina, few of the returnees complained about them. The majority already knew the problems beforehand, and economic problems did not diminish their will to return. Rather, the returnees appear to be affected by other factors which leave some partially reintegrated into the country, while others experience rejection or at least a more difficult readjustment into national life. The dozen in-depth interviews alone were much more important for constructing an analysis of these factors than were the quantitative results of the survey; nevertheless, the latter do provide a reference point for the analysis of the psychosocial adjustment of the returnees.

Characteristics and Context of Exile

In the sample of 134 families of political repatriates, almost 70 percent left Argentina between 1976-1978. Another 12 percent emigrated before the 1976 coup, that is, after 1974. The rest departed between 1979 and 1980. Most had remained in exile an average of six years. When the survey was conducted, the majority had returned for an average of 18 months, although the date of return varied from the middle of 1982 (after the Malvinas War) until the beginning of 1985. A few returned between 1980 and 1981.

At the time of the survey, two-thirds of the families consisted of a married couple with one or more children. Some 13 percent were divorced or without spouse and had children in their care. About 21 percent were single persons. Most were young at the time of exile: The average age was 27; about one-fourth were between 20 and 24; a few were barely adolescents. Many of the exiles were students, but more than three-fourths of the total were working prior to their departure. Of those who were working, only 14 percent had manual or low-skilled jobs; more than one-third had high-skilled jobs.

The departure from Argentina was preceded and accompanied in many cases by traumatic circumstances related to the Argentine political situation. It is difficult to capture the nature of the decision to become an exile without considering the situation that existed at the time.

Argentina experienced a fierce political battle characterized by guerrilla activity and repressive violence in the first half of the 1970s. In the economic arena, the demands of the popular sectors (principally industrial workers faced with the continual decline in employment and income) clashed against a stagnant and dependent economic system. The dominant economic groups not only failed to attend to these pressures, but also demanded a "rationalization" of the productive forces and greater "labor discipline". These objectives were very difficult to establish within the democratic framework existing in Argentina at that time.

In March 1976, the civilian government was deposed by a military coup which established a harsh dictatorship that lasted until 1983 under several military juntas. This authoritarian regime proposed and executed an economic plan based on financial deregulation and the abrupt opening of the economy after decades of strong protectionist policies. The plan greatly damaged the industrial sector that was established by way of import-substitution after World War II. The military regime also chose state terrorism to carry out the so-called "eradication of subversion" which was meant to include not only guerrilla rebels but also union protest and all expressions of dissent against the central program of the regime. State terrorism, which was applied to its maximum between 1976 and 1978, was characterized by a widespread show of repression which extended throughout the society. It considered subversive all ideological activities or positions that the military perceived as leftist or simply not overtly supportive of their self-appointed government, even when the people involved were clearly opposed to any revolutionary or guerrilla actions.

In the majority of cases, persons considered subversive were arrested by military forces acting in a paramilitary fashion. They became the "disappeared ones" and were taken to secret prisons and torture areas. In most cases, they were killed. The details of the repressive program have been examined carefully by the 1984 National Commission on Disappeared Persons (CONADEP). They were also probed in 1985 by the court empowered to try members of the military juntas for homicides, tortures, and other crimes.[3] The key elements in this repressive pro-

---

[3] The details of the trial, including a transcription of the testimony and the sentences can be found in successive issues of *El Diario del Juicio* published in Buenos Aires from the middle of 1985 until January 1986. Several former Junta members got heavy sentences, including life terms for Gen. Videla and Adm. Massera.

gram were the arbitrariness of repression, the uncertain future of the disappeared, and the repression extended to relatives of the presumed subversives — including the elderly and children

This environment of terror reached wide sectors of society, particularly those most likely to oppose the military: workers, students, intellectuals, political activists, *etc*. Some of the exiles managed to leave the country after having experienced some form of repression, that is, for example, after they were fired, threatened, blacklisted, or detained for a while. However, the majority chose exile as a way to escape imminent repression following the arrest or disappearance of family, friends, or colleagues.

Many who left the country avoided obtaining passports from police authorities; rather, they preferred to leave by going to a border country such as Brazil, where they needed only their identification card to enter. From there, they could renew their passport at consulates or request refugee status and assistance. Others had obtained a passport in Argentina before they had drawn the attention of the repressive state.

The climate of uncertainty and terror was an essential component in the repressive program. It extended a cloak of darkness and fog over the fate of the diappeared and, at the same time, over the precise legal status of the exiled, or for that matter, of anyone else.

No one could be certain if he or she was a suspect. The mere act of beginning an inquiry about such a matter might create a dangerous suspicion best to avoid. Those who had left the country for fear of being subjected to repression and those who chose "internal exile" by hiding in other parts of the country could never ascertain whether or not there was a clear danger, whether they could return, or what the extent of the charges were against them. These repressive policies influenced the very nature of the exile and indirectly the conditions for return.

The act of leaving the country was not a feasible option for all who were threatened by repression. Generally, it was an available option for the middle class and was not as feasible for workers and low-income sectors. In practice, intellectuals, professionals, and academics represented a high proportion of the emigrants not so much because of the social selectivity of the repression — which was much more indiscriminate — but because it was easier for them to leave the country.

The high cost of traveling was prohibitive for the poorer classes of society, especially when all the neighboring countries were dominated themselves by military dictatorships which did not welcome Argentine exiles. Furthermore, the middle class was already imbued with a migratory culture since most of their ancestors arrived in Argentina from the end of the nineteenth century to the end of World War II. Many of them also had relatives or friends abroad.

It is fitting to recall that, for those choosing exile, terror was not just a theoretical possibility or merely part of the social climate. Many of the exiles personally suffered from extremely traumatic experiences before they left the country. These experiences — assassinated family members, disappeared school or work colleagues, torture suffered personally or applied to relatives in their presence, long periods of solitary confinement or precarious, clandestine hiding — all indelibly marked the memory of the exiles during their period outside of the country and influenced the conflicts that arose when they considered the possibility of returning to Argentina.

Some Facts About Exile and Return Migration

Many of the persons interviewed experienced important changes in their lives while in exile. A high proportion (55 percent) continued their education; some began new careers which implied, upon returning, the need to enter a new professional community without relying on contacts that otherwise would have facilitated their professional success. One-third of those who were married when they emigrated were divorced, and half of these married again abroad (with Argentine and foreign spouses in equal proportions). Of those who were not married when they departed, two-thirds got married or formed free unions. One-third of these marriages or unions ended eventually in divorce or separations, which is remarkable, as the time span involved is relatively short.

Upon returning, the profile of the migrants had changed significantly in more than one respect. The average age was now 35; many had changed their marital status; many had had new children abroad; more than half had a higher level of education and often a new profession.

The decision to return sometimes generated conflicts in the families of the exiles. Such disputes occurred among 26 percent of the couples; disputes also arose among other couples once they had returned to Argentina. Children — especially teen-agers — frequently rejected the plan to return. For them, return represented a true exile to a country they did not know or that they no longer remembered. Some families broke up when their adolescent children (and in one case, a spouse) refused to return.

More than 60 percent returned without a formal job or a sure offer of employment. Nevertheless, they knew that the economic situation was difficult, and that finding a job would be a difficult affair; most consider, in retrospect, that they were not unduly optimistic.

Approximately 40 percent had made exploratory visits prior to their return. Some 57 percent of those surveyed returnees relied on financial assistance through UNHCR, ICM, or other institutions. It must be added, however, that the real proportion that sought such assistance must have been much less since our sample was strongly biased toward cases contacted through assistance agencies.

Two-thirds of the migrants shipped their personal belongings to the country; one-third came only with baggage. Of those who shipped cargo, one-third had their goods damaged or robbed or experienced customs problems upon entering the country. Some lost all of their belongings (sent as cargo), including many irreplaceable goods. For them, these losses added to the psychosocial strains associated with return.

More than 40 percent were housed with friends and relatives immediately upon returning to Argentina. At the time of the survey, when an average of 18 months had elapsed since their arrival, 45 percent were living in their own houses; 29 percent were renters; and 26 percent continued living with relatives and had not resolved their housing problem.

Eight percent of the heads of households and 15.9 percent of their spouses were unemployed. Both rates were well above the national rate of open unemployment. A contingent of repatriates survived with precarious and marginal jobs or received as their only income modest financial assistance from humanitarian organizations.

Although the jobs they were able to obtain were in many cases satisfying, in general, they were paid very low salaries. This was due to the decline in real wages throughout the economy, but often contrasted with the pay they had been earning abroad.

If the occupations carried out abroad and those obtained upon returning are grouped in three categories (high, middle, and low),[4] some 16 percent had moved up in category while 20 percent had descended. Those who ascended in level were mostly those who had a mid-level job abroad and occupied a high-level position when they returned. However, many of these high-level positions, such as scientific researcher or public official, currently pay low salaries. Those who dropped in occupational level were those who had a high level position abroad (international official, scientific research) and accepted mid-level positions (non-managerial public official or small business job) when they returned.

The amount of time that elapsed since returning did not influence the possibilities of ascending or descending in category, except for those who had low-level jobs abroad. While few migrants actually had low-level jobs abroad, two-thirds of that group obtained a mid-level position

---

[4] The high level includes highly skilled occupations, such as administrators and managers as well as businessmen, scholars, *etc.* The mid-level corresponds to non-manual, medium-skilled jobs, mainly clerks or small shopkeepers. The low-level includes manual jobs and low-skilled jobs in general.

less than one year after returning. This figure approaches 80 percent for those who had been in the country for more than two years.

While the possibility of living near relatives and friends was mentioned as an important factor among the motives influencing our informants' decision to return, no more than 57 percent indicated maintaining good relations with their families in Argentina; only a small proportion indicated those relations to be strong or satisfactory. Also, some 30 percent said that their current friends were principally other repatriates whom they met abroad or after having returned. Only one-fourth maintain a close relationship with friends they had before migrating. The rest maintain new friendships with persons who were not exiled or have groups of friends in which neither category predominates.

Nine out of ten respondents who mentioned social relations among the areas in which they noticed changes, indicated that these relationships generally have deteriorated from the time before they were exiled until now. The most frequently cited problems were aggressiveness, authoritarianism, and the lack of solidarity.

Finally, while the majority considered that returning was the correct decision and appeared to be basically content in having taken that step, about 40 percent declared a desire or intention to emigrate again when the opportunity presents itself. This does not include those who would migrate only in the case of a new military coup.

Having presented some of the basic characteristics, motivations, and intentions of the returnees in our sample, we can move on to develop an appropriate framework to interpret the reentry of the exiles. This framework takes into account the most important psychological and psychosocial factors involved in the process of return migration.

Toward an Interpretive Framework

The literature on return migration largely considers economic and demographic implications rather than psychological and psychosocial aspects. A good example of the dominance of economic and demographic studies is the collection of works included in Kubat (1984). These studies were originally presented at the First European Conference on International Return Migration. Very few studies presented at the conference addressed non-economic factors within a theoretical framework.

The study on Dutch return migration by Blauw and Elich (1984), for example, has some relevance to our analysis, even though it does not develop an appropriate theoretical framework. The Dutch who returned from Australia and New Zealand cited reasons that the authors group into two categories: cultural shock and personal problems. The former include aspects perceived as negative in the receiving society (vandalism, crime, and discrimination against women) as well as the difficulty in making friends, notwithstanding the cordiality exhibited by the local population. This is the common complaint from other migrants in different areas. Among the personal problems, the primary one mentioned was nostalgia for one's country in terms of family ties and familiar haunts. This category also included unemployment, dissatisfaction with work, and the breakup of marriage. After they had returned, the majority of the migrants maintained contact with the previous host country where they had friends and relatives; very few said they regretted migrating; only one-fifth regretted having returned home; and some wanted to re-emigrate. "Before they returned, many held idealized images of Holland, its friendly people, its warm social relations. After they returned, the picture was not as rosy as they had imagined" (Blauw and Elich, 1984:232).

The authors summarized their interpretation about the reasons for return migration in terms of the incapacity of the migrants to adapt to culture shock in the receiving country which reached a peak about two years after they had emigrated: "The economic reasons came to be much more secondary relative to the other reasons for emigrating or for returning. It is difficult to place these motives in a framework that makes economic motivations the primary cause of migration" (Blauw and Elich, 1984:232). As can be seen, these authors clearly show the presence of non-economic subjective factors, but they refrain from elaborating a more detailed alternative interpretation.

A study in the same book by Richmond (1984) tries to analyze the possible explanatory factors for return migration with few encouraging results: "The empirical studies on return migration have not managed to identify any consistent pattern that distinguishes migrants who remain and migrants who return" (Richmond, 1984:270). In reviewing some empirical studies, Richmond suggests that pull factors seem to be stronger than push factors (something that is confirmed in this study) and that the level of education also can influence the decision to return.

Richmond also cites Glaser (1978) on the return of foreign students from industrialized countries. In this case, return migration is caused by family and peer pressure as well as by patriotic feelings, rather than by other factors such as success in school or the temporary nature of their migration. The more capable and successful students are not more or less inclined to return than their colleagues. Many students who decide to remain abroad were originally temporary migrants.

With respect to exiles, Richmond points to the existence of an almost universal desire to return, what he calls "an ideology of return", although in practice these aspirations are often utopic.

Richmond concludes with an attempt to formulate general tendencies. First, he maintains that the dominant method of adaptation is "transilience": The migrant is integrated economically and has a high level of cognitive acculturation, but has little identification with the society in which he or she resides. This coincides with our findings. We observed that the problem of societal identification — tied to the migrant's own identity — seems to be a fundamental factor in the decision to return. Second, Richmond maintains that return migration will tend to increase when the host country experiences problems that affect upward social mobility or when these problems improve in the country of origin. In our study, the data do not seem to show a causal relationship between return migration and labor and social factors. This is the case for both exiles and non-political migrants (Maletta and Szwarcberg, 1985). Finally, Richmond indicates that there will be greater probability for return when the host country is more similar in language and culture to the country of origin and when communication is stronger between the two countries. This hypothesis, however, does not seem to have a sound basis.

Indeed, we find in the case of some very similar countries neighboring Argentina that the geographical vicinity and socio-cultural similarity appear to have reduced problems of adaptation. For example, these problems may be mitigated by frequent visits to the place of origin which short distances make easier. Contrary to Richmond's last proposition, our study discovered many cases of return migration from countries very different from Argentina. The reasons cited for return migration were the desire to recover inherent aspects of the country of origin (non-existent in the host country) or to be closer to the extended family.

Yet even in neighboring countries, identification eludes the migrant. This theme is tied to the migrant's own identity and does not appear to be related to cultural similarities between the two countries. For example, a recent study on Uruguayan immigrants in Argentina by Szwarcberg and Hensel (1985) showed that despite great similarities between these sending and receiving societies, Uruguayans demonstrated a strong need to return to Uruguay because the latter is their own country, and Argentina is not. The Uruguayans feel in Argentina exactly how Argentines felt in other countries, and they expressed this sentiment often with the same words. Richmond's conclusions about the relationship between similar cultural traits and return migration do not appear to play a prominent role here.

Rosemarie Rogers (1984) classifies possible reasons for return migration in various categories according to events that a) maintain ties with the guest country or country of origin; b) are produced at the macro or micro level; and c) are related or not to the original reason to migrate. This typology is useful in showing the diversity of reasons behind the decision to return, but it is not based on an explanatory framework. It is merely a taxonomy that does not allow for any one variable to assume a privileged analytical position within the framework.

A Psychoanalytical Approach to Migration, Exile, and Return

An interesting effort to address the problems of migration and exile psychoanalytically is found in the work of León Grinberg and Rebecca Grinberg (1984). The two researchers have worked for twenty years on the topics of migration, identity, and change. They adopt a psychoanalytical perspective which is influenced in particular by the writings of Klein (1952). They consider migration, even voluntary migration, to be a traumatic situation; this crisis, they maintain, produces a feeling of "abandonment", a feeling that would be related to the "loss of a protective mother", "to the loss of the containing object according to the terminology of Bion" (Grinberg and Grinberg, 1984:24-25).

The Grinbergs illustrate their work with clinical cases and with cases drawn from psychoanalytical literature. They attempt to relate latent aspects of the migratory process with certain "myths, which express sentiments crucial to the migratory experience" (Grinberg and Grinberg, 1984: 14-21). An example is the loss of Paradise in the biblical account of the origin of mankind.

A chapter of their work is dedicated to exile as a specific type of migration. Various features of exile are mentioned. First, there is a frequent absence of "good-byes" — a ritual that migrants could use to "protect" themselves when they leave, and which is often infeasible when one must flee suddenly and in danger:

> To all of their anxieties is added an anguish provoked by the lack of a formal or explicit good-bye, which makes them feel that their departure is like crossing the border between the kingdom of the living and the kingdom of the dead...All of the loved ones to whom they have not been able to say farewell and whom they fear they will not see again become dead persons with whom they feel unable to part satisfactorily . . . (Grinberg and Grinberg, 1984:189).

Secondly, the exile is marked by the impossibility of returning, at least while the reasons for leaving persist:

> Many of them can also suffer from the "survival syndrome" which has been studied in prisoners of Nazi concentration camps who managed to survive while their family and friends were tortured or exterminated. . . . The exiles can feel crushed by the guilt they

experience from having seen their companions fall or having heard their terrible cries from nearby cells. This state of mind is fertile ground for scepticism or disillusion, if not despair (Grinberg and Grinberg, 1984:190).

To integrate oneself totally in the receiving society and above all renounce a return is equivalent to "breaking the 'sacredness' which some attribute to exile and is felt as a loss of the identity that defines them" (Grinberg and Grinberg, 1984: 190-191). Their relationship with the country of refuge is complex; they did not come "to" it but rather fled "from" their own country. This marks their relationship with the place where they dwell but in which they do not "live" in the fullest sense of the word. Their stay in the country of refuge is lived as a mere waiting period between their previous (often retrospectively mystified) life and their future life. This future life is represented by the illusion of being able to return, "an illusion all the more idealized, the greater the impossibility to attain it" (Grinberg and Grinberg, 1984:191).

With respect to return migration, the Grinbergs indicate foremost that "to return is hard". It is a conflict even for those who during their exile lived in a state of waiting for the possibility of returning. The key idea here is that, in spite of everything, ties have been created in the host country even beyond the consciousness of the migrant. In testimony cited by the authors, some exiles confess: "I feel that I am neither from here nor there" (Grinberg and Grinberg, 1984:220).

Another feature of the Grinbergs' analysis is the contention that "return is a new migration" (Grinberg and Grinberg, 1984:222). No one exists who truly returns; everyone goes, enters something new, even when attempting to reincorporate into a known reality.

> [The exile returns] with expectations of recovering all things that were longed for...But the reality confronted by the migrant can be different. The acknowledgement of changes in persons, things, customs, habits, homes, streets, relations, and affections will make the exile feel like a stranger. Nor will the language sound the same; colloquial expressions will have changed; understandings that have mounted on so many words with implied meanings like winks of complicity between the initiated (Grinberg and Grinberg, 1984:222).

And again: "What is unavoidable is that no return is only a return; it is a new migration, with all the losses, fears, and hopes that are inherent in it" (Grinberg and Grinberg, 1984: 251).

With its many insights notwithstanding, the Grinbergs' work does not pay detailed attention to the specifics of return migration. It also does not study in sufficient depth the relationship between exiles and return migration. Their return observations, based on empirical evidence and case studies cited in the literature, are always sharp and revealing, but they do not have in this regard a sufficiently systematic theory or approach — a defect that lamentably will continue to be seen in the present study.

A word may be added here on the practical implications of studying return migration from a perspective rooted in psychology and psychoanalysis. The exploration of exile and return from this perspective can appear inadequate when the purpose is to develop state policies, or when the migrants show more urgent primary needs such as housing or food (which is the case for many streams of refugees all over the world). Yet in the Argentine case — which is probably repeated in other groups of exiles from Chile, Uruguay, and other parts of the world — the psychosocial problem occupies a prominent place when it comes to interpreting the situation of the exiles, their possible return, and its practical consequences. Here, the psychosocial approach has immediate application for mental health policy.

Human rights organizations that have worked with exiles who returned to Argentina have had valuable experiences dealing with their clients' psychosocial and psychological problems. In working with this population, human rights personnel have developed various therapeutic strategies and services. A similar case holds for exiles who have returned to Chile (FASIC, 1982). An outstanding example is the establishment of individual and group therapy services for maladjusted children in the exiles' families.

Obviously, the emphasis on psychological aspects is not meant to exclude other sociological or economic factors. As a matter of fact, all these psychological interpretations are based precisely on considering the psychological implications of experiences as directly tied to the social, political, and economic milieu. The type of identities that exile and return put into crisis are those that are tied to objects in the country of origin — one's family, profession, or political stand — those that are incomprehensible without reference to the macro-social reality that gave rise to them.

Even economic reality is constantly present though not in a mechanical or linear manner; the subjects do not react necessarily to market indicators (especially in the labor market) by applying some conventional economic calculations, but rather mix economic forces with other motivations. It is certain that if one adopted a neoclassical economic framework, such motivations could also receive an economic evaluation and treatment as in ordinary economic analysis of migration in terms such as human capital. However, such a treatment would probably trivialize the analysis without adding specific meaning.

Amid terror, uncertainty, assassinations, disappearances, and re-
prisals against family members — exile represents a traumatic cut or
wound in the lives of the individuals affected, a rupture that separates
their lives in two parts that they try to unite thereafter through several
means, including (when feasible) the quest for home, *i.e.*, return migration.

From a slightly different angle, return migration can be seen also as
an attempt to rebuild one's own identity which was mutilated by events
immediately prior to exile and by exile itself. The return thus represents from this point of view an attempt to recover the previous spatial
environment that operated as a support for that identity. To return to
his or her country (a geographical movement) thus acquires a temporal
and social meaning in the migrant's mind.

A third interpretation (that bears on and, thus, does not exclude the
other two views) emphasizes that exile is a forced migration, not one
that is chosen. Once the political conditions are adequate, return appears (for those exiles who decide to return) as a necessary movement
— an almost compulsive affirmation of the desire to live in one's
country. Perhaps, more importantly, it is an affirmation of the freedom
to occupy again a place in the social, political, and emotional milieu that
had formerly expelled the migrant. Only after accomplishing that
movement, a new kind of freedom can emerge; now one is able to
choose between remaining in the country or departing again, without
the choice having been imposed. This would explain the high percentage of returnees who are content with their decision to return, yet
at the same time intend to migrate again.

Age and Exile

The idea of exile as a trauma, a cut, or a wound acquires different
shades of meaning depending on the person's age when exiled and his
or her stage in life. At one extreme would be the sudden exile of adolescents, such as one interviewed youth who had to leave quickly after several of his high-school classmates "disappeared". He was sent by his
family to Israel alone, and found it very difficult to adjust there. Eight
years later he stated: "When one leaves, there is something that is cut,
something in me that is cut, something that was cut at the moment when
those tragic events occurred in the country".

His formative adolescent years, mutilated by exile, continued in Israel
under conditions totally divorced from the previous situation in Argentina. Now he does not feel a part of either of the spheres of socializa-
tion: "My sense of belonging is not fundamentally in one place, for my
history was cut off at a certain moment".

The interview with this young man was very difficult, since re-living the moments prior to his exile, speaking about his experience abroad and his decision to return produced such an intense emotional state that his ability to speak was completely blocked. A part of the terror which motivated the exile, the "cut" to which he alluded, is permanently with him. It prevents him from assuming Argentina as his own country, yet it also ties him to it. He cannot free himself from the past that was interrupted when he had to leave at 16 years of age.

His return came about almost compulsively, "without knowing why", when he was about to be married in Israel. The date of his return not only coincided with the reemergence of democracy in Argentina but also with the war between Lebanon and Israel. The sudden decision to return, not very well explained at the conscious level, was associated with a definite identification with two situations of danger: one in Argentina in 1976, the other in Israel in 1983. Another influencing factor was probably the coming need to commit himself in Israel through marriage, a decision that could have been painful. Later, this young man decided to return to Israel, and it remained clear in his answers that he did not feel he belonged in either country and that he could not easily commit himself to anyone or anything.

In the case of another young married couple, the woman had temporarily "disappeared" and afterwards both emigrated to Brazil at age 18 when she was granted a precarious condition of freedom. Their story expresses similar but less dramatic feelings: "We were nobody here in Argentina once our entire horizon was upset; groups of friends, political activities — all of this did not exist anymore because people had left or were dead. . . . Nor do we have an identity here at this time, except for the family and a few things that one identifies with the country". In fact, their own "history" began in exile, when they decided to live together and started seeking jobs.

This couple also returned without knowing why, as a compulsion to be reunited with the country they had left. The return marked for them the end of a transitory state in Brazil which they saw as leading nowhere. Their return seems like an opportunity to feel a sense of belonging in their own country, to do things, to achieve, without having in Argentina a specific environment that was waiting for them (except the expectation of regaining their civil legal status, to be discussed in the next section).

A journalist who was in exile for nine years said at age 35: "The factor that weighed particularly heavy on me in returning was the need to rebuild, to change the pattern of my life, to reconstruct it around a social and emotional environment".

The differential impact of exile at different ages is seen clearly when comparing these cases with those of older persons. A sixty-year-old man remarked upon returning: "Here in Argentina I began to recognize my entire life, which I recognize in small conversations, in the street, in the way of living, in the market, on the bus. With time, everything that had been cutoff was being reconstructed. . . . I only came back to visit and see, but I've been carried away by things, . . . and now I am staying. I feel my whole life here, where things and persons have meaning for me; far away in exile I did not know the history".

The contrast with the younger people is notable. For the Israel-bound teen-ager, the break with Argentina happened before his entire universe of meanings was formed. To the older man, the country is so familiar that upon recognizing it, he decides to stay. The former must live forever with his biographical wound, while the latter observes that "everything that had been cut off was being reconstructed". It is worth noting the frequent description of exile as a cut, a rupture, or a wound in the spontaneous wording of the interviewed exiles.

Exile was a break, and they return to rebuild a sense of continuity. The older one is, the greater the possibilities for a successful re-encounter and the more elements to mitigate the break. There is a sensation in younger persons of something beyond repair, a break with Argentina and now another break with the country where they concluded their adolescence. A rupture of that import in the formative years could do far more damage than in later stages of life.

For middle-age persons, not so young but yet not old, the past and the future, the country of origin and the world abroad are all more available. The possibility exists not only to rediscover the past but also to emigrate anew in search of a future project outside of the country. "My father", said a 45-year-old professional woman, "returned a short time ago saying he was old, that he returned irrespective of any problem he may encounter, to face things as they are. I also felt like coming here, but we (she and her husband) didn't come to stay irrespective of conditions. . . . We are very realistic". This same woman showed her displeasure at the distrustful indifference of her professional colleagues who had remained in the country. ("It seems I'm invisible".) She ultimately went abroad again. Meanwhile, her father remained in Argentina.

Legality and Belonging

To return often implies recovering a legal status and the possibility of re-integrating oneself into the pattern of social relations and institutions. The male member of the young couple who returned from Brazil (referred to earlier) stated in this regard:

The idea of recovering one's legal status is important, for in Brazil we recovered freedom without legality. We lived outside of the law, with expired documents, for many years. We got tired of the laborious process of renewing our visas each year and we simply stopped. We always lived on the margin, without being recognized. Here I feel recognition, although it is anonymous, for I have papers, a social security number, *etc.* I function within a social framework, I feel I belong to something. . . . When I get my salary and I see my social security number, I really get emotional.

In an interview this same young man, now working at a weekly magazine in Buenos Aires, remembered the emotion he felt when he saw his name on the list of union members. Having been exiled so young, having lived without legal status or fixed jobs in Brazil, this young couple had never seen their names written anywhere — not on a bank account, a social security card, a union list. To return, for this couple, was like returning from a "civil death".

Identity and Rediscovery

The break represented by exile can also be interpreted as a threat or wound to the substance or integrity of one's identity. Thus, Grinberg and Grinberg (1984:155) define "the feeling of identity as the capacity of the individual to continue to feel oneself amid the succession of changes" (Grinberg and Grinberg, 1984:155). According to the authors, this feeling of identity results from the interaction of three bonds of integration: spatial, temporal, and social. The first refers to the ability to perceive oneself as separate and distinct; the second refers to the capacity to perceive oneself as the same in the course of time; the third refers to identifications between subject and external objects (either persons or things).

It is not within the scope of this chapter to analyze this or other concepts of identity. Rather, we intend to use the concept of identity heuristically in order to formulate some hypotheses.

It should be remembered that the concept of identity is virtually absent in Freudian vocabulary and that it has been imported into social psychology by later psychological and psychoanalytical currents.

The very term *Identität* is not common in Freud's work. It only appears in a letter he wrote to the B'nai B'rith in 1926. There, Freud used it to refer to a typically social identity, that of the Jewish people: "The clear conscience of an internal identity, the familiarity of *possessing* the same internal construction".[5] Here, identity has a relative sense and points to a cultural identity. It has an ethnic, social identity based on the similarities ("the same internal construction") more than on individual differences.

The concept of identity in Erikson's work (1963) and Melanie Klein's corresponding concept of "the self" share an idea of "integrity"; the subject continuously builds an integrated synthesis of his multiple identifications, and forms it through different stages (Klein, 1952).

For other psychoanalytical approaches, especially those stemming from Lacan, the idea of an integrated identity is an illusion, a myth or ideal pursued by the individual. In this view, there is a basic break or split that never disappears and that forms a constituent part of the person. This is a notion taken from Freud himself, who, at the end of his work, wrote about the "splitting of the Ego". The Ego pursues the illusion of becoming a whole, of achieving a union of its basic division. It places that illusion in goals that embody the ideal self that each individual pursues at a particular moment, without ever reaching that unity, even though the goals that one transitorily pursues are attained. Depression resulting from achieving a goal, very often observed in clinical experience, is seen as a manifestations of this duality: The goal is achieved, but not the unity itself. The depression persists until the person adopts a new goal. The concept of identity is thus tied to the Ideal Ego and to the complex theme of "narcissism".[6]

Voluntary emigration expresses precisely the attempt to reach a goal (say, economic or professional success) which the individual pursues. In exile, on the other hand, political persecution cuts or mutilates the individual and collective projects of political militants and their families, and removes the material basis for the identity based on those projects.

Moreover, the specific type of persecution unleashed in Argentina that massively struck circles of friends and family also violently broke the deepest emotional ties amidst an atmosphere of terror and uncertainty that adds even greater anguish than is expected in exiles who fled from other kinds of persecution.

In a normal migration, as the Grinbergs (1984:189) indicate, the ritual of farewell and subsequent communication (as well as the fact that migration is connected to personal projects and does not represent a break) put a strong protective mantle on departure and separation. By

---

[5] Translated directly from the original German: "...die klare Bewusstheit der inneren Identität, die Heimlichkeit der gleichen inneren Konstruktion". *See*, Freud 1941, Vol. XVI.

[6] *See*, "The Splitting of the Ego in Melancholy", "On Narcissism", and "Ego and Id", in Freud (1941). *See also*, Lacan 1966.

contrast, the exile often leaves without saying good-bye, has lost some family or friends beforehand, does not know the whereabouts of others, and does not know if he or she will ever see them again. Subsequent communication is temporarily or definitely interrupted until the return, or even after the return, when former relationships are dispersed or disappeared.

The study of exile, return, and identity must also be enriched by adding a temporal component which could be called "the disparity of time". The exile, like any emigrant, has been absent for a certain period of time. This commonplace fact encompasses many levels of meaning. On the one hand, events have continued in the exile's absence; the country has continued to exist and change without the exile (a clear indication for the expatriate that his or her presence is not necessary). This aspect of absence is one of the most anguishing for the exile, because it evokes and implies the most sinister idea in death: "The world (*viz*, country) can continue to exist without me".

Not only have things continued to happen, but they have modified reality. Upon returning, the exile finds a different country to whose changes he or she is foreign. The country is no longer his or hers since the exile was not present, did not influence, nor was affected by the events as they occurred (except affected indirectly upon learning about them in newspapers, *etc.*)

The emigrant thus has not shared in events that occurred to his or her compatriots. Meanwhile, some things also have occurred to the migrant that cannot be shared with others who remained in the country. The exile changed, grew, and reoriented ideological preferences (perhaps not in the same direction as his/her compatriots). The individual returned perhaps with a new profession or family, and his/her appreciation of the home country is probably indelibly marked by the experience abroad. This experience often leads one to compare and relativize that which for others may seem obvious, natural, or inevitable.

Many of the persons we interviewed noticed these "differences" and asked: "Am I the one who changed or is it the country? Is the country only different from my ideals or is the country also different from the one I left behind?" One individual mentioned:

> a very ambivalent sensation: that of having recovered something I desired for a long time and only to have lost it at the moment I recovered it. Because I longed to return to Argentina, but to my Argentina, and upon returning I notice that it does not exist anymore and will not exist forever; I do not even have here what I had abroad: hope. . . . It's like a mirage that disappears when you touch it.

In general, facing those changes makes one's own country seem strange and new. Those who return "in order not to feel like foreigners" feel different and, as one returnee put it, "a stranger in his own country". In other return migrations, the principal changes accrue to the migrant, but in the last decade in Argentina, political, social, and economic events have been so intense that it is also possible to register macro-social changes that make identification difficult, not to mention the micro-social changes that affect the immediate context (family, professional, emotional) of the migrant.

To analyze those macro-social changes is not within the scope of this chapter. Nevertheless, some notions of change in the country come from the exiles' own words.

One of the most recurring topics aired is the deterioration of social relations, conviviality, and solidarity. This observation could correspond to the real changes that occurred in their absence. Argentina, and in particular, Buenos Aires (where 70 percent of the families we interviewed resided) have always been tough and competitive places, but the years of military dictatorship undoubtedly accentuated this characteristic.

Indiscriminate repression created fear of every association with persons possibly dangerous to the regime or perceived as a threat. Fear created a tendency to take refuge in one's privacy and family, in trivial and apolitical matters, and in daily subsistence in order to forget about, and keep aside from, social problems or ideological matters.

Together with fear went a stark economic reality. Argentina's GDP per capita in 1985 was lower than in 1975, and income distribution has become even more unequal. The labor market shrank, and a large fraction of the labor force maintained two jobs in a double workday, accepted jobs beneath their skill level, and received very reduced wages. This added up to stress and reduced opportunities for leisure and friendships.

The military regime established a fiercely speculative financial system that appeared until the date of our survey as the only way to make money. This occurred in the middle of an inflationary spiral that reached 1000 percent a year, although it did decline drastically in the second half of 1985. In an atmosphere such as this, the interviewed returnees said that economic uncertainty and unending concern over daily subsistence eliminate many possibilities of placing value on non-income-producing activities; there is no free time, no spiritual tranquility to dedicate oneself to friendship or conviviality; one lives often in a permanent environment of aggressiveness and ill-will.

Nonetheless, there is the possibility that the experience abroad has sensitized the returning migrants to the lack of solidarity or to certain traits of intolerance and authoritarianism that perhaps existed in the country at the moment they began their exile.

Moreover, the exiles are disturbed by the reception provided them. They felt as if their compatriots would have preferred that they had not returned. The exiles observed that people pretended to ignore the causes which originally caused the returnees' departure from the country.

We interviewed a psychoanalyst who had lived ten years in exile. In referring specifically to his colleagues as a professional group, he said:

> The first thing to notice is their inability to talk about what happened, to avoid talking about recent political experience. Even when the past is approached, it is in a very banal and frivolous manner combined with amnesia. There is an extreme and persistent concern about money and economic survival. Our professional colleagues do nothing else but concentrate on their work, to try to defend their privileges which are scarcely defensible as they lose them day by day. . . . Then there is a sort of fragmenting of reality. There is a kind of ignorance not only about what happened but also about what is occurring to other social sectors. The middle class has managed to put on blinders in order not to see, understand, or know what is happening.

The exile comes into this context with a critical view, willing to examine the dictatorship, review its economic results, and learn about social concerns, only to find that his or her colleagues do not listen. Thus, the exile is a voice from the past, incomprehensible and annoying for those who remained behind, in a country isolated behind barriers of ideological and cultural backwardness.

Some exiles returned from countries where for years they felt foreign to their culture and customs. There they experienced an excessive individualism that contrasted to fantasies of solidarity and warmth they expected to find at home. "I left a united society when I went to exile, and I returned to a now cannibalistic society", said a working-class woman after returning from exile. Perhaps this woman idealized the level of solidarity that existed before her exile. "We returned to the maternal womb, but it was dry and rotten", was the metaphor of a professional who lived in Italy for several years.

At the micro-social level, exile freezes the image the exile held of others who remained, and *vice-versa*. The return abruptly puts them face to face with the changes that have occurred in both. The duration of Argentine exile (an average of six to eight years) is long enough for significant changes to occur, but not so long as to avoid the illusory expectation that everything remains the same.

One micro-social arena where changes are noticed immediately is in the family. "When I left, my parents were supporting me; now they are retired and ill and I must care for them", was one answer expressed about changes in the family. Many exiles left at one stage in life and returned in another completely different one. Changes have occurred in the family setting; the parents may have died; siblings may have married or no longer live together.

There are also seemingly trivial changes in the physical environment that cause strong emotional reactions. In some cases, the exile's former house has been abandoned; furniture is no longer there; old china or wall decorations have been lost or replaced; the family library has been sacked by the repressive forces. Other changes are more subtle, such as a modification in the way of living or relationship with one's parents. "It's like coming home to find everything there, but with different places for the furniture; at each step one stumbles upon something that was not there before". One returns to the familiar, the things that are known, but at the same time everything is different in a spatial environment that is not the same, just like the migrant who returns is not the same anymore.

Apart from the changes in family and friends, the exile may suddenly perceive that he or she has also changed and is different than the others. People may tell the exile that he speaks with a new accent. The exile's most trivial ideas can be shocking or novel to others. The exile's point of view about the family, the profession, politics, and about him- or herself may have changed. Some changes are visibly noticed: The exile may return with a new spouse, new children, or a new profession that involves a new identity unknown to friends and colleagues.

Moreover, the mere fact of having lived abroad or having participated in another society makes the exile distance himself from some native things which, for others, are so immediate that they are indisputable; migrating is in a sense the "end of innocence", the end of an immediacy with one's country that will never be attainable again by the returning migrant.

The returnee looks at the country with different eyes and relativizes it in comparisons that are impossible for others who did not migrate. Even the non-migrant's occasional tourist excursions abroad do not allow for adequate knowledge of other realities, at least not enough to distance oneself from one's own reality.

The new things the exile brings, of course, also could be seen as positive contributions to enrich the national society. In fact, one of the exiles' main motivations for return is that of "being useful and to contribute something to my country". This desire to be useful, of integrating oneself into the society can often be an attempt to generate a new goal, a support for the identity the exile wishes to rebuild.

These expectations of being useful implicitly involve the assumption (often unwarranted) that people in the home country are actually willing to receive the contributions of those who return from exile. In fact, that idea was nourished by the official pronouncement of the new democratic government which called for the return of Argentines since late 1983, arguing that "the country needed them".

In many cases, however, a sense of frustration emerges, due to what is perceived as a cold indifference toward the possible contributions of those who return. Feelings of rejection are better treated under the "stigma of exile" — a topic which is discussed in the next section. Here, we want to mention only that rejection undermines the fantasies that nourish the self-image of the returning migrant and that maintain the expectations of rebuilding his or her identity.

The one who comes back with the desire to "be useful" often finds a response of "disqualification". Offering a contribution is interpreted by others as a request or demand rather than giving or sharing. Two examples of actual dialogue reported by persons interviewed will illustrate this point:

Migrant (by telephone): "I would like to meet to talk after so many years and to tell you how it went for me".

Colleague (current director of an institution): "Before anything, I want to say that I cannot offer you a job here".

In another case, the migrant (a scientist) went to a research center in his field and spoke to a person he had not known previously:

Migrant: "I am aware that the Institute has worked on the topic. I had valuable experience on the same topic in Europe, and I would like to exchange some ideas on it".

Colleague: "The library of this institution has all of the material we have produced on that theme; you can consult it there". (The person also gave the migrant a book on the subject published by the institute; he did not show the least interest in listening to the migrant on the topic itself.)

In both cases, the migrants encountered responses that had a clear meaning: Your contribution is not needed. Before they can express themselves, they are placed in an inferior position with no evaluation of their experience or possible contribution. Obviously, these disqualifying responses (as they are defined in communication theory) form part of a defensive tactic by those who have not emigrated against someone who is seen as a competitor.

The exile thus faces a panorama of indifference, not hostility. Instead of feeling welcomed "at home" and perceiving that his or her presence is desired and needed, the returnee finds that he is often viewed as almost an intruder. To recall Freudian terminology, this tactic is an attack on narcissism. In those individuals who have converted the need to be useful into a central part of their identity (according to the frame of mind that earlier carried them into political militancy and eventually into exile), this type of aggression produces a devastating effect.

It must also be re-emphasized that this matter is tied to the general crisis of political identities in Argentina of the 1970s. That situation affected those who emigrated as well as those who remained in the country, but it prevented the exiles who returned from inserting themselves directly into a known sociopolitical environment. The opposite seems to have occurred for exiles who returned in recent years to Brazil, Uruguay or Chile, where old political alignments remain strong in spite of the changes.

This contributes to undermining the mental state of the former exile and of the family group as a whole. In that context, the desire to emigrate again emerges very easily, above all when the economic reality does not add favorable arguments for remaining, but contributes even more to the existing anguish.

The Stigma of Exile

The fact of having been exiled can be a negative factor in the biography (the social identity) of the individual, for many reasons related to the specific context in which exile occurred and the form in which the dictatorship ended.

One of the manifestations of the "stigma" is simply an ideological suspicion, which is not applied only to former exiles, but to all who, in one way or another, are suspected of an extremist political position. An exile for instance, can be seen as potentially dangerous by the personnel manager of a private company who tries not to hire troublesome persons, agitators, or subversives.

In Argentina, the anti-subversive harangue of the military dictatorship made every protest evil to such an extent that even at the time of our survey (1985) there was a strong distrust of anyone associated with those persecuted by the military. During the years of dictatorship, those with clean conscience consoled themselves upon learning about a disappearance: "Surely", they thought, "that person must have done something". The same idea emerges upon facing a former exile whose need to leave the country can be attributed, in the mind of the other person, to having belonged to some terrorist organization or to having at least supported an extremist ideology. Thus, an exile would be a "dangerous" person with whom one had to be careful, and whose ideas should still be distrusted.

A sixty-year-old man who was a former exile sharply perceived this problem: "When I arrived it seemed that there were persons who did not know that I had been exiled... As if one had gone who knows where, as if one had disappeared like an angel and had returned. This is apart from those who thought that if I were in exile, there must have been a reason". His friends accepted him again but distrusted his opinions and preferred to keep the years of exile in a shroud that was hardly mentioned:

> Some old friends from the school invited me to dinner; they had selected a speaker who did not show up; someone thought that I wanted to speak in his place and said to me: "Not you, you are forbidden to speak....They saw me arrive after seven or eight years....and no one asked me "Where were you? What happened to you?" It was understood that my exile was a shrouded time, and....no further questions were asked.

The origin of this attitude from his former colleagues seemed very clear to him: "Those of us university authorities who were in charge in 1973-1975 were masked", he said upon recalling his actions prior to the military coup.

In 1985, on the other hand, the strength of democracy in Argentina was still precarious. Frequent political events reminded the citizenry that the repressive apparatus still existed and that another coup could be possible in the future. The distrust of many was also a precaution for that uncertain future.

Since the middle of 1985, the feeling of mistrust has been muted somewhat. This is a result of the trials of the military junta as well as a consequence of democracy growing stronger. Testimony at those trials brought out more clearly in the public view the nature of the atrocities and the arbitrariness of the repression. Upon probing into the repressive aberrations of the regime, it was admitted that many had been innocent victims of the repression. But this process of clarifying the past, which is not yet complete (1986), had barely begun to unfold at the time of our survey. This contributed to the political prejudice against the exiles.

Another dimension of the stigma appears among those ideologically closer to the exiles but who feel somehow threatened by their return. During the early part of 1984 the Argentine intellectual community debated over "those who went" and "those who stayed". The debates produced a false dichotomy. The former feared being accused of cowardness, and having enjoyed a golden exile while their colleagues suffered. The latter feared being accused of collaborating with the regime. Each group perceived the other as a danger to their own legitimacy. That period of public debate was surpassed in a few months and was generally recognized as a mistaken way of approaching the issue. But, perhaps, it raised doubts and fears that still linger.

Another side of the exile stigma is the sense of being the object of professional mistrust or misgivings — a stigma that arises in the context of a saturated labor market. This appears to hold especially in the social sciences, journalism, university teaching, theater, politics, and unions; in these fields the political legitimacy of one's own position plays an important role in defining affiliations and opportunities for professional success. This aspect, related to competition in the professional marketplace, usually did not become explicit, nor even acknowledged, at least among "those who stayed". However, the reticence to incorporate the exiles in various activities, or the belief that they were obtaining privileges because of their condition of having been in exile, appeared frequently in conversations with the exiles and with other informants. One of the most frequent manifestations was the indifference with which the exiles' experience abroad was received. We alluded to this in the previous section.

That indifference was reported mostly by professionals and by scientific researchers. There seem to be two origins of this attitude. The first is a professional jealousy in the face of dangerous competition in a reduced labor market for Argentine scientists. One tactic is trying to undervalue or ignore academic and professional credentials obtained abroad. A second tactic, most common in the field of social sciences, is to rationalize the matter by way of arguing against the relevance of other national experiences with respect to their usefulness in interpreting the Argentine case. This last contention, be it valid or not, is connected to the previous one because it helps to overvalue the professional experience in Argentina *vis-à-vis* that acquired abroad.

The problem of stigma, and professional mistrust in particular, tends to disappear over time. This occurs as the former exiles are integrated in one way or another in their respective professions. With time the fear based on fantasies leads to a confrontation with reality in which the fact that a person was in exile loses relevance.

Faced with these various instances of the exile stigma, many repatriates choose to hide their condition, as best as possible, in an attempt to submerge themselves in the mainstream and pass by unperceived. In one of the cases we studied, a young woman refugee who left the country as a primary school teacher succeeded in obtaining an advanced university degree in early childhood education in Sweden. In Argentina she found out that her Swedish degree was equivalent to a confession of her refugee status. She found it difficult to get a job in private education (oriented to the most affluent and conservative sectors of society) or in public education directed by a rigid and traditional bureaucracy. In an act that could be considered a classic Freudian slip, one fine day, this woman inadvertently lost her Swedish diploma.

The End of Return

When the phenomenon of the stigma is added to the preceding considerations about the meaning of return migration, it is fitting to ask how long the status of "return migrant" lasts? When does one stop being a returnee?

We studied migrants who had returned between five months and five years prior to the interviews. The vast majority had returned between six months and two years before. The duration of return did not seem to be a very decisive factor in determining the nature of the exiles' reinsertion into the labor market. However, it did influence the exile's perception about his or her problems and position in society.

What marks the end of return is the disappearance of the status of "returnee" as a significant element in one's own definition and in the perception others have about the person. Some of those we interviewed were clearly in this stage. They did not attribute their economic problems to having been in exile but rather to the problems of the country. They had reconstructed a normal life in all respects, including some who had married or had children, or had begun successfully a new professional activity, perhaps different from that which they had before their exile.

The survey was carried out between March and June 1985, a little more than a year after the installation of the democratic government. Those who returned earlier (for example, at the end of the 1982 war) had left many problems of re-insertion pending during the final period of the dictatorship; they only began to resolve these problems once the constitutional government was established. Therefore, perhaps this survey does not permit one to see clearly the theme of "the end of return" which would require more time to pass.

Nevertheless, the responses obtained in this research suggest that the end of return could have been reached with relative speed in many cases. This is not incompatible with the fact that 40 percent of those interviewed showed an intention or readiness to emigrate again. To return, as was defined in this study, constitutes a way of affirming one's own freedom, of repairing the arbitrary will that expelled them from the country and prevented them from returning for many years. Once their identity is reconstructed in their own land and the wounds of exile are healed, there can be another decision to migrate. This time, however, it is the result of free choice tied to their own personal growth and it is a step that does not weaken the validity of the act of returning.

The same feeling occurs among those who did not return. Although we do not know their number, it is estimated that perhaps between one-third and one-half of the exiles have not returned to Argentina. Many of these individuals remain abroad as a result of an internal conflict that implies changing their identity from political exiles to simple immigrants and abandoning a status with which they have lived for a long time.

The decision to remain abroad, when it is correctly elaborated, is also a way to exercise freedom of choice, which is made possible by the existence of a democratic order, by the end of political and ideological persecutions, and by the end of fear. This occurs even when one has not passed over the stage — that others consider necessary — of facing return and rediscovering one's own roots.

REFERENCES

Argentina — Instituto Nacional de Estadística y Censos
1983 *Censo nacional de población y vivienda 1980. Serie D-Población.* Buenos Aires.

Bertoncello, R., A. Lattes, C. Moyano, and S. Schkolnik
1985 "Los argentinos en el exterior". Buenos Aires: Centro de Estudios de Poblacicn.

Blauw, W. and J. Elich
1984 "The Return of Dutch Emigrants from Australia, New Zealand and Canada", *The The Politics of Return:* Edited by D. Kubat. New York: Center for Migration Studies.

CONADEP (Comisión Nacional sobre la Desaparición de Personas)
1984 *Nunca mas — Informe de la Comisión Nacional sobre la Deseparición de Personas.* Buenos Aires: Eudeba.

Erikson, E.
1963 *Childhood and Society.* New York: W.W. Norton & Company Inc., Second Edition.

Freud, S.
1941 *Gesammelte Werke.* London: Imago Publishing Co., Ltd.

FASIC (Fundación de Ayuda Social de las Iglesias Cristianas)
1983 "Estudio psico-social de 25 familias retornadas", *Migraciónes Internacionales en las Américas,* 2(2): 97-118.

Glaser, W. (with G. Habers)
1978 *The Brain Drain: Emigration and Return.* Oxford: Pergamon Press.

Grinberg, L. and R. Grinberg
1984 *Psicoanálisis de la migración del exilio.* Madrid: Alianza Editorial.

Gurrieri, J. (and collaborators)
1983 *Escasez de recursos humanos calificados y migraciones internacionales en la Argentina.* Buenos Aires: Dirrección Nacional de Migraciónes.

Houssay, B.
1986 *La emigración de científicos, profesionales y técnicos de la Argentina.* Buenos Aires: Consejo Nacional de Investigaciones Científicas y Técnicas.

Klein, M.
1952 *Developments in Psycho-Analysis.* London: The Hogarth Press.

Kubat, D., ed.
1984 *The Politics of Return: International Return Migration in Europe.* New York: Center for Migration Studies.

Lacan, J.
1966 *Ecrits.* Paris: Editions du Seuil.

Maletta, H. and F. Szwarcberg
1985 *Migración de retorno a la Argentina: Problemas económicos y psico-sociales.* Geneva: Hemispheric Migration Project, ICM/CIPRA, Georgetown University.

Marshall, A.
1986 "Argentine Migration to the United States: Composition of Labor Flows". Chapter 6 in this volume.

Oteiza, E.
1971 "Emigración de profesionales, técnicos y obreros calificados argentinos a los Estados Unidos: Análisis de las fluctuaciones de la emigración bruta, julio 1950 a junio 1970". Buenos Aires: *Desarrollo Económico*, 10:429-484.

Richmond, A.H.
1984 "Explaining Return Migration", *The Politics of Return.* Edited by D. Kubat. New York: Center for Migration Studies.

Rogers, R.
1984 "Return Migration in Comparative Perspective", *The Politics of Return: International Return Migration in Europe.* Edited by D. Kubat. New York: Center for Migration Studies.

Rogers, R. AND P. Pessar
1986 "Trends and Policy Implications of Return Migration", *Proceedings of the Washington, D.C.: Inter-American Conference on Migration Trends and Policies.* Georgetown University, Center for Immigration Policy and Refugee Assistance, Hemispheric Migration Project.

Szwarcberg, F. and P. Hensel
1985 "Un proyecto de colonización rural v generación de empleo para migrantes de retorno al Uruguay. Análisis de las características de uruguayos residentes en la Argentina, exiliados retornados con apoyo de ACNUR, y potenciales de retorno con experiencia rural". Buenos Aires: ILO-ICM Project "Migraciones Internaciónales para el Desarrollo en América Latina".

CONTRIBUTORS

PATRICIA Y. ANDERSON is a demographer at the Institute for Social and Economic Research at the University of the West Indies in Mona, Jamaica. In 1988, Dr. Anderson will be a visiting professor at the State University of New York at Plattsburgh.

HAROLD BRADLEY, S.J., is director of Georgetown University's Center for Immigration Policy and Refugee Assistance and is a specialist in U.S. immigration history and policy.

JORGE DANDLER is an anthropologist who has directed research on migration and rural development for the Centro de Estudios de la Realidad Económica y Social in La Paz and Cochabamba, Bolivia. Dr. Dandler now is an advisor on rural development and indigenous populations for the Latin American regional office of the International Labor Organization in Lima.

HECTOR MALETTA is a sociologist and economist working with the United Nations Development Program in Buenos Aires. His research has focused on labor migration and agrarian problems in Peru and Argentina.

LELIO MÁRMORA is the director of the Buenos Aires office of the Intergovernmental Committee for Migration (ICM). For over ten years, he has directed Latin American research programs on labor migration and refugee movements for ICM and the International Labor Organization.

ADRIANA MARSHALL is currently directing a research project at the Geneva headquarters of the International Labor Organization, while on sabbatical from the Facultad Latinoamericana de Ciencias Sociales in Buenos Aires. Dr. Marshall has conducted research on the economic impacts of international migration on selected European, North American, and Latin American countries.

CARMEN MEDEIROS is a doctoral candidate in anthropology at the Graduate Center of the City University of New York. She had conducted field work on Bolivian migrant families for the Centro de Estudios de la Realidad Económica y Social based in Bolivia.

FRANK L. MILLS is a demographer. He is the assistant director of the University of the Virgin Islands' Caribbean Research Institute. Dr. Mills' research applies statistical methods to social science problems, such as labor migration.

JOSEPH O. PALACIO is an anthropologist at the Belize City campus of the University of the West Indies. Dr. Palacio's research has focused on Central American refugees and Belizean family life and community participation.

PATRICIA R. PESSAR is the research director of Georgetown University's Center for Immigration Policy and Refugee Assistance and director of the Hemispheric Migration Project. Dr. Pessar, who is an anthropologist, has published widely on the role of the household in migration and the impact of migration on Caribbean development.

ROSALIA SCHNEIDER is a clinical psychologist and professor of psychology at the Universidad Nacional de Buenos Aires.

FRIDA SZWARCBERG is a sociologist who has conducted research on family aspects of rural-urban migration in Peru and Argentina.

ELISABETH UNGAR BLEIER is a professor of political science at the Universidad de los Andes in Bogotá, Colombia. In addition to labor migration, she has studied the effectiveness of social services in Colombia.

Index